WRITINGS OF THE LEFT

General Editor: RALPH MILIBAND

Professor of Politics at Leeds University

MICHAEL BAKUNIN

SELECTED WRITINGS

MICHAEL BAKUNIN
SELECTED WRITINGS

Edited and Introduced by

ARTHUR LEHNING

Editor Archives Bakounine, *International Institute of Social History, Amsterdam*

Translations from the French by

STEVEN COX

Translations from the Russian by

OLIVE STEVENS

JONATHAN CAPE
THIRTY BEDFORD SQUARE
LONDON

THIS COMPILATION FIRST PUBLISHED 1973
INTRODUCTION AND COMPILATION © 1973 BY ARTHUR LEHNING
TRANSLATIONS BY STEVEN COX AND OLIVE STEVENS © 1973 BY
JONATHAN CAPE LTD

JONATHAN CAPE LTD, 30 BEDFORD SQUARE, LONDON WCI

Hardback edition ISBN 0 224 00893 5
Paperback edition ISBN 0 224 00898 6

PRINTED IN GREAT BRITAIN
BY EBENEZER BAYLIS AND SON LTD
THE TRINITY PRESS, WORCESTER AND LONDON
BOUND BY G. & J. KITCAT LTD, LONDON

GENERAL EDITOR'S PREFACE

It is often claimed nowadays that terms like Left and Right have ceased to mean very much. This is not true: the distinction endures, in as sharp a form as ever, between those who, on the one hand, accept as given the framework, if not all the features, of capitalist society; and those who, on the other, are concerned with and work for the establishment of a socialist alternative to the here and now. This, ultimately, is what the Left is about.

But the Left is itself endlessly fragmented over matters great as well as small. It always has been. But it is probably true that the Left has never been more divided than now. This is not surprising. For the great certitudes represented by the traditional mass movements of the Left — social democracy and orthodox communism — have, for different reasons, long ceased to be acceptable to the generations which came to political consciousness in the fifties and sixties. This is why those years have, for so much of the Left, been marked by extreme confusion, division and search.

Such a situation has many negative aspects. But it would be wrong to think of it as altogether negative. For the confusions, the divisions and the uncertainties betoken also a very healthy rejection of easy answers to complex problems; and no one on the Left who thinks at all seriously can now doubt that the creation of what could properly be called a socialist society is a very complex enterprise indeed.

It is precisely the awareness of its complexity which has led, in recent years, to a rediscovery — the term is not too strong — of a revolutionary literature, much of which had earlier been all but submerged in a great ideological freeze. None of this literature provides 'answers' to the questions which are posed by the socialist project. But what is best in it does at least suggest how the questions have been approached and tackled by successive generations of men and movements of the Left.

In the last decade or so, a fair amount of this heritage of the revolutionary Left has become more easily available than

5

before. But much of it, as far as the English reader is concerned, remains too little known, and for one reason or another difficult to get at. 'Writings of the Left' is intended to fill the gaps. Each of the volumes in this series will deal, by way of selected texts, either with the work of individual thinkers; or with particular episodes in the history of the Left; or with specific themes in socialist thought. These volumes will speak, not in the voice of the Left (there is no such voice) but in the many different voices of the Left, and on matters which remain central to socialist theory and practice.

RALPH MILIBAND

CONTENTS

INTRODUCTION

Michael Bakunin, the greatest of the Russian revolutionaries of the nineteenth century, played an important role in the democratic movements and revolutions of Western Europe. He began to formulate his anarchist and atheist ideas in 1864, and propagated them from 1868 onwards in the International Working Men's Association—the First International. In France, Russia, French-speaking Switzerland, Italy and, above all, Spain, his ideas were widely circulated and gained converts. Bakunin's main historical achievement lies in his having linked the libertarian ideas of anarchism with the movement for the emancipation of the working classes, and in his having sown the seeds of anti-authoritarian socialism and of the theory and practice of anarcho-syndicalism.

Making a meaningful selection of his written work is, however, a difficult task. During his lifetime Bakunin wrote a great deal, generally without much apparent concern for cohesion. In his standard biography of Bakunin, E. H. Carr wrote: 'There are few whose life and thought have exerted such immense influence on the world as Michael Bakunin, and yet who left such an inadequate and confused account of their views.' This cannot be denied. The turbulent life of this revolutionary did not take place in the reading-room of a great library. To a large extent, his influence was the result of his enormous epistolary activity. He could write some twenty-four letters in one day—many of them having the proportions of a pamphlet.* His writings were nearly always part of his activities as a revolutionary, whether propagandist or organizer. The greater part of them remained unpublished during his lifetime. Even now, the process of editing has not been completed; but when all his works are accessible, it should be

* Unfortunately most of his correspondence from 1864 to his death in 1876 is lost—nearly all his letters to Spain, Italy, the Jura, and an important part of his Russian correspondence. Because of their revolutionary activities, Bakunin and his friends had to destroy letters and documents on several occasions.

9

evident that they constitute a coherent social philosophy, with a complementary theory of revolutionary practice.

In connection with the philosophical depth and originality of Bakunin's revolutionary writings, it may be useful to remind the still sceptical reader of two points. One, all too obvious, is that, especially in English-speaking countries, few of the agencies which have had the responsibility of disseminating revolutionary ideas have had much knowledge of Bakunin; and when they did have the knowledge, they lacked the incentive to analyse or propagate his works. The other point is that Bakunin, being primarily a man of action, *always* wrote for men and women whom he was trying to trigger into acting, or else to guide while they were acting. And this *souci d'efficacité* meant that his style, his words themselves, had to be adapted to his immediate audience. Thus the difficulty that we experience in ascertaining the meaning of many of his paragraphs, especially when comparing them with others, stems largely from the fact that he is speaking to different audiences, rather than from his supposedly incoherent mind. Furthermore, the apparent lack of cohesion in his system is partly to be accounted for in terms of his eventful life, which did not allow him much respite for polished theoretical works.

If the reader wants to understand Bakunin's influence in his own time, he must go beyond the written word and meet the propagandist. His personality was perfectly fitted to the demands of the task. 'Impossible', wrote E. H. Carr, 'to convey to posterity that sense of overwhelming power which was always present to those who knew him in life.' Bakunin had the rare gift of persuading people to devote their lives to his cause, and of quickly forming intimate bonds with them if they seemed useful to him for his revolutionary purpose. The sceptical and critical Alexander Herzen recognized in Bakunin's character an exceptional quality, even greatness, in that, having grasped two or three characteristics of his environment, he detached from it the revolutionary current and immediately set about propelling this further, intensifying it, making it a passionate, vital question.

The eldest son of a Russian aristocrat of eighteenth-century liberal culture, a career diplomat who had lived for years in

Florence and Naples, Michael Aleksandrovič Bakunin was born on May 30th, 1814, at the estate of Premukhino, in the province of Tver, to the north-west of Moscow. An army career was planned for him, and he entered the Artillery School at St Petersburg; but at the age of twenty-one he resigned from the army and started to study philosophy in Moscow. In 1836 he translated Fichte's *Lectures on the Vocation of the Scholar*—his first publication—but soon became an ardent disciple of Hegel and, in 1838, published a translation of the latter's *Gymnasial Lectures*, with an introduction. It was the first of Hegel's works to appear in Russia.

In 1840 Bakunin went to Berlin to further his studies, and here he came under the influence of the Hegelian Left. In 1842 he moved to Dresden, where he made friends with the radical poet Georg Herwegh and with Arnold Ruge, who was then editor of the Left Hegelian paper, *Deutsche Jahrbücher für Wissenschaft und Kunst*, in which Bakunin published a pseudonymous article, 'The Reaction in Germany, A Fragment by a Frenchman', which aroused wide interest, and created a sensation in revolutionary circles.

Beneath the Hegelian jargon, understood by the intelligentsia of that time, the quintessence of this essay was the 'negation' of an abstract dialectic and a call to revolutionary practice. In contrast to Hegel's primacy of the positive in the dialectical process, Bakunin here sees the negative as the creative driving force. This means the ruthless destruction of everything positive, no 'mediation', no reconciliation between thesis and antithesis. There is no question here of the Hegelian trichotomy. The historically new emerges through the complete destruction of the old. In these revolutionary 'antithetical' dialectics Bakunin gave a precise and definite philosophical expression to what had been developing among the Hegelian Left during the past five years; at the same time, however, he was first to draw from this development the inference that this antithesis, being in reality the act of destruction, was the *sine qua non* of historical progress.

Thus he added, even before Marx, a new dimension to the Hegelian dialectic: the revolutionary philosophy of action, a social philosophy of the unity of theory and practice.

The famous statement, 'The passion for destruction is a

creative passion, too', is the concluding sentence of this article.
This sentence, the most often quoted (and often misquoted)
of his work, must be understood within the context just
described.

Already, then, Bakunin viewed the goal of history as liberty,
the liberation of man and human dignity. This is attainable
only through revolution and a total break. Revolt and liberty
are correlatives. Liberty is the source and the goal of life, but if
man is to achieve real self-awareness he must act, and he must
oppose all those who hold authority over him.

While he was still in Dresden, in 1842, Bakunin read Lorentz
von Stein's classic work, the first extensive survey of French
socialist theories and social movements. Soon afterwards he
went to Zurich with Georg Herwegh, where he met, in May
1843, Wilhelm Weitling, who had written in 1838 the first
communist programme for a secret organization of German
proscrits, the 'League of the Just'. This body had close connections with the secret revolutionary republican societies of a
Babouvist character that were led by Auguste Blanqui and
Armand Barbès; after Marx and Engels had joined the secret
League in 1847, it took the name of Communist League,
propagating its ideas mainly through the German Workers'
Education Society in London. The latter published in 1848,
by order of the League, the *Manifesto of the Communist Party*.

Bakunin was much impressed by Weitling's striking personality and his famous *Guarantees of Harmony and Freedom*,
from which he quoted enthusiastically the remarkable statement, 'The perfect society has no government but only an
administration, no laws but only obligations, no punishments
but only means of correction.' Nevertheless, he was critical of
Weitling's communist society, of which he wrote to Herwegh:
'His is not a free society, a really live union of free people, but
a herd of animals, intolerably coerced and united by force,
following only material ends, utterly ignorant of the spiritual
side of life.'

Bakunin knew Buonarroti's famous book of 1828, *Babeuf's
Conspiracy for Equality*, with its detailed description of communist aims and the revolutionary techniques of Babeuf's
attempt to overthrow the post-Thermidorian government in

1796. Bakunin stressed its historical importance and spoke with admiration of Buonarroti as 'the greatest conspirator of his age', *'un homme de fer, un caractère antique'*, but he rejected his theory of establishing equality through the force of the State. Babeuf and his friend, wrote Bakunin, possessed the cult of equality 'to the detriment of liberty', they were 'Jacobin socialists'. The State would confiscate all private property, administer it in the general interest, divide upbringing, education, livelihood and pleasures into equal shares for all, and require physical or mental initiative in the world; all liberty would disappear. The whole of society would present a picture of monotonous and forced uniformity. The government would exercise an absolute power over all members of society.

As a result of Weitling's arrest, and after an unheeded request by the Russian government to return to Russia, Bakunin left Switzerland in February 1844 and went by way of Brussels to Paris. There he met Marx and Proudhon, among many other prominent figures of the democratic and republican camp. Because of a speech he made on November 29th, 1847, at a banquet commemorating the Polish insurrection of 1830, in which he advocated the independence of Poland, he was expelled from France at the request of the Russian ambassador. This speech made him famous throughout Europe, and his expulsion was one of the highlights, and perhaps also an important contributing event, in the chain of events leading to the outbreak of the February Revolution in France.

Bakunin now moved to Brussels, where he again met Marx and became acquainted with his circle. After the February Revolution he returned to Paris, but in April 1848 left for Germany. When the revolutions in Berlin and Vienna took place, he wanted to set off an insurrection in Poland, and tried to do so. In June he attended the Slav Congress in Prague. An uprising there brought the Congress to an unexpected end and Bakunin went back to Germany.

Here, in the autumn of 1848, he wrote his *Appeal to the Slavs*, in which he advocated a coalition between the Slavs of Austria, the Hungarians and the democratic Germans, to liquidate the Austrian Empire and to ally with the Poles in their strivings for an independent Poland and a revolution in Russia. The

social liberation of the masses and the emancipation of the
suppressed nationalities should, in his view, lead to a universal
federation of European republics.

Marx and Engels disagreed with this policy. Engels denied
that there were any good grounds for wishing for the national
independence of any Slav country, except perhaps Poland.
This view, and Marx's Russophobia, were certainly to be
factors in the political antagonism between Marx and Bakunin
which became manifest in the late 1860s.

In May 1849 Bakunin became one of the leaders of the
democratic revolution in Dresden. The democratic workers,
wrote Friedrich Engels, found in him a 'capable and cool-
headed leader'. Arrested in Chemnitz, condemned to death
in Saxony, extradited to Austria, again condemned to death,
Bakunin was finally handed over to Russia, where, without
trial, he was imprisoned first in the dungeons of the Peter and
Paul Fortress (until 1854) and then in Schlüsselburg. In 1851
he wrote a *Confession*, addressed to the Tsar, a carefully worded
account of his activities and ideas, by which he hoped to gain
an improvement of his situation. But he remained in prison
until 1857, when he was exiled to Siberia. There he married a
young Polish girl, Antonia Kwiatkowska. In June 1861 he
escaped, and, travelling by way of Japan and North America,
arrived in London in December, where he met again his old
Russian friends Alexander Herzen and Nikolaj Ogarev.

As already noted, it was not until 1864–5 that Bakunin
definitely formulated the anarchist theory with which his
name is associated.

He believed that revolutionaries should aim at a society
where the greatest possible development of local, collective
and individual liberties could be brought about. The experience of the French revolutions of six decades had taught
him that it was not possible to achieve liberty without economic equality and the abolition of all economic privileges—
not only of the political ones. Equality was, for him, the first
condition; liberty was possible only after this, in this and
through this. Without equality, every liberty would constitute a privilege, the sovereignty of a minority and the
slavery of the vast majority.

On the other hand, equality without liberty was for Bakunin an irredeemable fraud, 'perpetuated by deceivers to deceive fools'. Equality must be created by 'the spontaneous organization of the work and the common property of the manufacturing associations and by the equally spontaneous federation of the communities, not by the supreme and paternal activity of the State'. Equality without liberty meant to him the despotism of the State, and in his opinion the State could not survive for a single day 'without possessing an exploiting and privileged class: the bureaucracy'. Babeuf's conspiracy and all similar attempts to establish a socialist society were bound to fail, because in all these systems equality was associated with the power and authority of the State, and in consequence liberty was excluded.

The most sinister alliance imaginable would combine socialism with absolutism — that is to say, the aspirations of the people for economic liberation and material prosperity with dictatorship and the concentration of all political and social forces in the State:

> May the future preserve us from the benevolence of despotism, and may it also save us from the damaging and stultifying consequences of authoritarian, doctrinaire or institutional socialism. Let us be socialists, but let us never become sheep. Let us seek justice, complete political, economic and social justice, but without any sacrifice of liberty. There can be no life, no humanity, without liberty, and a form of socialism which excluded liberty, or did not accept it as a basis and as the only creative principle, would lead us straight back to slavery and bestiality.

Only after the abolition of the State — the first, the essential condition for real freedom — could society be reorganized, but not from above, not according to some visionary plan, nor by decrees spewed forth by some dictatorial power. This would simply lead, again, to the establishment of a State and to the formation of a ruling 'aristocracy' — i.e. a whole class of people who had nothing in common with the masses, and who would begin to exploit and suppress the people all over again under the pretence of acting in the general interest, or in order to save the State. 'The victory of the Jacobins or the Blanquists would mean the death of the revolution.'

A radical revolution could be brought about only by an attack on all established institutions, and by the abolition of property and its associate, the State. Then it would not be necessary to destroy people and thereby provoke the inevitable reaction which the massacre of the people always causes in every society. Bakunin clearly implied that, once the social, economic and political basis of oppression was destroyed, it would be obvious to nearly all that the new society was good, and impossible for die-hard reactionaries to seize a weapon strong enough to destroy (or even seriously to threaten) the new society.

For Bakunin, revolution had to begin with the dissolution of the State; the disbanding of the army and the police; the abolition of the courts, the burning of all bonds, bills and securities; the repeal of those bourgeois laws which sanctioned private property and their replacement by expropriation. The entire social capital — including public buildings, raw materials, the property owned by Church and State — would be put in the hands of the workers' organizations. At the outbreak of revolution the community would be organized by the 'Permanent Federation of the Barricades'. The council of the revolutionary community would consist of one or two delegates from each barricade, one from each street or neighbourhood; these deputies, with a binding mandate, would always be responsible to the people, and subject to recall.

Bakunin did not mean that there could be a revolution without violence, but that this should be directed against institutions rather than against persons. The revolution should, however, not develop a new authority, i.e. the right to coerce. Those who carried out the repression would do so with the approval of the revolutionaries; this would be the only legitimation for violence in a revolution, since law did not exist. The unavoidable violence should be short, and not lead to an organization invested with authority to repress. In all his writings Bakunin rejected the idea of a 'revolutionary government', of 'Committees of Public Safety', including the so-called 'dictatorship of the proletariat'. For such a new authority, such a 'proletarian State', in theory representing the workers, would lead in practice to a new ruling class.

Revolution meant to overthrow the State because social revolution must put an end to the old system of organization based upon sustained violence, giving full liberty to the masses, groups, communes and associations, and likewise to the individuals themselves. It would destroy once and for all the historic cause of all violence — the power and the very existence of the State, the downfall of which would carry away with itself all the iniquities of juridical right and all the falsehoods of the diverse religious cults, which were simply the consecration, ideal as well as real, of all the violence represented, guaranteed and furthered by the State.

Poverty and despondency were not sufficient to provoke a social revolution. They might lead to local revolts, but were inadequate to arouse whole masses of people. Only when the people were stirred up by a universal idea rooted in the depths of the popular instinct and clarified by events and experience, only when they had a general idea of their rights, could revolution take place. On the other hand, one could not aim at destruction without having at least a vague concept of the new order that should succeed the existing one — the more vividly that future was visualized, the more powerful was the drive to destruction. And, to Bakunin, the nearer that visualization conformed to the developing conditions of the actual society, the more salutary could the results of destructive action be. Hence the importance of social analysis.

But here Bakunin was very cautious: he viewed the pretensions of science with a particularly critical eye. Of course he considered scientific knowledge very useful as a way of transforming the world, but this transformation was not to be directed by an 'academy of scientists'. He sharply opposed 'scientific despotism' as demoralizing to an even higher degree than the despotism of violence, because it corrupted man's thought at its source. The most degrading slavery to which mankind could ever be subjected would be a society ruled by pedants.

We might sum up Bakunin's views on this matter by saying that he expected the scientists to provide the know-how — something of enormous importance to him, in that he regarded science as having a crucial liberating function in society. But he was always categorical in his insistence that it was not the scientist but the free individual who had the right to decide priorities.

Looking back in 1873 to his Hegelian period, Bakunin described the Hegelian universe as a *fata morgana*, suspended between heaven and earth, which was designed to convert the life of its inhabitants into an unbroken chain of somnambulistic fictional constructions. By forcing upon them a metaphysical ideal, they were made unfit for life, or else condemned to do in the real world the reverse of what they hoped for most dearly. Even the materialistic heirs of the Hegelian Left, like Marx, were in the grip of metaphysical abstraction.

Bakunin's social philosophy culminates in the concept of freedom, which for him is not an abstract or metaphysical matter. In this connection he found the idea of God detestable, in contradiction with human freedom. His programme states the negation of God and the principle of authority, divine or human, and also of any tutelage by a man over men. He denies the existence of free will and the right of society to punish, since every human individual, with no exception whatever, is but an involuntary product of natural and social environment. The negation of free will, however, does not connote the negation of freedom. On the contrary, freedom represents the corollary, the direct result, of natural and social necessity. Man can gradually free himself from the natural hostility of the external world with the aid of thought, with the aid of his rational will.

Man starts with animality in order to arrive at humanity, but he is a social animal. He does not create society by means of a free agreement; he is born in the midst of nature, and apart from it he could not live as a human being. Social solidarity is the first human law, freedom is the second. Both interpenetrate and are inseparable from each other, thus constituting *toute l'humanité*, the very essence of humanity. Freedom is not the negation of solidarity; it represents, on the contrary, the development and, so to speak, the humanization of the latter.

The individual freedom of every man becomes actual and possible only through the collective freedom of society, of which man constitutes a part by virtue of a natural and immutable law. Thus respect for the freedom of others is the highest duty of man. To love his freedom and to serve it, this is the only virtue. This is the basis of all morality, and there can be no other.

Bakunin's atheism is therefore not that of an ordinary free-thinker; to him, godlessness is a *sine qua non* of freedom, linked up with his anarchist socialism. The classic exposition of these views is to be found in his best-known and most widely diffused work, *God and the State*.

After his arrival in London at the end of 1861, Bakunin immediately took up his revolutionary propaganda work with regard to Polish and Russian affairs. In 1863 he tried to go to Poland to take an active part in the insurrection that had broken out, but in this he failed. In January 1864 he went to Italy, where he lived for the next three years.

After the failure of the Polish insurrection and — as is now clear from his manuscripts of 1864 — before he turned his attention to Italian affairs, Bakunin lost his belief in national liberation movements as a social and revolutionary force. From now on he advocated a social revolution on an international scale. He was of the opinion that the fall of the Napoleonic Empire would inaugurate a new 1848, and that preparations should be made for this. His main task he now saw as finding revolutionaries to work intimately together to influence coming events and to avoid the mistakes of 1848. To this end he created in Florence in 1864 a secret society, the *Fraternité*, to which he soon gave international ramifications. It consisted only of men and women who temporarily worked together with him on the basis of his programme. The main significance of Bakunin's societies is that they allow us to follow the evolution of his ideas. That they never functioned as organizations is of no consequence. Most of the drafts, pro-grammes and projects that he wrote for these rather ephemeral or even non-existent bodies are a fundamental source of his political and social ideas; they were not meant to be ideological or theoretical discourses. They reflect and are connected with his revolutionary activities for a decade.

Bakunin hoped that the inner and secret circle around him —recruited from among those who most faithfully accepted his programme—could crystallize into a 'moral academy', as it were, the members of which would be completely immune from ambition for power. He hoped that they would be 'invisible pilots in the thick of the popular tempest'. It is an all too frequent misconception to attribute to Bakunin a purely spontaneous strategy. His revolution needed leaders; he even spoke of an 'invisible dictatorship'. But what he denied was that even these selected revolutionaries should have any right to demand from the masses respect or obedience in the name of some mysterious authority of theirs. It would be one of the cardinal functions of the leaders to inculcate in their followers the principle that they should, through the foundation of free associations, prevent all consolidation of authority.

Numbers mean nothing if forces are not organized; the workers' unions could create that conscious will without which no victory was possible. Three men united in organization already formed a serious beginning of strength, but even several hundreds did not constitute an adequate revolutionary force when organized apart from the people.

Bakunin never thought that these small groups could or should start a revolution. Revolutions, he wrote, cannot be brought about either by individuals or by secret societies. They derive from circumstances, from the inevitable course of events, and they can be successful only if they have the support of the masses, the only army of the revolution. There are moments in history when revolutions are impossible and others when they are unavoidable. They ferment for a long time in the depths of the instinctive consciousness of the masses; then they explode, often triggered off by apparently trivial causes. But propaganda and action can prepare the revolution.

All that a well-organized secret society can do is first to assist the birth of the revolution by sowing ideas corresponding to the instincts of the masses, then to channel the revolutionary strength of the people. The revolutionaries are to be without ambition or vanity, capable of acting as intermediaries

between the revolutionary idea and the popular instinct.
A real revolution, Bakunin held, is only that which is made
by the people and not on behalf of the people. Any revolution in which the people are not completely involved, while
remaining the masters of their own decisions, can be successful
only when based on a privileged class, and consequently
should be regarded as a counter-revolutionary movement.
Bakunin also denied that the organization of a mass movement
by a revolutionary nucleus, on the premise that they know
better, imposed a centralized dictatorial authority. Here lies
the difference between Bakunin's 'conspiratorial' methods and
all kinds of 'Blanquist' tendencies and self-styled *avant-garde*
political parties.

In September 1867 the First, and founding, Congress of the
League of Peace and Freedom was held at Geneva. Bakunin
had hoped to use the League to propagate his socialist ideas,
which he proclaimed openly for the first time in his speech at
the Congress. Subsequently, these ideas were laid down in a
'Motivated Proposal to the Central Committee' of the League,
now known by the title *Federalism, Socialism and Anti-theologism*.
When the Second Congress took place, at Berne in September
1868, it became clear, however, that the liberal, democratic
majority would not accept Bakunin's ideas and refused to
include economic and social equality in its programme.
Bakunin then broke away from the League and founded, with
a socialist minority of the Congress, the 'International Alliance
of Socialist Democracy', which decided to adopt the programme of the International and to adhere to it. The Alliance
consisted, for some time, of a public and a secret organization;
the latter, however, was soon disbanded. After correspondence
with the General Council of the International, the International Alliance too was dissolved and its Geneva branch
entered, with a slight change in the original programme, into
the International as an independent section, taking the name
of 'Alliance of Socialist Democracy'.

In the Jura Bakunin participated actively as a propagandist
and an editor of the official organ of the French-speaking
Swiss International. He was a delegate at the Fourth Congress
of the International at Basel in 1869, where he advocated,

against the Marxist thesis, the abolition of the right of inheritance. Already in 1868 an Italian friend and comrade of Bakunin, Giuseppe Fanelli, had founded the first sections of the International in Spain; and soon the Spanish Federation, the largest organization in the International, was to accept Bakunin's collectivist and federalist programme.

Ever since Bakunin had become a member of the International in the summer of 1868, he had rejected the Marxist theory that the working class should be organized in a political party with the purpose of obtaining political power, and by 1872 large parts of the International had come to accept his view. Its historical expression was laid down in the resolution Bakunin drafted for the Congress of Saint-Imier in September 1872, in which it was stated that the proletariat, by seizing political power, would itself become a dominating and exploiting class; therefore, the destruction of all political power was its first duty.

Bakunin held the view that dictatorship — *any* dictatorship, of whatever brand — could have no aim but self-perpetuation, and that it could beget only slavery for the people tolerating it. Freedom could be created only by freedom. The new social organization should be set up by the free integration of workers' associations, villages, communes and regions from below upwards, conforming to the needs and instincts of the people. That was what Bakunin meant by federalism. Smaller groups would federate into greater units. Of course he was well aware that a certain economic centralization was inevitable, as a consequence of the development of large-scale production, but he rejected the view that economic problems could be solved only by political centralization. He insisted on the need for social ownership of property and argued that if the authoritarian State, with its unnatural centralization, became the basis of social organization, the unavoidable result would be the destruction of the liberty of the individual man and of smaller groups, and this would lead to new exploitation and to endless wars.

Bakunin was certainly influenced by the federalist ideas of Proudhon, but the latter had, according to Bakunin, remained an incorrigible idealist all his life, immersed in the

Bible, in Roman law and in metaphysics. Marx, as a thinker, was on the right path. He had established the principle that juridical evolution in history is not the cause but the effect of economic development, and, though he did not originate it, to him belongs the credit for giving it a solid base. On the other hand, remarked Bakunin, Proudhon understood the concept of liberty much better than Marx. Proudhon, when not obsessed with metaphysical doctrine, was revolutionary by instinct — he worshipped Satan and proclaimed anarchism. Quite possibly Marx could have constructed a still more rational system of liberty, 'but he lacks the instinct of liberty; he remains from head to foot an authoritarian.'

According to Bakunin's theory, free productive associations, having become their own masters, would one day expand beyond national frontiers and form one vast economic federation, with a kind of economic council, informed by detailed statistics on a world scale, that would decide and distribute the output of world industry among the various countries, so that there would no longer, or hardly ever, be industrial crises, stagnation, disasters and waste of capital. It goes without saying that these ideas provided the matrix from which was moulded the ideology of the Bakuninist federations, especially those of Italy and Spain, which officially adhered to what came to be known as 'collectivism', or the view that society should consist of free federations of free associations of free workers.

From the Congress in Basel onwards, the word 'collectivism' became a current expression in the International, and the Jurassiens, the Belgians and the French used it as synonymous with anti-State or non-authoritarian communism.

When in July 1870 the Franco-Prussian War broke out, Bakunin immediately realized the revolutionary potentialities of the situation. He believed that a German victory would delay socialism in Europe for at least half a century. After the first victories of the Prussian armies, he feverishly started a campaign with a view to rallying the masses of the French people to continue the fight against the invader and, by using the confusion caused by the defeat of the French and the serious weakening of the French State, to start a revolutionary movement. This, he hoped, might very well spread to Italy and Spain, and could, via the Slav peoples of Austria, extend to Poland and the Ukraine, finally to reach the Russian peasant masses.

In September 1870 Bakunin wrote his *Letters to a Frenchman*, in which he expounded his views of the path the revolutionary movement ought to take. In the existing circumstances, he wrote, the revolution could not be led or organized by Paris, which was absorbed in its own defence. The best and only thing that Paris could do, also in order to save itself, would be to proclaim and encourage the absolute autonomy and spontaneity of all the provincial movements. The provinces, in order to save France and Paris itself, would have to rebel and spontaneously organize themselves, independently of Paris. In this respect, Bakunin thought in the first place of the southeast of France: Marseilles and especially Lyons, the second town of France and traditionally revolutionary. It was here that Bakunin took part, in September, in the insurrectionary movement which proclaimed a 'Federation of Communes'. This was immediately suppressed and he had to flee the country.

In his *Letters to a Frenchman* Bakunin gave practical advice on how to overcome the antagonism between workers and peasants. He regarded the peasants generally as a revolutionary force, though historically the essential role belonged to the proletarians of the cities.

In order to win over the peasants to the side of the revolution, it would be necessary to use great prudence, for ideas and propaganda accepted by the workers could have the opposite effect on the peasants. The fatal antagonism of workers and peasants had to be eliminated, otherwise the revolution would be paralysed. It would be necessary to undermine in fact, and not in words, the authority of the State.

He advocated that delegates should be sent to the villages to promote a revolutionary movement amongst the peasants. Communism or collectivism should not be imposed on them, even if the workers had enough force to do so, because such an authoritarian communism would need the organized violence of the State, and this would lead to the re-establishment of authority and a new privileged class.

What should the revolutionary leaders do (and there should be as few of them as possible) to organize and spread the revolution? They must promote the revolution not by issuing decrees—Bakunin declared himself above all an absolute enemy of revolution by decree, a concept which he considered to be reaction disguised as revolution—but by stirring the masses to action. They must under no circumstances foist any artificial organization upon the masses; on the contrary, they should foster the self-organization of the masses into autonomous bodies, federated from the bottom upward. This could be done through pressure on the most intelligent, the most influential individuals in each locality, to ensure that these organizations, as far as possible, conformed to revolutionary principles. 'Therein', he wrote, 'lies the secret of our triumph.'

After his flight from Lyons Bakunin returned to Locarno. From here he followed eagerly the course of events in France; in particular, of course, the development of the Paris Commune, this 'henceforth historic negation of the State', as he put it.

Mazzini's attack on the vanquished Commune and the persecuted International aroused Bakunin's indignation, and he wrote in four days, at the end of July 1871, his brilliant *Risposta d'un Internazionale a Giuseppe Mazzini*, published in Milan, which made a considerable impression in Italy. Thanks to Bakunin's personal magnetism, which allowed him to cast a spell over visiting young Italian revolutionaries, as well as to his inexhaustible energy in maintaining an extensive correspondence with remote and unusually receptive connections, the International made quick progress in Italy, and an Italian Federation was founded at Rimini in August 1872. By then, of course, his fight with Marx had for some time been quite open. It is worth while to consider briefly the nature of the debate between Bakunin and Marx.

It was after the Fourth Congress of the International at Basel in September 1869 that the controversy between Marx and Bakunin had come plainly into the open. Already before the Congress, Marx, alarmed by Bakunin's increasing influence in the International, which he imagined to be a danger to his theoretical and personal supremacy, had written to Engels: 'If this Russian doesn't take care, he will be excommunicated.' From then on, Marx would see in every opposition to the General Council the hand of Bakunin, the 'intrigues of the Alliance' and of the '*fripouille alliancistè*', and he started an underhand, slanderous campaign against his rival. On the other hand, Marx and Engels underestimated Bakunin's real influence, not only in Switzerland, but also in Italy and Spain, where he had played a decisive role in the foundation of the International — in fact, it was on the collectivist and anti-Statist principles of Bakunin that the political and economic programme of these federations was based.

In his appreciation of the international scene, Bakunin differed from Marx and Engels, not only with regard to the role of the Slavs, but also on the political future of Europe, and he was far from agreeing with them that Bismarck and Victor Emmanuel in their striving towards the unification of their respective countries did useful work for socialism. National unity, with its consequences of political and economic centralization, was, in Marx's view, a prerequisite of socialism. Bakunin, by contrast, feared that this development would lead to a new Caesarism, and after the Franco-Prussian War he predicted an era of endless wars and the danger of the 'Prusso-Germanization' of Europe.

There was also behind the clash between Marx and Bakunin a profound difference in their respective ways of conceiving propaganda methods and revolutionary strategy. This is well known. But to regard the antithesis between Marx and Bakunin as one between organization and conspiracy is erroneous. It is perfectly clear that Bakunin was by no means an enemy of organization. On the contrary, for a successful revolution, he wrote, 'brought about through the force of circumstances', a real force, one that knows what has to be done, is necessary: a serious international organization of workers' organizations in all countries, capable of replacing the political and economic world of the State and the bourgeoisie.

The issues at stake in the discussion were of quite another, deeper nature. To put it shortly, while both Marx and Bakunin agreed on the final aims (a Stateless, classless society), Bakunin thought Marx wrong on quite obvious grounds. Marx's model of the path to revolution was primarily based on a notion of economic inevitability; in Marx's model, none of the steps revolutionaries had to take were to be seen as socialist in their apparent qualities—they were to be seen as socialist only in that future results would prove them to have led to socialism. Bakunin doubted that all this, especially the dictatorship of the proletariat, would necessarily lead to socialism. He advocated socialist (i.e., libertarian) means in order to achieve a socialist (i.e., libertarian) society.

The practical side of this theoretical controversy was glaringly obvious after the Conference of London in September 1871, where Marx tried to transform the International, till then a confederation of autonomous federations, into an organization of political parties. A resolution to that effect— that the working class should organize itself into a political party with a view to the conquest of political power—as well as the arbitrary methods of the General Council, of which Marx was the dominating figure, led to a protest, first from the Jura Federation and then from other national federations as well.

At the Fifth Congress of the International at The Hague in 1872, a majority decided to make the principle of the conquest of political power obligatory for the whole International. By a majority vote Bakunin was expelled from the International. An investigating committee concluded that he had 'tried to establish and perhaps succeeded in establishing a society in Europe named the Alliance, with rules on social and political matters entirely different from those of the International'. This 'amazing document', a 'blend of naivety and irrelevance' as E. H. Carr put it, missed the point, however. In fact, the International had no official programme. The Provisional Rules of 1864 and the Statutes of 1866 were vague enough to admit all kinds of organizations and schools of thought. The policy of the International was worked out at its congresses and by its federations.

The accusation that Bakunin wanted to replace the programme of the International by that of the Alliance was likewise

unjustified.* Again and again Bakunin stressed the point
that it was very important that the programme of the International should be general enough to unite the workers of all
countries. It is true that the Bakuninist programme was not in
accordance with the Marxian resolution on the conquest of
political power adopted at The Hague. But this resolution had
to be confirmed by the federations, and in this case it was
rejected by the overwhelming majority of the International.

Another fact was added to the charge, quite beyond the
committee's terms of reference. It consisted in a letter written
in February 1870 by Sergej Nečaev in the name of a non-
existent foreign bureau of a quite imaginary Russian revolutionary centre; this rather threatening letter ordered the
representative of a Petersburg editor, for whom Bakunin was
translating the first volume of *Das Kapital*, to release the latter
from his obligations, though advance money had been paid.
Marx had got hold of this document and read it in a secret
session of the committee, implying that it had been sent on
Bakunin's instigation. In fact, however, Bakunin was not
responsible for its composition and was wholly unaware of its
contents. When Marx produced the letter in order to discredit
Bakunin, he was informed of this fact, but may have thought
that the end justified the means.

On September 15th, 1872, an Extraordinary Congress of the
Jura Federation was held at Saint-Imier; here all the resolutions of the Hague Congress were rejected and a proposal was
made to elaborate a free and federative pact between all
federations. One hour after this Congress closed an International Congress opened in the same room, attended by
delegates from the Italian, Spanish and Jura Federations and
representatives of French and American sections. Five resolutions, partly drawn up by Bakunin, were passed, in which the
broad outlines of this 'pact of friendship, solidarity and
mutual defence' were sketched, the conclusions of the Hague
Congress condemned, and the new General Council rejected.

* If Bakunin inserted his atheist principles in his Alliance programme—
an often-repeated charge against him—this had no sectarian implications.
He had no intention of enforcing his programme on the International; but,
on the other hand, as has already been pointed out, atheism was an integral
part of his social philosophy.

The Congress declared that the destruction of all political power was the first duty of the proletariat and added that to organize a new political power, besides being deceitful, would be just as dangerous for the proletariat as any existing government. The proletarians of all countries, it was stated, should reject every compromise with bourgeois politics, including parliamentarism.

At its Congress in Brussels in December 1872, the Belgian Federation adhered to the Saint-Imier pact. Within a few months the Spanish, Italian and Jura Federations confirmed their statements, and the Sixth Congress of the International was held at Geneva in September 1873.

Marx had continuously lost ground in the International to Bakunin and his ideas. The decision of the Hague Congress to remove the General Council to New York meant the end of the Marxian International, and its next Congress was a debacle.

Bakunin, for his part, was worn out. His health now steadily deteriorated; he was tired and depressed after the catastrophe in France, as well as by the slanderous campaign against him, and not very optimistic about even distant revolutionary prospects. He died in Berne on July 1st, 1876.

In one of his last manuscripts he had written: 'My name will live on, and to this name will attach the real, legitimate glory of having been the pitiless and irreconcilable adversary, not of their own persons, but of their authoritarian theories and ridiculous, odious pretensions to world dictatorship.' He was right in attributing a lasting quality to his work. Bakunin's collectivist anarchism, and his theory of revolution, ultimately formed the ideological and theoretical basis of anarcho-syndicalism, and of democracy based on workers' councils. The Russian soviets of 1917 and the Spanish anarcho-syndicalist experiment of 1936, to mention only the two best-known examples, showed that the doctrines of Bakunin made sense, to say the least. The problems of State and revolution, socialism and dictatorship, revolutionary strategy and tactics, will be studied infinitely more profitably with the knowledge of Bakunin's work.

Amsterdam, Autumn 1972   ARTHUR LEHNING

I   FROM A LETTER OF BAKUNIN TO HIS SISTERS

This extract is taken from Jurij Steklov's edition of M. A. Bakunin, *Sobranie Sočinenij i Pisem 1828–1876*, vol. I, 'Dogegelianskij Period, 1828–1837' (Moscow, 1934), pp. 325–31. It is here translated from the Russian by Olive Stevens.

Tver, August 10th, 1836

My splendid, my delightful friend Tanyusha, you have no idea what an impression your letter made on me. I am sure you cannot feel all the sweetness and harmonious happiness which I experienced as I read it. And you ask me whether I need your friendship, whether it can contribute to my happiness! Does this mean that you do not realize, you do not see, that to separate myself from you would, for me, be tantamount to breaking with the one and only expression of my inner life? At last I have found this heavenly harmony within my family, I have found this pure and sacred tranquillity, a tranquillity so full of energy, so full of love, a tranquillity which has in it all the future that I have been seeking. And so you belong to me, so you are my sisters, not only by the instinctive laws of nature, but by the life led by our kindred spirits and the identity of our eternal aims.

Oh, now I no longer fear the external world! I have found in it what was essential for me; I have found in it more than it usually gives: the echo of your hearts, and your selfless, sacred love. I have found in it golden souls, that belong to eternity rather than to this world. If all external misfortunes and assaults were rolled into one, and tried out their strength on me, they could not wreck my bliss. My bliss cannot be influenced by them, for it is not of this world! My inner life is strong because it is not founded on vulgar expectations or on worldly hopes of outward good fortune; no, it is founded on

NOTE. In the texts that follow, the asterisked footnotes are Bakunin's own, unless otherwise stated. The editor's explanatory notes are in a numbered sequence and will be found at the back of the book.

the eternal purpose of man and his divine nature. Nor is my inner life afraid, for it is contained in your love, and our love is as eternal as our purpose. Oh, I no longer fear the external world; I will find the means to carry out the plans I have in mind. Now I am not alone, my spirit has been sanctified by your sacred, selfless love. And yet you ask me if I really need your love! It has sanctified and exalted me, it has made me worthy of my calling, and, with its mighty strength, has drawn me on to my everlasting aim. Love is the mighty rod which brings out living water from the rock. Yes, I am happier than I deserve; I am now more than ever under an obligation; I delight in what I have not deserved, and I must deserve the joy given me by providence. Yes, I understand that a sacred duty has been laid upon me, and I will carry it out; I am stronger than I have ever been, I am strengthened by your love!

The earth, my friends, is no longer our inheritance. Our happiness is in heaven and so is our life. Our spiritual activities do not seek the earth or its delights: no, they have already been captivated by true delight, and are indifferent to all that is earthly. Our religion, my friends, is eternal, it contains within it all that is most beautiful, all that is noble. It has nothing in common with what is physical or dead. Our religion gives life to everything, and burning passion and high ideals are sanctified by it: art, learning, all that is noble in man, all that can excite his soul, all this comes from religion, all this is sanctified by the holy baptism of love that is divine and not of this world, and must reveal the eternal approach of the divinity in man to the divine purpose, to that which has neither end nor beginning, and yet both begins and ends in all that exists. My friends, my religion has made our hearts eternal, it has given us love, love to all mankind; our personal love and our personal life strive to flow into the absolute love and into eternal life.

At this moment I do not hate anybody. I bless everybody. Let us have pity for those who have still not reached our state of bliss. Let us hate only evil, and not the unhappy victims of evil, for they are human beings, and, although they have noi fully developed themselves, they too have the right to their divine inheritance, and they alone exclude themselves from it.

They are miserable; we must pity them, we must increase our efforts to tear them out of this condition of death and apathy. We must not allow failure to drive us to despair: when will has moral force behind it, it is all-powerful. The moral will of man is the will of God, and nothing can stop its plans being carried out.

And so, my friends, having conquered the moral world, we have at the same time conquered the omnipotent. We desire Good, and Good must prevail in spite of all the onslaughts of Evil. This is our purpose: to widen more and more the sphere of our activity, and at the same time the sphere of our love and our happiness; to cleanse our hearts of all that is worldly, and, continually ennobling them, make them worthy sacrifices of eternal Love; to carry the eternal heaven of our souls into the external world, and in this way to raise the earth up to heaven; ever to put into practice, in the external world, ideas that are fine, lofty and noble; ever to draw nearer to a sacred world, and to be united in a mutual purpose, mutual hopes and mututal sacred love; ever to increase and ever to purify our personal love and our personal joy. My friends, what can stop us, what can make us despair? External, passing sufferings cannot quell the determined soul, and in fact have the opposite effect on it, purifying and ennobling it. Man is never so ready to accept the truth as when he is spiritually sad and in a condition of suffering. It is sorrow that calls up eternity, armoured in finality, and it is sorrow that reveals on high the divinity of man. But sorrow must be conscious, and then it can turn into joy. It is only terrifying for those who have no spiritual life, and who are still not acquainted with heaven. He who has not suffered cannot truly love, because suffering is an act of liberation for man from all earthly expectations, and from his bondage to instinctive, unconscious delights. Therefore, he who has not suffered is not free, and without freedom there is no love, and without love there is no happiness and no bliss.

Therefore, my dear Varya, let not your outward wretchedness lead you to despair. It should, on the contrary, be the basis of your happiness, of your true, divine happiness, of a happiness that is beyond the reach of profanation. Your wretchedness sanctifies you, my dear friend; and if you will

2

allow it to penetrate your consciousness, it will illuminate you and set you on high. Let religion become the basis and reality of your life and your actions, but let it be the pure and single-minded religion of divine reason and divine love, and not that religion which you used to profess, not that religion which strove to disassociate itself from everything that makes up the substance and life of truly moral existence. This religion is not the restricting whim of some capricious god, nor is it a narrow, icy feeling which opposes all that is perfect in the world of morals and intellect, and threatens to sink itself in a pathetic sphere of activity containing neither ideas nor feelings nor love. At least it is not that religion which was totally inconsistent with true love, and which might have destroyed a soul as full of fire and as thirsting for love and all that is highest as yours, so that it could not have been revived by any moral force. No, my dear friend, let yourself be penetrated by true religion, by the religion of Christ, for ever free of the defiling touch of those who, in attempting to understand it, inevitably tried to lower it to their level. Look at Christ, my dear friend; He suffered so much, and did not even have the joy of being completely understood by those around Him, and yet He was happy, for He was the Son of God. His life was divine through and through, full of self-denial, and He did everything for mankind, finding His satisfaction and His delight in the dissolution of His material being and in the fact that He was the saviour of mankind. He is the Son of God for He belongs to all men, He is the Son of Man, and He is our pattern. And if we were able to rise up to Him, or rather if we had sufficient faith, sufficient strength, sufficient moral and intellectual breadth to desire this—for indeed we could do this, because we should, and because we *All* should, then Nothing is impossible —if we could at last attain even a distant impression of the bliss and divine love which He tasted, we should behave as He did, for His suffering was indeed bliss.

This is what religion does. Outward sufferings proceed from the outer world independent of our will. If we are conscious of ourselves without possessing an inner life, then we become the victims of outward sufferings, and we suffer without the possibility of being saved by any sort of outward miracle. But if religion and an inner life appear in us, then we become conscious of our strength, for we feel that God is within us, that same God who creates a new world, a world of absolute freedom and absolute love. Because we have been baptized in this world and are in communion with this heavenly love, we feel that we are divine creatures, that we are free, and that we have been ordained for the emancipation of humanity, which is still enslaved, and of the universe, which has remained a victim of the instinctive laws of unconscious existence. Everything that lives, that exists, that grows, that is simply on the earth, should be free, and should attain self-consciousness, raising itself up to the divine centre which inspires all that exists. Absolute freedom and absolute love — that is our aim; the freeing of humanity and the whole world — that is our purpose.

Pagan stoicism was strong and stoical only because of the instincts of human nature; but let us be strong in the knowledge of our divine nature and of our purpose. Love and eternal bliss create the strength that is within us.

Have a careful look at this religion; be assured that all that is perfect in man — art, learning, feeling, thought — belong to it, and that all these varied aspects of human life merely express its different forms. Understand thoroughly that every moment of human life is the revelation of the Holy Spirit, the sole and absolute spirit which speaks in man and forms his consciousness, and that, finally, the gospel is the main source of revelation, and Jesus Christ is above all the Son of God. If you understand all this thoroughly, your life, instead of being poor and restricted, as it was, will become rich and eternal, and the life of all mankind, past and present, will become yours. You will find kindred souls who will no longer be able to remain strangers to you, since you and they will have the same origins. Their purpose, their suffering, their hopes, their moments of extreme joy, will be yours, and will belong to you as they do to them. That is the only and indivisible, harmonious entity, which strives towards absolute harmony and absolute love.

These are the feelings and these are the ideas which you ought to develop in yourself. Let all your actions, even the smallest thing that engages your attention, come under the eternal influence of this absolute idea, or, to put it more accurately, let your actions always reproduce this absolute idea. And then you will be happy and strong. Your husband, with his insignificant and limited ideas, will have to recognize this strength, even if he does not understand you. You will reproduce yourself in your son, who will owe his rebirth and his new life to you, and, having given him this divine life, you will make him yours for ever. For as divine life does not end and is no other than eternal consciousness, and as all consciousness begins with consciousness of its own origins, your son will acknowledge you as his mother throughout eternity, and the bonds uniting you will take on more and more of a divine character and will become the source of undying bliss.

And we too, my dear friends, will never be parted, since all that is connected with consciousness is eternal. The good we render each other is the framework and earthly part of our divine life, and that is why we can never be parted, for all that enters into the divine life is as eternal as that life itself. But why should I talk of parting? Since all human development is progressive, our mutual love will become stronger; since all who are brothers and sisters in the Lord will continue thus for ever, the bonds uniting them will become more and more holy. In this way, our life is not, and never will be, exclusively an inner life. We have our individual ways of expressing ourselves, and we always shall have. Are we not completely happy, as happy as it is possible to be, considering that we live in an imperfect world and that our faculties are still imperfectly developed? But our aim is perfection, and as we are preordained for perfection, our mutual love and with it our common happiness will also become perfect...

II THE REACTION IN GERMANY

A Fragment from a Frenchman

'Die Reaktion in Deutschland. Ein Fragment von einem Franzosen' first appeared in Arnold Ruge (ed.), *Deutsche Jahrbücher für Wissenschaft and Kunst*, nos. 247–51 (Leipzig, October 17th–21st, 1842). This translation by Mary-Barbara Zeldin, first published in James M. Edie, James P. Scanlan and Mary-Barbara Zeldin (eds.), with the collaboration of George L. Kline, *Russian Philosophy* (Chicago: Quadrangle Books, 1965), vol. I, pp. 385–406, is reprinted by permission of Quadrangle Books. Copyright © 1965 by Quadrangle Books, Inc.

Freedom, the realization of freedom: who can deny that this expression today stands at the head of the agenda of history? Friend and foe must admit it; indeed, no one dares openly and fearlessly to profess that he is an *enemy* of freedom. But the expression, the profession, does not make the reality, as the Gospel well knows. Unfortunately, there is still a multitude of people who in fact, in their innermost hearts, do not believe in freedom. And so, for freedom's sake, it is worth our while to concern ourselves with these people. They are of very different kinds.

First of all we encounter high-placed, aged and experienced people who in their youth were themselves dilettantes in political freedom—a distinguished and rich man takes a piquant pleasure in speaking about freedom and equality, and so doing makes him twice as interesting in business. These men now try to hide their physical and spiritual laxity under the veil of that much abused word, 'experience', now that their former interest has left them along with their capacity for youthful vitality.

There is no profit in speaking with these people: they were never serious about freedom and freedom was never for them a religion which offers the greatest pleasure and the highest bliss only by means of the most extreme conflicts, of the bitterest griefs, and of complete, unconditional self-denial. There is no profit in speaking with them, if only because they are old and are going to die soon *bon gré mal gré*.

There are also, unfortunately, many young people who share the same convictions or, rather, lack of any conviction. These belong either, and for the most part, to the aristocracy which in its essence has long been politically dead in Germany, or to the burgher, commercial and officer classes. There is nothing you can do with these either, and, indeed, even less than with the first category of prudent and aged people whose death is already so near. Those had at least a glimmer of life, but the latter are lifeless and dead men from the very beginning. Completely involved in their paltry, vain, or monetary interests, and completely occupied by their commonplace concerns, they have not even the slightest conception of life and of what goes on around them. Had they not heard something of history and of the development of the spirit in school, they would apparently believe that nothing in the world had ever been different from the way it is now. They are colorless, ghostly beings. They can do neither good nor ill. We have nothing to fear from them, for only that which is alive can be effective, and, since it is no longer fashionable to associate with ghosts, we too shall not waste our time with them.

But there is still a third category of adversaries of the principle of revolution: that is the *Reactionary party* which emerged all over Europe soon after the Restoration. In politics it is called *Conservatism*, in jurisprudence the *Historical School*, and in the science of speculation, *Positive Philosophy*. With these we want to speak. It would be poor taste on our part if we ignored their existence and acted as if we considered them insignificant. On the contrary, we shall honestly admit that they are now everywhere the ruling party. And more still: we want to concede that their present power is not due to a play of chance but has its deep ground in the development of the modern Spirit. Anyhow, I concede no true power to chance in history—history is a free, but consequently necessary, development of free Spirit, so that if I wanted to call the present supremacy of the Reactionary Party a chance event I would, in so doing, render the worst possible service to the democratic creed which uniquely and alone is founded on the unconditional freedom of Spirit. Such an evil, deceitful sedative would be much more dangerous for us: unfortunately we are as yet still far from understanding our position and, in the only too frequent misunderstanding of the true source of our power and of the nature of our enemy, we must either wholly lose our courage, depressed by the dreary picture of daily drudgery, or—and this is perhaps still worse—since a vital human being cannot long tolerate despair, there comes upon us a groundless, boyish, and fruitless exuberance. Nothing can be more useful to the Democratic party than the recognition of its weakness and of the relative strength of its adversary at this stage. Through this recognition the Democratic party first steps out of the uncertainty of fantasy and into the reality in which it must live, suffer, and, in the end, conquer. Through this recognition its enthusiasm becomes discreet and humble. Only if it first comes to an awareness of its holy, priestly office through this painful contact with reality; only if it recognizes through the endless difficulties which stand everywhere in its way and which flow not only from the obscurantism of its adversaries, as it often seems to imply, but also and rather from the fullness and totality of human nature which cannot be exhausted in abstract theoretical propositions—only if it first recognizes through these difficulties the inadequacy of its whole present existence and thus comes to understand that its enemy is at hand not only externally but also and much more internally, and that it must therefore begin by conquering its internal enemy; only if it first convinces itself that Democracy not only stands in opposition to the government and is not only a particular constitutional or politico-economic change, but a total transformation of that world condition and a herald of an original, new life which has not yet existed in history; especially only if it first comes to understand that Democracy is a religion, if it thus through this awareness itself becomes religious, that is, *permeated* by its principle not only in thought and reasoning, but true to it also in real life down to life's smallest manifestations, only then will the Democratic party really conquer the world.

Consequently, we want to admit candidly that the present power of the Reactionary party is not contingent but necessary.

It has its ground not in the inadequacy of the Democratic *principle* — this is indeed that of the equality of man realizing itself in freedom and thus also is the most intrinsic, universal, and all-embracing, in a word the unique essence of the Spirit self-operating in history. The present power of the Reactionary party is due, rather, to the inadequacy of the Democratic party which has not yet reached an affirmative consciousness of its principle and therefore exists *only* as the *negation* of the prevailing reality. As such, as mere negation, the whole fullness of life is necessarily external to it; it cannot yet develop this fullness out of its principle which it conceives almost wholly negatively. Consequently, it has up to now been only a party and not yet the living reality; it has been the future, not the present. This fact, that the democrats constitute only a party — and, indeed, a weak party so far as its external existence is concerned — and that their being only a party presupposes the existence of another, opposed, strong party — this fact alone should already give them an explanation of their true, essential, inherent deficiency. With respect to its essence, its principle, the Democratic party is the universal, all-embracing one, but, with respect to its existence, it is only a particular one, the Negative, against which stands another particular one, the Positive. The whole significance and the irrepressible power of the Negative is the annihilation of the Positive; but along with the Positive it leads itself to destruction as this evil, particular existence which is inadequate to its essence. Democracy does not yet exist independently in its affirmative abundance, but only as the denial of the Positive, and therefore, in this evil state, it too must be destroyed along with the Positive, so that from its free ground it may spring forth again in a newborn state, as its own living fullness. And this self-change of the Democratic party will not be merely a *quantitative* change, i.e., a broadening of its present particular and hence evil existence: God save us, such a broadening would be the leveling of the whole world and the end result of all of history would be absolute nothingness — but a *qualitative* transformation, a new, vital, and life-creating revelation, a new heaven and a new earth, a young and magnificent world in which all present discords will resolve themselves into harmonious unity.

The inadequacy of the Democratic party can still less be

mitigated by transcending the one-sidedness of its existence as
a party through an eternal mediation with the Positive—this
would be a vain endeavor, for the Positive and the Negative
are once and for all incompatible. Insofar as it is isolated in its
contradiction to the Positive and is taken for itself, the Negative
appears at first to be empty and lifeless; and this apparent
emptiness is also the principal reproach which the Positives
make to the Democrats—a reproach which, however, rests
only on a misunderstanding. In fact, as a thing in isolation,
the Negative is not at all; as such it would be nothing. It
exists only in contradiction to the Positive. Its whole being, its
content and its vitality are simply the destruction of the
Positive. 'Revolutionary propaganda,' says the Pentarchist,
'is, in its deepest essence, the *negation* of the existing conditions
of the state; for, with respect to its innermost nature, it has no
other program than the destruction of whatever order prevails
at the time.' But is it possible that that whose whole life is
only to destroy should externally be reconciled with that
which, according to its innermost nature, it must destroy? Only
half-men who seriously take sides neither with the Positive nor
with the Negative can argue in such a fashion.

There are two major divisions within the Reactionary
party today: to the one belong the pure *Consistent* reactionaries,
and to the other the inconsistent, *Compromising* reactionaries.
The first interpret the contradiction in its pure form; they feel
indeed that the Positive and the Negative get along no more
than fire and water; and, since they do not see in the Negative
its affirmative aspect and so cannot believe in the Negative,
they quite rightly conclude that the Positive must be maintained through a complete suppression of the Negative. That
they do not perceive that the Positive is as such a Positive which
they defend only insofar as the Negative opposes it, and that
consequently, in the event of a complete victory over the
Negative, it would no longer be the Positive but rather its
contradictory, the completion of the Negative—that they do
not perceive this must be forgiven them, since blindness is the
main characteristic of all that is positive and insight belongs
only to the Negative. We must be very grateful to these
gentlemen, however, in our evil and unscrupulous times, when
so many seek out of cowardice to conceal from themselves

the strict consequences of their own principles in order thus to escape the danger of becoming disturbed in the artificial and weak system of their pretended convictions. These gentlemen are sincere, honest; they want to be whole men. One cannot talk much with them, for they never want to enter into a sensible conversation. It is so difficult for them now, since the dissolving poison of the Negative has spread everywhere; it is so difficult, indeed almost impossible, for them to maintain themselves in pure Positivity that they withdraw from their own reason and must be afraid of themselves, of the slightest attempt to demonstrate, which would be to refute, their convictions. They feel this strongly and hence also speak crossly when they must speak. And yet they are honest and whole men, or, more correctly, they want to be honest and whole men. Just like us, they hate everything that is half-hearted for they know that only a whole man can be good and that halfheartedness is the putrid source of all evil.

These fanatical reactionaries accuse us of heresy. If it were possible they would perhaps even call out of the arsenal of history the subterranean power of the Inquisition in order to use it against us. They deny us all that is good, all that is human. They see in us nothing other than embodied Anti-christs, against whom every means is permitted. Shall we repay them with the same coin? No; it would be unworthy of us and of the great cause whose agents we are. The great principle in whose service we have pledged ourselves gives us, among many other advantages, the fine privilege of being just and impartial without, by so being, harming our cause. Nothing partial can use truth itself as a weapon, for truth is the refutation of all one-sidedness; whereas all one-sidedness must be partial and fanatical in its utterance, and hate is its necessary expression, for it can maintain itself in no other way than by opposing, through a violent repulsion, all other one-sidedness, even if as legitimate as itself. One-sidedness by its very presence presupposes the presence of other one-sidednesses, and yet, as a consequence of its essential nature, it must exclude these in order to maintain itself. This conflict is the curse which hangs over one-sidedness, a curse innate to it, a curse which transforms into hatred in their very utterance all the good sentiments that are innate in every man as man.

We are infinitely more fortunate in this respect. As a party we indeed stand in opposition to the Positives and fight them, and all evil passions are awakened also in us through this fight. Insofar as we ourselves belong to a party, we are also very often partial and unjust. But we are not only this Negative party set in opposition to the Positive: we have our living source in the all-embracing principle of unconditional freedom, in a principle which contains in itself all the good that is contained only in the Positive and which is exalted above the Positive just as over ourselves as a party. As a party we pursue only politics, but as a party we are justified only through our principle; otherwise we would have no better ground than the Positive. Hence, we must remain true, even contrary to our self-preservation, to our principle as the only ground of our power and of our life; i.e., we must eternally transcend ourselves as this one-sided, merely political existence in the religion of our all-embracing and all-sided principle. We must not only act politically, but in our politics also act religiously, religiously in the sense of freedom of which the one true expression is justice and love. Indeed, for us alone, who are called the enemies of the Christian religion, for us alone is it reserved, and even made the highest duty even in the most ardent of fights, really to exercise love, this highest commandment of Christ and this only way of true Christianity.

And so we want to be just also with respect to our enemies, we want to recognize that they *are striving really* to want the good, that indeed in their nature they are called to the good, to a vital life, and that they have deviated from their true destiny only owing to an incomprehensible misfortune. We are not speaking of those who have joined their party only in order to be able to give vent to their evil passions. There are, unfortunately, many Tartuffes in every party; we are speaking only of the sincere defenders of Consistent Positivism. These strive after the good, but they cannot effectively will it; this is their great misfortune, they are divided in themselves. In the principle of freedom they see only a cold and prosaic abstraction — to which many prosaic and dry defenders of freedom have greatly contributed. They see only an abstraction which excludes all that is vital, all that is beautiful and holy. They do not perceive that this principle is by no means to be confused with its current evil and merely negative existence, and that it is only as a living self-affirmation which has transcended the Negative as well as the Positive that it can conquer and that it will realize itself. They believe — and this belief is unfortunately still shared by many adherents of the Negative party itself — that the Negative tries to diffuse itself as such, and they think, just as we do, that the diffusion would be the leveling of the whole spiritual world. At the same time, in the directness of their feeling, they have a wholly justified endeavor toward a vital full life, and, since they find in the Negative only its leveling, they turn back to the past, to the past as it was before the birth of the contradiction between the Negative and the Positive. They are right insofar as this past really was in itself a living whole and as such appears much more vital and much richer than the divided present. Their great mistake, however, consists in this, that they think that they can re-create it in its past vitality; they forget that the past totality can by now appear only in the amorphous and cracked reflection of the present inevitable contradiction which that totality entails, and that the totality, as positive, is only its own corpse, with its soul torn from it, i.e., the corpse as delivered up to the mechanical and chemical processes of thought. As adherents of blind Positivism they do not understand this, whereas with respect to their nature as vital men they feel this deficiency of life full well. And since they do not know that by the very fact that they are Positive they have the Negative within them, they throw onto the Negative the whole blame for this deficiency, and the whole weight of their urge for life and truth, by this impotence to satisfy itself, turns into hate. This is the necessary inner process in every Consistent Positivist, and therefore I say also that they are really to be pitied, since the source of their endeavor is yet almost always honest.

The *Compromising* Positivists hold an entirely different position. They distinguish themselves from the Consistent Positivists in the first place in that, more rotted than these by speculative disease of the time, they not only do not condemn the Negative unconditionally as an absolute evil but concede to it a relative, transitory justification; and, in the second place, in that they do not possess the same energetic purity, a purity for which the Consistent, ruthless Positivists at least strive and which we have designated as the characteristic of a full, complete, and honest nature. The standpoint of the Compromisers we may in contrast designate as that of *theoretical dishonesty*; I say theoretical because I would rather avoid any practical, personal accusation and because I do not believe that a personally evil will could really intervene obstructively in the development of Spirit; although it must be admitted that theoretical dishonesty by its very nature almost always reverts into a practical one.

The Compromising Positivists are cleverer and have more insight than the Consistent ones. They are the clever men, the theorists *par excellence*, and to that extent they are also the chief representatives of the present time. We can apply to them what was said in a French journal at the beginning of the July Revolution about the *Juste-milieu*: The Left says, 2 times 2 are 4; the Right, 2 times 2 are 6; and the *Juste-milieu* says, 2 times 2 are 5. But they would take this amiss. Hence we want to try to investigate their unclear and difficult essence in all earnestness and with the deepest respect for their wisdom. It is much more difficult to deal with them than with the Consistent ones: the latter have the practical energy of their convictions; they know and they speak in clear words and say what they mean to say; they hate, just as we do, all uncertainty, all confusion, for as practically energetic beings they can breathe only in a pure and clear air. With the Compromisers, however, it is a curious matter. They are wily; oh, they are clever and wise! They never permit the practical impulse toward truth to destroy the meticulously patchworked edifice of their theory. They are too experienced, too clever, to grant a gracious hearing to the beseeching voice of simple, practical conscience. From the height of their position they look down on it with condescension and, if we say only the simple is true and real because only such a thing can work creatively, they maintain in reply that only the composite is true, for it has cost the greatest pains to piece such a thing together and because it is the only characteristic by which one can distinguish them, the clever people, from the stupid and uneducated mob. Consequently it is very difficult to deal with them, because all is known to them; because, as worldly-wise people, they consider it an unforgivable weakness to let themselves be astonished by anything; because they have by their thinking penetrated every corner of the natural and spiritual universe, and because, after this long and laborious speculative journey, they have reached the conviction that it is not worth the bother to enter into real, vital contact with the real world. It is difficult to come to an understanding with these people, since, just like the German constitutions, they take back with the right hand what they offer with the left. They never answer 'yes' or 'no'; they say: 'To a certain extent you are right, but, yet ...' and, if they have nothing left to say, they say: 'Yes, it is a curious thing.'

And yet we want to try to contend with them. The party of the Compromisers, despite its inner lack of principle and its inability to effect anything on its own, is today a powerful, indeed the most powerful party—numerically, of course, not with respect to its content. It is one of the most important signs of the times, and so we dare not ignore it and bypass it.

The whole wisdom of the Compromisers consists in this, that they maintain that two opposing trends are as such one-sided and therefore untrue; but, they argue, if the two members of the contradiction are untrue when taken abstractly in themselves, then the truth must lie in their middle, and so one must inter-correlate them to arrive at the truth. This reasoning at first appears irrefutable: indeed, we have ourselves admitted that the Negative, insofar as it is opposed to the Positive and is self-oriented in this opposition, is one-sided. Then does it not necessarily follow from this that the Negative is essentially fulfilled and completed by the Positive? And are not the Compromisers right in wanting to reconcile the Positive and the Negative? Yes, if this reconciliation is possible; but is it really possible? Is not the annihilation of the Positive the only meaning of the Negative? If the Compromisers ground their position on the nature of contradiction, namely on the fact that two opposing one-sidednesses are as such mutually dependent, then they must accept and recognize each nature to its full extent; they must do this for the sake of consistency, in order themselves to remain true to their own position. For the side of the contradiction which is favorable to them is inseparable from its unfavorable side; but this unfavorable side consists in this, that it is not positive but *negative*, destructive, to give priority to one member over the other. The gentlemen are to be referred to Hegel's logic, where the category of contradiction is so beautifully treated.

Contradiction and its immanent development constitute a keynote of the whole Hegelian system, and since this category is the chief category of the governing spirit of our times, Hegel is unconditionally the greatest philosopher of the present time, the highest summit of our modern, one-sided, *theoretical* cultural formation. Indeed, just like this summit, just by the fact that he has comprehended and thus resolved this category, just by this fact is he also the beginning of a necessary self-resolution of modern cultural formation: as this summit he has already gone above theory — granted that at the same time he is still within theory — and has postulated a new, practical world which will bring itself to completion by no means through a formal application and diffusion of theories already worked out, but only through an original act of the practical autonomous Spirit. Contradiction is the essence not only of every specific, particular theory, but also of theory in general, and so the dialectical phase of its comprehension is simultaneously the phase of the fulfilment of theory; but its fulfilment is its self-resolution into an original and new, practical world, into the real presence of freedom. But this is not yet the place to develop this further, and we want to turn again to the discussion of the logical theory of contradiction.

Contradiction itself, as the embracing of its two one-sided members, is total, absolute, true. One cannot reproach it with one-sidedness or with the superficiality and poverty which are necessarily bound up with one-sidedness, since it is not only the Negative, but also the Positive, and since, as this all-embracing thing, it is total, absolute, all-inclusive fullness. This entitles the Compromisers to forbid that one of the two one-sided members be taken in the abstract, and to require that they be comprehended as a totality in their necessary union, in their inseparability. Only the contradiction is true, they say, and either of its opposed members, taken by itself, is one-sided and thus untrue; hence we have to grasp the contradiction in its totality in order to have truth. But this is just where the difficulty begins. Contradiction is indeed truth, but it does not exist as such, it is not there as this totality; it is only a self-subsisting, hidden totality, and its existence is just the conflicting cleavage of its two members, the Positive and the Negative. Contradiction as the total truth is the inseparable unity of the simplicity and cleavage of itself in one; this is its implicit, hidden, but thus also at first incomprehensible nature, and just because this unity is a hidden one, contradiction exists also one-sidedly as the mere cleavage of its members. It is present only as Positive and Negative, and these mutually exclude each other to such an extent that this mutual exclusion constitutes their whole nature. But then how are we to comprehend the totality of contradiction? Here there appear to remain two ways out: either we must arbitrarily abstract from the cleavage and flee to the simple totality of the contradiction, which totality is prior to the cleavage—but this is impossible, because the incomprehensible is simply incomprehensible, and because contradiction in itself exists immediately only as cleavage, without this it is not at all; or we must in a maternal way try to reconcile the opposed members. And in this consists the whole effort of the Compromiser School. Let us see whether they really succeed.

The positive appears at first to be the restful, the immobile. It is Positive indeed only because it rests in itself without disturbance and because it contains nothing that it could negate;* only because it contains no movement, since every movement is a negation. The Positive is just the sort of thing in which immobility as such reposes, the sort of thing which is reflected in itself as the absolutely immobile. But reflection on immobility is inseparable from reflection on mobility; or rather they are one and the same reflection, and so the Positive, absolute rest, is positive only in contrast to the Negative, absolute unrest. The Positive is internally related to the Negative as its own vital determination. Thus the Positive has a double place in relation to the Negative: on the one hand it rests in itself and in this apathetic self-sufficiency contains nothing of the Negative; on the other, however, and just because of this rest, as something in itself opposed to the Negative, it actively excludes the Negative; but this activity of exclusion is a motion

* ' ... *in sich nichts hat, was es negieren konnte*'—does Bakunin perhaps mean 'that could negate it'?—TRANS.

and so the Positive, just because of its positivity, is in itself no longer the Positive, but the Negative; in that it excludes the Negative from itself, it excludes itself from itself and drives itself to destruction.

Consequently, the Positive and the Negative do not, as the Compromisers think, have equal justification. Contradiction is not an equilibrium but a preponderance of the Negative, which is its encroaching dialectical phase. The Negative, as determining the life of the Positive itself, alone includes within itself the totality of the contradiction, and so it alone also has absolute justification. What, someone will perhaps ask me; have you not yourself admitted to us that the Negative, taken in itself abstractly, is just as one-sided as the Positive, and that the diffusion of its evil existence would be a leveling of the whole world? Yes, but I was speaking only of the present existence of the Negative, of the Negative insofar as, excluded from the Positive, it is peacefully self-oriented and so is positive; as such it is also negated by the Positive, and the Consistent Positivists, in denying the existence of the Negative, its peaceful self-orientation, are performing both a logical and a holy service — although they do not know what they do. They believe that they are negating the Negative while, on the contrary, they are negating the Negative only insofar as it is making itself Positive; they awaken the Negative from its Philistine repose, to which it is not fitted, and they lead it back to its great calling, to the restless and ruthless annihilation of every positively existing thing.

We shall grant that the Positive and the Negative, if the latter is peacefully and egoistically self-oriented and so untrue to itself, have equal justification. But the Negative should not be egoistic; it should lovingly surrender to the Positive in order to consume it and, in this religious, faithful, and vital act of denial, to reveal its inexhaustible and pregnant nature. The Positive is negated by the Negative and the Negative in turn is negated by the Positive: what, then, is common to both and overlaps both? Denial, destruction, passionate consumption of the Positive, even if this latter seeks slyly to hide itself in the guise of the Negative. The Negative is justified only as this ruthless negation, but as such it is absolutely justified, for as such it is the action of the practical Spirit invisibly present in the contradiction itself, the Spirit which, through this storm of destruction, powerfully urges sinful, compromising souls to repentance and announces its imminent coming, its imminent revelation in a really democratic and universally human religion of freedom.

This self-resolution of the Positive is the only possible reconciliation of the Positive with the Negative, for it is the immanent, total motion and energy of the contradiction itself, and thus any other means of reconciling them is arbitrary, and everyone who intends another reconciliation merely proves in so doing that he is not permeated with the Spirit of the times and thus is either stupid or unprincipled; for a man is really intelligent and moral only if he surrenders himself whole-heartedly to this Spirit and is permeated by it. Contradiction is total and true—the Compromisers themselves grant this—but as total it is wholly vital and the energy of its all-embracing vitality consists, as we have already seen, just in this in-cessant self-combustion of the Positive in the pure fire of the Negative.

What do the Compromisers do now? They grant us this whole thing; they acknowledge the totality of contradiction just as we do, except that they rob it, or rather want to rob it, of its motion, of its vitality, of its whole soul, for the vitality of contradiction is a practical power incompatible with their impotent half-souls, but by this fact superior to their every attempt to stifle it. The Positive, as we have said and demon-strated, has no justification if taken in itself; it is justified only insofar as it negates the rest, the self-orientation of the Negative; insofar as it unconditionally and determinately excludes the Negative and thus maintains it in its activity—thus far it becomes actively negative. This activity of negation to which the Positivists are raised through the unsurmountable power of contradiction invisibly present in every living being and which constitutes their only justification and the only characteristic of their vitality—it is just this activity of negation which the Compromisers want to prohibit them. As a consequence of a singular incomprehensible misfortune, or rather from the whole comprehensible misfortune of their practical lack of principle, their practical impotence, they acknowledge in the Positive just that which is dead within themselves, rotten, and worthy only of destruction—and they reject that which constitutes their whole vitality: the vital fight with the Negative, the vital presence in them of contradiction.

They say to the Positives: Gentlemen, you are right in approving the rotted and withered remains of conventionality; one lives so prettily and comfortably in these ruins, in this irrational rococo world whose air is as healthful for our consumptive souls as the air of a cow barn is for consumptive bodies. So far as we are concerned, we would have settled ourselves in your world with the greatest pleasure, a world where not reason and the reasonable determination of the human will, but long existence and immobility are the measure of the true and the holy, and where consequently China, with its mandarins and its bamboo sticks, must obtain as absolute truth. But what can we do, Gentlemen? The times are bad; our common enemies, the Negatives, have won much ground. We hate them as much as and perhaps even more than you do yourselves, since, in their lack of restraint, they permit themselves to scorn us; but they have become powerful and one must willy-nilly be mindful of them in order not to be wholly destroyed by them. So don't be so fanatical, Gentlemen; grant them a little space in your society. What matters it to you if they succeed in your* historical museum to some ruins which, though very venerable, yet are wholly fallen into decay? Believe us, entirely pleased by the honor which you thus render them, they will conduct themselves very quietly and discreetly in your honorable society, for, in the end, they are but young people who, 'embittered by poverty and a lack of carefree conditions,' shout and make so much noise only because they hope thus to obtain a certain importance and a comfortable place in society.

Then they turn to the Negatives and say to them: your endeavor is honorable, Gentlemen. We understand your youthful enthusiasm for pure principles and we have the greatest sympathy for you, but, believe us, pure principles in their purity are not applicable to life; life requires a certain dose of eclecticism, the world cannot be conquered as you wish to do it, you must yield something in order to be able to mold it; otherwise you will wholly damage your position in

* Reading *'Ihrem'* for *'ihrem'*—TRANS.

it. And, as one tells of the Polish Jews, that in the last Polish war they wanted at the same time to serve both warring parties, the Poles as well as the Russians, and were hanged by both, so these poor souls vex themselves with the impossible business of external reconciliation, and for thanks are despised by both parties. It is too bad that present times are too weak and too listless to apply the Law of Solon to them!

People will reply: these are mere phrases. The Compromisers are mostly honest and scientifically educated people. There are a great many universally esteemed and highly placed persons among them, and you have presented them as unintelligent and unprincipled men! But what can I do about it, since it is so true? I do not want to attack anyone personally; the inner man is for me an inviolable sanctuary, something incommensurable, on which I shall never permit myself a judgment; this inner core can have infinite worth for the individual himself, but for the world it is real only insofar as it expresses itself and it is only that which does express itself. Every man is really only what he is in the real world, and you surely don't expect me to say that black is white.

Yes, people will retort, their endeavor seems to be black to you, or rather grey; but in fact the Compromisers want and aim only at progress and they further it far more than you do yourself, for they go to work prudently and not excessively as do the Democrats who want to blast the whole world to pieces. But we have seen what such people imagine the progress intended by the Compromisers to be; we have seen that the Compromisers want nothing else but the stifling of the only vital principle of our present time, otherwise so poor: the stifling of the creative and pregnant principle of resolving motion. They perceive just as we do that our time is a time of contradiction. They grant us that this is an evil, internally torn condition, but, instead of letting it turn over into a new, affirmative, and organic reality through the completion of the contradiction, they want, by means of an endless gradation, to preserve it eternally in its present shabby and consumptive state. Is that progress? They say to the Positives: 'Hang on to the old, but permit the Negatives at the same time to resolve it gradually.' And to the Negatives: 'Destroy the old, but not all at once and completely, so that you will always have something to do. I.e., each of you remain in your one-sidedness, but we, the elect, will prove the pleasure of totality for ourselves.' Wretched totality with which only wretched souls can be satisfied! They rob contradiction of its moving, practical soul and rejoice that they can command it arbitrarily. The great present-day contradiction is not for them the practical power to which every vital man must ruthlessly surrender himself in order to remain vital, but only a theoretical toy. They are not permeated by the practical Spirit of the times, and hence they are also immoral men. Yes, they who so glory in their morality are immoral men, for morality is impossible outside the religion of free humanity which alone brings heavenly joy. One must repeat to them what the author of the Apocalypse said to the Compromisers of his own day:

I know thy works, that thou art neither cold nor hot. I would thou wert cold or hot.

But because thou art lukewarm, and neither cold nor hot, I will begin to vomit thee out of my mouth.

Because thou sayest: I am rich, and made wealthy, and have need of nothing: and knowest not, that thou art wretched, and miserable, and poor, and blind, and naked.*

But, people will say to me, are you not, with your irreconcilable extremes, relapsing into the abstract position long ago refuted by Schelling and Hegel? Did not Hegel, whom you value so highly, himself make the quite correct observation that just as little can be seen in pure light as in pure darkness, and that only the concrete unity of the two makes vision possible at all? And does not Hegel's greatest service consist in his having demonstrated how every vital existence is vital only because it has negation not outside itself but within itself as an immanent condition necessary to its vitality; and how, if it were only positive and had its negation outside itself, it would be motionless and lifeless? I know that very well, Gentlemen! I grant you that a vital organism, for instance, is vital only in that it carries the germ of death within it. But if you want to quote Hegel to me, then you must quote him in full. Then you will observe that the Negative is the condition necessary for the life of this particular organism only so long as it is present in it

* *Rev.* 3:15–17—TRANS.

merely as a dialectical phase asserted in that phase's totality; that there comes a point, however, when the gradual effect of the Negative is suddenly interrupted in such a manner that the Negative is transformed into an independent principle, and this moment is the death of this particular organism, a dialectical phase which in Hegelian philosophy is characterized as the transition of nature into a qualitatively new world, into the free world of Spirit.

The same is repeated in history. The principle of theoretical freedom, for instance, already made itself felt in the deceased Catholic world from the start of that world's existence; this principle was the source of all heresies in which Catholicism was so rich. But without this principle Catholicism would have been motionless, and so it was at the same time the principle of its vitality, though only so long as the principle was maintained in its totality as pure dialectical phase. Protestantism also arose gradually: it had its beginning in the beginning of Catholicism itself; but once this gradualness was interrupted, the principle of theoretical freedom raised itself to a self-sustaining, independent principle. Then the contradiction was revealed in its purity for the first time, and you well know, Gentlemen, you who call yourselves Protestants, what Luther answered to the Compromisers of his day as they offered their services to him.

You see, my view of the nature of contradiction is susceptible not only of logical, but also of historical corroboration. But I know that no proof will avail since, in your lifelessness, you undertake no occupation so willingly as the mastery of history. It is not for nothing that you have come to be called dry arrangers.

'We are not yet defeated,' the Compromisers will probably reply to me. 'All that you say about contradiction may be true, but there is just one thing we cannot grant you, namely, that things are now, in our time, so bad as you maintain. Of course, there are contradictions in the present day, but they are not so dangerous as you assert. Look, there is tranquility everywhere, everywhere movement has subsided. No one thinks of war, and the majority of nations and of men now strain every nerve to preserve peace, for they well know that the material interests which today appear to have become the main concern of politics and of universal culture cannot be promoted without peace. How many important inducements to war and to the dissolution of the present order of things have there not been since the July Revolution! In the course of these twelve years there have been such entanglements that no one could possibly have expected them to be peacefully unraveled; moments when a universal war seemed almost inevitable and when the most fearful storms threatened us; and yet all difficulties were gradually resolved, all remained quiet, and peace seems to have established itself on earth for ever.'

Peace, you say. Yes, what is now called peace. I maintain in reply, however, that contradictions have never been so sharply presented as now, that the eternal contradiction, which is the same at all times except that it increases in intensity and develops itself ever more in the course of history, that this contradiction of freedom and unfreedom has advanced and soared to its last and highest summit in our time, otherwise a time so similar to the period of dissolution of the heathen world. Have you not read the mysterious and awesome words, *Liberté*, *Égalité* and *Fraternité* on the foreground of the Temple of Freedom erected by the Revolution? And do you not know and feel that these words intimate the complete annihilation of the present political and social world? Have you heard nothing of the storms of the revolution, and do you not know that Napoleon, this so-called tamer of Democracy, diffused its leveling principles over all of Europe, like a worthy son of the Revolution? Have you not also perhaps heard something of Kant, Fichte, Schelling, and Hegel, or do you really know nothing of a philosophy which established the same leveling revolutionary principle in the intellectual world—namely, the principle of the autonomy of Spirit? And do you not comprehend that this principle stands in the highest contradiction to all current positive religions, to all present-day churches?

'Yes,' you will answer, 'but these contradictions belong to past history; the Revolution was most recently subdued in France itself by the wise reign of Louis-Philippe, and modern philosophy by one of its greatest originators, by Schelling himself. Contradiction is now everywhere dissolved, in all spheres of life.' And do you really believe in this dissolution, in this subjugation of the Spirit of revolution? Are you then blind and deaf and have you no eyes or ears for what goes on around you? No, Gentlemen, the Spirit of revolution is not subdued, it has only gone back into itself again, after having convulsed the whole world in its foundations by its first appearance; it has only sunk into itself in order soon to reveal itself again as an affirmative, creative principle, and right now it is burrowing—if I may avail myself of this expression of Hegel's—like a mole under the earth. And that it is not working for nothing you can see from the many ruins with which our religious, political, and social flooring is covered. You speak of resolution, of reconciliation! Just look around you and tell me what has remained alive of the old Catholic and Protestant world. You speak of the subjugation of the Negative principle! Have you read nothing of *Strauss*, *Feuerbach* and *Bruno Bauer*, and do you not know that their works are in everyone's hands? Do you not see that the whole of German literature, books, brochures, newspapers, indeed, the works of the Positivists themselves, are unwittingly and unwillingly permeated by this negative Spirit? And you call this reconciliation and peace!

You well know that humanity, owing to its high calling, can be satisfied and pacified only by the adoption of a universally practical principle, by a principle which intensely concentrates within itself the thousand different manifestations of spiritual life. But where is this principle, Gentlemen? You must surely now and then experience vital, human moments during the course of your existence, otherwise so dismal; moments when you cast aside the petty concerns of your daily life and yearn for the true, for the noble, for the holy. Answer me honestly, now, your hand on your heart, have you ever anywhere found something vital? Have you ever discovered under the ruins which surround us this world you long for, where you could wholly surrender yourselves and be once more born anew in this great communion with all humanity? Is this world perchance Protestantism? But Protestantism is abandoned to the most ghastly anarchy: into how many different sects is it not rendered? 'Without great, universal enthusiasm there are only sects and no public idiom,' says Schelling; but the current Protestant world is as far from being permeated with a general enthusiasm as heaven is from earth; it is rather the most prosaic world one can imagine, Well, then, is it perchance Catholicism? But where is Catholicism's ancient splendor? Has Catholicism, which formerly ruled over the whole world, now not become an obedient tool of an alien, immoral policy? Or do you perhaps find your peace of mind in the contemporary state? Yes, that would really be a fine peace of mind! The state is currently in the throes of the deepest internal conflict, for without religion, without a powerful universal conviction, the state is impossible. Just look at France and England if you want to convince yourselves of this; I shall not say anything about Germany!

Finally, study yourselves, Gentlemen, and tell me honestly, are you pleased with yourselves, and can you be pleased with yourselves? Are you not, without exception, dismal and shabby appearances of our dismal and shabby times? Are you not full of conflicts? Are you whole men? Do you really believe in anything? Do you really know what you want and can you want anything at all? Has modern speculation, the epidemic of our time, left a single sound part in you, and are you not permeated by this disease and paralysed and broken by it? In fact, Gentlemen, you must confess that our times are dismal times and that we are all its still more dismal children!

On the other hand, however, visible appearances are stirring around us, indicating that the Spirit, this old mole, has brought its underground work to completion and that it will soon come again to pass judgment. Everywhere, especially in France and England, social and religious societies are being formed, wholly alien to the present political world, societies which derive their life from new sources quite unknown to us and develop and diffuse themselves in silence. The people, the poor class, which without doubt constitutes the greatest part of humanity; the class whose rights have already been recognized in theory; which, however, up to now is still condemned by its birth, by its ties with poverty and ignorance, as well, indeed, as with actual slavery—this class, which constitutes the true people, is everywhere assuming a threatening attitude and is beginning to count the ranks of its enemy, weak as compared to it, and to demand the actualization of the rights already conceded to it by everyone. All peoples and all men are filled with a kind of premonition, and everyone whose

vital organs are not paralysed faces with shuddering expecta-
tion the approaching future which will speak out the redeem-
ing word. Even in Russia, in this endless and snow-covered
kingdom which we know so little and which perhaps a great
future awaits, even in Russia dark clouds are gathering,
heralding storm. Oh, the air is sultry and filled with lightning.

And therefore we call to our deluded brothers,
    Repent, repent, the Kingdom of the Lord is at hand!

To the Positivists we say: open the eyes of your mind; let the
dead bury the dead, and convince yourselves at last that the
Spirit, ever young, ever newborn, is not to be sought in fallen
ruins! And we exhort the Compromisers to open their hearts to
truth, to free themselves of their wretched and blind wisdom,
of their intellectual arrogance, and of the servile fear which
dries up their souls and paralyses their movements.

Let us therefore trust the eternal Spirit which destroys and
annihilates only because it is the unfathomable and eternally
creative source of all life. The passion for destruction is a
creative passion, too.

III FROM A LETTER OF BAKUNIN TO HERZEN AND OGAREV

These extracts are taken from M. Dragomanov's edition of Bakunin's letters, *Pis'ma M. A. Bakunina k A. I. Gercenu i N. P. Ogarevu* (Geneva, 1896), pp. 169–87. There exists a good German translation, *Michail Bakunins Sozial-politischer Briefwechsel mit Alexander Iw. Herzen und Ogarjow* (Stuttgart, 1895); in this the letter is printed on pp. 116–33. These extracts are here translated from the Russian by Olive Stevens.

Ischia, July 19th, 1866

... Now let us turn to our affairs. You reproached me with inactivity at a time when I was more active than at any other; I refer to the last three years. The one thing I was engaged in was the foundation and organization of a secret international social revolutionary society. I already know that temperamentally you are unable to undertake anything of this sort, and also that your efforts are directed elsewhere, but I believe absolutely in the strength and honesty of your character, and therefore I am sending you the complete programme, and a statement of the principles and the organization of the society, in a special sealed packet which the Countess will give you.[1] Pay no need to the literary defects of the work, but consider the essence of the matter. You will find a lot of unnecessary detail, but remember that I wrote surrounded by Italians, who, alas, are almost unacquainted with socialist ideas. In particular I had to struggle against so-called national feelings and ideas, and against the loathsome patriotic bourgeois rhetoric which extols Mazzini and Garibaldi. After three years' hard work I managed to achieve positive results. We have friends in Sweden, Norway and Denmark, in England, in Belgium, in France, in Spain and in Italy; there are also the Poles, and there are even a few Russians. In southern Italy the greater part of Mazzini's organization, the Falangia Sacra, have come over to us. I append herewith a short programme of our Italian national organization.[2] In one of his dispatches to his

59

friends in Naples and Sicily, Mazzini formally denounced me, calling me, incidentally, *il mio illustre amico Michele Bakunin.* This attack on me is rather inconvenient, as there are many government agents among Mazzini's falanges, especially in Sicily, and he could seriously compromise me. Fortunately the government here does not yet understand the socialist movement and consequently is not afraid of it. In this they show their stupidity, for after the complete shipwreck of all the other parties, ideas and motives, there is only one possible live force in Italy, and that is the social revolution. All the people, especially in southern Italy, are pouring to us in their masses, and what we lack is not raw material, but educated people, able and devoted enough to give shape to this material. There is a great deal to be done; we are hindered by backwardness, and the absence of financial resources is awful, but in spite of all this, in spite even of the diversion of war, we are in no way cast down, we do not lose patience (and we need a lot of it), and, although slowly, every day we move forward ...

Believe me, Herzen, your notorious 'change of front', which you were so proud of, and with which you intended to prove to us 'theoretical revolutionaries' your practical and tactical expertise, was an utter failure. Your concessions to the decadent upper-class literary opinion of Russia, which you imagined to be united in spirit and ferociously ready to defend the integrity of the empire over the Polish question, would have been a mistake even if all the people of Great Russia were of this opinion. Can it be that truth and right stop being truth and right simply because a whole nation is against them? There are moments in history when people and parties, strong in the principles and truth that inspire them, must have the courage to stand alone for the sake of the common good and their own honour, and they must be certain that sooner or later the truth will draw to them new and living forces, and not old bald-headed renegades whose return always damages the cause. Truth is not abstract, and it is not arbitrarily produced by an individual; it is the most absolutely logical expression of those principles which live and move in the masses. Sometimes, because of shortsightedness and ignorance, the masses are deflected from the straight road leading right to their goal, and they often fall into the hands of governmental and privileged classes, and become tools for the achievement of aims directly opposed to their real interests. Surely people who understand the position, and who understand what one can do and what one cannot do, should not become involved and tell lies for the sake of being popular. Is this what our notorious practicality consists of? Is not this the same practicality that forced Mazzini to emasculate the republican banner in 1859, to write to the Pope and the King and seek a bargain with Cavour, so that concession after concession led to the complete, self-inflicted demolition of the republican party in Italy. It is this practicality that turned the national hero Garibaldi into the silent servant of Victor Emmanuel and Napoleon III. They say that Mazzini and Garibaldi had to bow to the will of the people. The whole point is that they did not bow to the will of the people, but that they bowed to the will of a small bourgeois minority that had taken upon itself the right to speak in the name of a people indifferent to all these political changes. The same thing has happened with you. You took the wailing of literary landowners as an expression of national feeling and you were scared, and this is what caused the change of front, the flirtation with bald-headed friends and deceivers, and new petitions to the Tsar, as well as articles like the one of the first of May of this year, which I would not have signed for anything in the world.[3] Not for anything in the world would I have thrown a stone at Karakozov, or called him, in the press, a fanatic or an upper-class man with a chip on his shoulder, just at the time when all the mean, boot-licking upper-class literary bureaucrats of Russia are cursing him, and in cursing him hope to gain favour with the Tsar and the government—just at the time when our bald-headed friends in Moscow and in Petersburg are saying with delight, 'Now Mikhail Nikolaevich will put him on the rack,' and when he is enduring all Muravyev's torments with incredible courage. We have no right whatsoever to judge him without knowing anything about him or the causes that led him to his well-known action. Like you, I think that no good can come of regicide in Russia, and I am even ready to agree that it would be definitely harmful, for it would arouse a reaction favourable to the Tsar, but I am not at all surprised that not everybody is of this opinion, and that in the stress of the present situation, which may well be intolerable, a man has come forward who is less philosophically sophisticated and therefore has more energy than we have, and who imagines that the Gordian knot can be cut with one stroke. I sincerely respect him for thinking this and for accomplishing his purpose ...

To sum up, there is no doubt that at the present time your propaganda has not even a tenth of the influence it had four years ago. The chimes of your *Bell*[4] ring out and are lost nowadays in empty space, hardly drawing any attention to themselves. It is clear that it rings out to no purpose and does not publish what it should. There are only two ways open to you; either you should close down the *Bell*, or you should give it a new angle. You must make a decision. What should the new angle consist of? The first thing to decide is for whom are you writing. Who is your public? The people do not read, therefore it is impossible for you to influence the people directly from abroad. You should guide those whose position enables them to influence the working class, in fact precisely those people whom you have systematically estranged by your practical concessions and your attitude to the establishment and to the bald-headed friends and deceivers. And first of all you should renounce any pretensions, hopes or intentions of influencing the course of events, the Tsar or the government. No one listens to you there; the fact is that they laugh at you. Everybody there knows where they are going and what they want, and they also know that the Government of All the Russias cannot exist by any other aims or methods than those of St Petersburg. If you turn your attention to that world, you will only lose precious time and compromise yourself to no purpose. Seek a new public among the young people, among the half-educated pupils of Chernyshevsky and Dobrolyubov, among the Bazarovs and the Nihilists, for they have life and energy and strong, straightforward determination ... This is the public that needs a blaze of light, and you cannot frighten it by telling the truth. Preach practical discretion and caution to it, but give it the whole truth, so that in the light of this truth it may know where it should go and where it should lead the people. Free yourselves, rid yourselves of elderly fears and elderly conceptions, of all flanking movements, tactics and exercises; stop being followers of Erasmus, become Lutherans, and you will regain the faith you gave to the cause and your former eloquence and your former strength; then, and only then, will the prodigal children who deserted you return to you in penitence, seeking to be taken back, because they will have heard again in your voice the voice of the leader, and woe unto you, if you consent to take them back.

IV PRINCIPLES AND ORGANIZATION OF THE INTERNATIONAL BROTHERHOOD

This manuscript of 1866 was published in Max Nettlau, *The Life of Michael Bakounine. Michael Bakunin. Eine Biographie*, vol. I (London, 1896–8), pp. 221–33 and 209–13. It is here translated from the French by Steven Cox.

I. *Aim of the society*

1. The aim of this society is the triumph of the principle of Revolution in the world, and consequently the radical overthrow of all presently existing religious, political, economic and social organizations and institutions and the reconstitution first of European and subsequently of world society on the basis of *liberty, reason, justice* and *work*.

2. This kind of task cannot be achieved overnight. The association is therefore constituted for an indefinite period, and will cease to exist only on the day when the triumph of its principle throughout the world removes its *raison d'être*.

II. *Revolutionary catechism*

1. *Denial of the existence of a real, extra-terrestrial, individual God*, and consequently also of any revelation and any divine intervention in the affairs of the human world. *Abolition of the service and worship of divinity*.

2. In replacing the worship of God by *respect* and *love for humanity*, we assert *human reason* as the one criterion of truth; *human conscience* as the basis of justice; *individual and collective liberty* as the only creator of order for mankind.

3. *Liberty* is the absolute right of all adult men and women to seek no sanction for their actions except their own conscience and their own reason, to determine them only of their own free will, and consequently to be responsible for them to themselves first of all, and then to the society of which they are a part, but only in so far as they freely consent to be a part of it.

4. It is quite untrue that the freedom of the individual is

bounded by that of every other individual. Man is truly free only to the extent that his own freedom, freely acknowledged and reflected as in a mirror by the free conscience of all other men, finds in their freedom the confirmation of its infinite scope. Man is truly free only among other equally free men, and since he is free only in terms of mankind, the enslavement of any one man on earth, being an offence against the very principle of humanity, is a denial of the liberty of all.

5. Every man's *liberty* can be realized, therefore, only by the *equality* of all. The realization of liberty in legal and actual equality is *justice*.

6. There is only one dogma, one law, one moral basis for men, and *that is liberty*. To respect your neighbour's liberty *is duty*; to love, help and serve him, *virtue*.

7. *Absolute rejection of any principle of authority and of raison d'État.* Human society, which was originally a natural fact, prior to liberty and the awakening of the human mind, and which later became a religious fact, organized on the principle of divine and human authority, must now be reconstituted on the basis of liberty, henceforward to be the sole determinant of its organization, both political and economic. *Order in society must be the outcome of the greatest possible development of all local, collective and individual liberties.*

8. The political and economic organization of society must therefore not flow downwards, from high to low, and outwards, from centre to circumference, as it does today on the principle of unity and enforced centralization, *but upwards* and *inwards*, on the principle of free association and free federation.

9. *Political organization.*
It is impossible to determine a concrete, universal and compulsory norm for the internal development and political organization of nations, since the existence of each is subordinate to a host of variable historical, geographical and economic factors which never permit of the establishment of an organizational model equally applicable and acceptable to all. Furthermore, any undertaking of this nature, being utterly devoid of practical utility, would militate against the richness and spontaneity of life, which delights in infinite diversity, and would in addition be contrary to the very principle of liberty. Nevertheless, there do exist *essential, absolute conditions* without

3

which the practical realization and organization of liberty will always be impossible. These conditions are:

9(*a*). *The radical abolition of all official religion and every privileged or State-protected, -financed or -maintained Church.* Absolute freedom of conscience and propaganda for all, each man having the unlimited option of building as many temples as he pleases to his gods, whatever their denomination, and of paying and maintaining the priests of his religion.

9(*b*). Seen as religious corporations, Churches shall enjoy none of the political rights which will belong to productive associations, shall be unable to inherit or possess wealth in common, excepting their houses or establishments of prayer, and shall never be allowed to participate in the upbringing of children, since their sole aim in life is the systematic negation of morality and liberty, and the practice of sorcery for profit.

9(*c*). *Abolition of Monarchy, Republic.*

9(*d*). *Abolition of class, rank, privilege and distinction in all its forms. Complete equality of political rights for all men and all women; universal suffrage.*

9(*e*). *Abolition,* dissolution and moral, political, legal, bureaucratic and social bankruptcy of the *custodial, transcendental,* centralist *State,* lackey and alter ego of the Church, and as such the permanent source of poverty, degradation and subjugation among the people. As a natural consequence, *abolition of all State universities*—public education must be the exclusive prerogative of the free communes and associations; *abolition* of *State magistracy*—all judges to be elected by the people; abolition of the *criminal and civil codes currently in force in Europe*—because all of these, being equally inspired by the worship of God, State, family as a religious and political entity, and property, are contrary to human rights, and because *only by liberty* can the code of liberty be created. *Abolition* of *banks,* and *all other State credit institutions. Abolition* of *all central administration, bureaucracies, standing armies* and *State police.*

9(*f*). Immediate and direct election of all public officials, both civil and judicial, as well of all national, provincial and communal councillors or representatives, by popular vote, which is to say by the universal suffrage of all adult men and women.

9(*g*). *Reorganization* of each region, taking as its basis and starting point *the absolute freedom of individual, productive association and commune.*

9(*h*). *Individual rights.*

(i) The right of every man or woman to be completely supported, cared for, protected, brought up and educated from birth to coming of age in all public, primary, secondary, higher, industrial, artistic and scientific schools at the expense of society.

(ii). The equal right of each to be advised and assisted by the latter, as far as possible, at the outset of the career which each new adult will freely choose, after which the society which has declared him completely free will exercise no further supervision or authority over him, decline all responsibility towards him, and owe him nothing more than respect and if necessary protection for his liberty.

(iii). The liberty of every adult man and woman must be absolute and complete freedom to come and go, openly to profess any shade of opinion, to be idle or active, immoral or moral, in other words to dispose of his own person and his own belongings as he pleases and to be answerable to no one; freedom either to live honestly, by their own labour, or shamefully, by exploiting charity or individual trust, given that such charity and trust be voluntary and be proffered by adults only.

(iv). Unconditional freedom for every variety of propaganda, whether through conversation, the press or in public or private meetings, without any constraint but the natural corrective power of public opinion. Absolute liberty of associations, not excepting those whose aims may be or seem to be immoral, and even including those whose aim is the corruption and [destruction] of individual and public liberty.

(v). Liberty cannot and should not defend itself except by means of liberty, and it is a dangerous misconception to advocate its limitation under the specious pretext of protection. Since morality has no other source, incentive, cause and object than liberty, and is itself inseparable from liberty, all restrictions imposed on the latter with the intention of safeguarding the former have always turned against it.

Psychology, statistics and the entire course of history prove that individual and social immorality have always been the necessary consequence of bad public and private education, of the absence or breakdown of public opinion, which never develops or improves its moral level except by way of liberty alone, and above all of defective social organization. As the famous French statistician Quetelet has pointed out, experience shows that it is always society which prepares the ground for crime, and that the wrongdoer is only the predestined instrument of its commission. It is pointless, therefore, to level against social immorality the rigours of a legislation which would encroach upon the freedom of the individual. On the contrary, experience shows that repression and authoritarianism, far from preventing its excesses, have always deepened and extended it in those countries so afflicted, and that private and public morality have always gained or lost to the extent that the freedom of individuals has broadened or narrowed. So that in order to moralize present-day society, we must first embark upon the outright destruction of that entire political and social organization which is based upon inequality, privilege, divine authority and contempt for humanity. And once having rebuilt it on the basis of the utmost equality, justice, work and an education inspired exclusively by respect for humanity, we should provide it for its guardian with public opinion, and for its soul with the most absolute liberty.

(vi). Yet society must not remain totally defenceless against parasitic, mischievous and dangerous individuals. Since labour is to be the basis of all political rights, society — a province, a nation, each within its individual borders — will have the power to remove [these rights] from all adult individuals who, being neither sick, disabled nor old, live at the expense of public or private charity, together with the obligation to restore them as soon as they begin to live by their own labour once again.

(vii). Since the freedom of every individual is inalienable, society shall never allow any individual whatsoever legally to alienate his freedom or to engage upon any contract with another individual on any footing but the utmost equality and reciprocity. It shall not, however, have the power to disbar a man or woman so devoid of any sense of personal dignity as to contract a relationship of voluntary servitude with another individual, but it will consider them as living off private charity and therefore unfit to enjoy political rights *throughout the duration of that servitude*.

(viii). All persons who have been deprived of their political rights shall likewise lose the right to rear and keep their children. In case of infidelity to a freely contracted commitment, or in the event of an overt or proven infringement of the property, the person or especially the liberty of a citizen, whether native or foreign, society shall apply those penalties specified by its laws against the offending native or foreigner.

(ix). Absolute abolition of all cruel and degrading sentences, corporal punishment and the death penalty as sanctioned and enforced by the law. Abolition of all those indefinite or protracted punishments which leave no hope and no real possibility of rehabilitation, since crime ought to be considered as sickness, and punishment as cure rather than social retaliation.

(x). Any individual condemned by the laws of any society, commune, province or nation shall retain the right not to submit to the sentence imposed on him, by declaring that he no longer wishes to be part of that society. But in such a case the society in question shall have the concomitant right to expel him from its midst and to declare him outside its warrant and protection.

(xi). Having thus reverted to the natural law of an eye for an eye, a tooth for a tooth, at least inside the territory occupied by that society, the individual shall be liable to robbery, ill-treatment and even death without any cause for alarm. Any person will be able to dispose of him like a dangerous animal, although never to subject him or use him as a slave.

9(*i*). *Rights of Associations.*

Working men's co-operative associations are a new development in history; we are witnessing their birth at this moment, and can only imagine but not determine the vast expansion they will undoubtedly undergo and the new political and social conditions to which they will give rise. It is possible, indeed highly probable, that eventually, bursting the bounds of the present-day communes, provinces and even States, they will provide the whole of human society with a new constitution, no longer divided into nations but into different industrial groupings, and organized according to the requirements not of politics but of production. That is for the future to decide. As for ourselves, we can only assert this absolute principle, that *whatever their purpose, all associations, like all individuals, must enjoy absolute liberty*. No society, and no part of society, be it commune, province or nation, has the right to prevent free individuals from freely associating, for no matter what purpose, be it religious, political, scientific or artistic, not even if it proposes to corrupt that society and exploit the innocent and the gullible, *except in the case of minors*.

Resisting charlatans and harmful associations is strictly a matter for public opinion. But society has the right and duty to refuse the social guarantee, legal recognition and political and civic rights to any association, as a collective body, which by virtue of its purpose, rules and statutes runs counter to the fundamental principles of the social constitution and whose membership stands in any other relationship but that of total equality and reciprocity. Nevertheless, society could not disbar the members themselves solely because of their participation in associations not regularized by the social guarantee. The difference between regular and irregular associations will therefore be as follows: associations legally recognized as collective bodies will by the same token have the right to bring charges against all individuals, whether members or outsiders, as well as all other regular associations defaulting on commitments towards them. Associations not recognized by law will not possess this right in their capacity as collective bodies, and will therefore be exempt from any legal responsibility, since all their commitments must be null and void in the eyes of a society which has not sanctioned their collective existence (although none of their members will be exempt from any individual commitments they may undertake).

9(j). The division of a country into regions, provinces, districts and communes, or into departments and communes, after the French model, will naturally depend on the pattern of each country's historical customs, present requirements and special nature. So there can only be two common and obligatory principles for any country which seriously intends to organize liberty within itself. *The first is that all organization must proceed upwards, from the commune to the central unit of the country, the State, by way of federation. The second is that between commune and State there must be at least one autonomous intermediary — the department, region or province.* Otherwise the commune, in the narrow sense of that term, would always be too weak to withstand the uniformly and despotically centralizing pressure of the State, which would necessarily reduce every country to the despotic level of monarchist France, as we have twice seen demonstrated in that country, because despotism has always been rooted far more in the centralized organization of the State than in the naturally despotic inclinations of kings.

9(*k*). The basis of any country-wide political organization must be *the absolutely autonomous commune, always represented by the majority vote of all the inhabitants — adult men and women alike.* No authority has the right to interfere in its life, legislation and domestic administration. It appoints and dismisses, by election, all civil servants — administrators and judges — and administers communal property and finances without supervision. Each commune will have the undisputed right to devise its own legislation and constitution, independent of any higher sanction. But in order to join the provincial federation and to become an integral part of a province its individual charter must fully comply with the fundamental principles of the provincial constitution and be subject to the sanction of that province's parliament. It will also have to submit to the rulings of the provincial court and to those measures decided by the government of the province after being sanctioned by the vote of the provincial parliament. Otherwise it will be excluded from the solidarity of the guarantee, by placing itself beyond the pale of provincial law.

9(*l*). *The province must be nothing other than a free federation of autonomous communes.* The *provincial parliament* may consist either of a single chamber seating the representatives of the communes or of two chambers, one composed of these representatives, the other of representatives of the entire provincial population, irrespective of commune. While it will in no way interfere with the domestic running of the communes, the *provincial parliament* will have to draft the fundamental principles behind the *provincial charter*, and these will be binding upon all communes wishing to participate in the provincial parliament. [Assuming the principles of the present catechism as a basis,] the parliament will modify provincial legislation in terms both of the respective rights and duties of individuals, associations and communes, and of the forfeits to which each shall be liable in the event of infractions of the laws it establishes. The communal legislatures, however, will retain the right to deviate from provincial legislation on secondary but never on essential issues, thereby tending towards a real organic unity rather than uniformity, and relying for the formation of a still closer unity upon experience, time and the development of life in common and the communes' own convictions and needs—in other words, upon liberty and never upon pressure or violence from the provincial centre, for even truth and justice become lies and inequity when enforced by violence.

The provincial parliament will establish *the constitutional charter of the federation of communes*, their respective rights and duties, and also their duties and rights in relation to the provincial parliament, court and government. It will vote on all the laws, arrangements and measures required either for the needs of the province as a whole or as a result of resolutions carried in the national parliament, but without ever bypassing provincial and communal autonomy. While it will never interfere with the domestic administration of the communes, it will decide each commune's quota of the provincial and national taxation. This quota will be divided among all able-bodied adults by the commune itself. Lastly, it will examine all the bills and accept or reject all the proposals of the *provincial government*, which will of course always be elective. The *provincial court*, also elective, will be the court of last appeal in all disputes between individuals and communes, associations and communes, and between one commune and another, and will be the court of first instance in all disputes between the commune and the provincial government or parliament.

9(*m*). *The nation must be nothing other than a federation of autonomous provinces*. The *national parliament* (consisting either

of a single chamber made up of representatives of each province, or of two chambers, one composed of these representatives, the other of the representatives of the entire national
population, irrespective of province) will in no way interfere
with the administration and internal political life of the
provinces, but will have the task of establishing the *fundamental
principles* that are to constitute the *national charter* and will be
binding upon all provinces wishing to participate in the
national pact. The *national parliament* will draft the *national
code*, allowing provincial codes to deviate on secondary but
not on essential issues. It will establish *the constitutional charter
of the federation of provinces*, pass all the laws, arrangements and
measures elicited by the needs of the nation as a whole, fix
the national taxation, dividing it among the provinces but
leaving them the function of re-allocating it among their
respective communes, and lastly will supervise all the bills
and adopt or reject the proposals of the *national executive
government* (which will always be elective, with a limited term
of office). It will negotiate the national alliances, make peace
or war, and have the exclusive right to order (always for a
predetermined period) the formation of a national army. The
government will be nothing more than the executant of its
wishes. The *national court* will be the court of final appeal in all
disputes between provinces and individuals, associations and
communes, as well as in all disputes between provinces. In
disputes between province and State, which will also be subject
to its rulings, the provinces will be able to appeal to the
international court, should it be eventually established.

9(*n*). The *international federation* will comprise all those
nations united upon the bases elaborated above and below. It
is probable, and highly desirable, that when the hour of the
great revolution strikes once more, all those nations which
follow the star of popular emancipation will join hands in a
close and permanent alliance against the coalition of countries
which will rally to the banners of reaction. This alliance will
have to form what will initially be a limited federation, the
seed, so to speak, of the *universal people's federation* which must
eventually embrace the whole world. The *international federation*
of revolutionary peoples, with its own parliament, court and
international guiding committee, will naturally be based upon

the very principles of revolution. Applied to the sphere of international politics, these principles are:

(i). Each land, each nation, each people, great or small, weak or strong, each region, province and commune has the absolute right to decide its own fate, determine its own existence, choose its alliances, unite and separate according to its needs and wishes without any heed to the so-called historic rights and the political, commercial and strategic laws of States. In order to be true, rich and strong, the fusion of the parts into a single whole must be absolutely free. It must arise solely out of local domestic needs and out of the mutual attraction of the parts—attractions and needs which these parts alone may judge.

(ii). Absolute abolition of so-called historic rights and of the abominable right of conquest, as being contrary to the principle of liberty.

(iii). Absolute rejection of the policy of State expansion, power and glory, a policy which, by turning every land into a fortress excluding the rest of mankind, as good as forces it to see itself as the be-all and end-all of mankind, to be utterly self-sufficient, to organize within itself a world apart from all human solidarity, and to measure its power and glory by the damage it inflicts on other nations. A conquering country is of necessity a country of internal enslavement.

(iv). The glory and greatness of a nation depend solely on the development of its humanity. Its strength and unity and the vigour of its domestic life are measurable only by its degree of liberty. From the starting-point of liberty, union is a necessary consequence, but it is difficult, if not impossible, to arrive at liberty from unity. And if it is attained, it will only be through the destruction of a unity built on something other than liberty.

(v). The prosperity and the liberty of nations, as of individuals, are totally interdependent, and there must consequently be absolute freedom of trade, exchange and communication among all federated countries. Abolition of frontiers, passports and customs. Every citizen of a federated country must enjoy all the civic rights of every other member country, and be able easily to obtain the title of citizen and all political rights in that country.

(vi). Since the liberty of all, individuals and collective bodies alike, is interdependent, no nation, province, commune or association may be oppressed without all the rest having their liberty jeopardized and feeling it to be so. All for one and one for all, this must be the sacred and fundamental rule of the *international federation*.

(vii). No federated country may retain a standing army or any institution setting soldier apart from citizen — As well as being the cause of domestic strife, corruption, brutalization and tyranny, standing armies and the soldier's profession are a threat to the prosperity and independence of all other lands. Every able-bodied citizen must, if necessary, become a soldier in defence of his home or of liberty. Material armament must be organized by commune and province in each country, much as it is in the U.S.A. and Switzerland.

(viii). The *international parliament* (comprising either a single chamber made up of each nation's representatives, or two chambers, the first including these representatives, the second the direct representatives of the entire population of the international federation, without distinction of nationality) will establish the international pact and the *federal legislation* which only this parliament will have the right to develop and modify, according to the needs of the times.

The *international court* will function only as the court of final appeal between States and their various provinces. In the event of any differences arising between two federated States, these can only be judged in the first and last instance by the *international parliament*, which again will rule without appeal on all questions of common policy and war, in the name of the entire revolutionary federation which opposes the reactionary coalition.

(ix). No federated State may ever make war on a fellow State. Once the *international parliament* has given its ruling, the offending State must submit to it. If not, then all the other States of the federation must break contact and set it beyond the pale of federal law, solidarity and the federal communion, and, in the event of any hostile move, oppose it with a unified armed front.

(x). All States belonging to the revolutionary federation

must play an active role in any war waged by any of its members upon an unfederated State. Before declaring war, each federated State must notify the international parliament, and only make its declaration if the latter rules that there is adequate cause. If it so rules, the federated executive directory will take up the cause of the offended State and request prompt reparation from the foreign aggressor State in the name of the whole revolutionary federation. If, however, the parliament rules that there has been no aggression and no genuine offence, it will advise the plaintiff State not to embark on war, giving warning that if it does so, it will act alone.

(xi). It is to be hoped that in the course of time the federated States will reject the ruinous luxury of separate representation and be content with federal diplomatic representation.

(xii). The *limited international revolutionary federation* will always be open to peoples wishing to join at a later stage, on the basis of the principles and militant, active revolutionary solidarity indicated above and below — but without the slightest concession of principle to any people. Consequently, only those peoples accepting all the principles recapitulated in this catechism shall be admitted into the federation.

10. *Social organization.*

Without political equality there is no true political liberty, but political equality will only become possible when there is *economic and social equality*.

10(*a*). Equality does not mean the levelling down of individual differences, nor intellectual, moral and physical uniformity among individuals. This diversity of ability and strength, and these differences of race, nation, sex, age and character, far from being a social evil, constitute the treasure-house of mankind. Nor do economic and social equality mean the levelling down of individual fortunes, in so far as these are products of the ability, productive energy and thrift of an individual.

10(*b*). The sole prerequisite for equality and justice is *a form of social organization such that each human individual born into it may find — to the extent that these are dependent upon society rather than upon nature — equal means for his development from infancy and adolescence to coming of age, first in upbringing and education, then in the exercise of the various capacities with which each is endowed by nature. This equality at the outset,* which justice requires for all, will never be feasible as long as the right of succession survives.

10(*c*). Justice, as well as human dignity, demands that *each individual should be the child of his own achievements, and only those achievements.* We hotly reject the doctrine of hereditary sin, disgrace and responsibility. By the same token, we must reject the illusory heredity of virtue, honours and rights — *and of wealth also.* The heir to any kind of wealth is no longer the complete child of his own achievements, and in terms of initial circumstance he is privileged.

10(*d*). *Abolition of the right of inheritance.* As long as this right continues, hereditary differences of class, rank and wealth — in other words, social inequality and privilege — will survive in fact, if not in law. But it is an inescapable social law that *de facto* inequality always produces inequality of rights: social inequality necessarily becomes political. And we have already stated that without political equality there is no liberty in the universal, human and truly democratic sense, while society will always remain split into two uneven halves, with one vast section, including the entire mass of the people, suffering the oppression and exploitation of the other. Therefore *the right of succession is contrary to the triumph of liberty,* and a society wishing to become free must abolish it.

10(*e*). *This right must be abolished because, relying as it does upon a fiction, it runs counter to the very spirit of liberty.* All individual, political and social rights belong to the real, the living individual. Once dead, his will does not exist any more than he himself does, and it is a fictitious will that oppresses the living in the name of the dead. If the dead person sets such store by the enforcement of his wishes, let him stand up and enforce them himself, if he can, but he has no right to ask society to bend all its strength and law to the service of his non-existence.

10(*f*). The legitimate and positive function of the right of succession has always been that of securing for subsequent generations the means to grow and to become men. Consequently, *only the trust for public upbringing and education will have the right to inherit,* with the matching obligation to make equal provision for the maintenance, upbringing and education of every child from birth to coming of age and emancipation. In this way, all parents will be equally confident in their children's future, and since equality for all is a fundamental pre-condition of morality for all, and all privilege is a cradle of immorality, parents whose love for their children is rational enough to be inspired not by vanity but by human dignity will prefer them to be brought up in strict equality, even if they do have the means to leave an inheritance which would place them in a privileged position.

10(g). Once the inequality produced by the right of inheritance has been abolished, there will still remain (but to a far lesser degree) the inequality that arises from differences in individual ability, strength and productive capacity — a dif-ference which, while never disappearing altogether, will be of diminishing importance under the influence of an egalitarian upbringing and social system, and which in addition will never weigh upon future generations once there is no more right of inheritance.

10(h). Labour is the sole producer of wealth. Everybody is free, of course, either to die of starvation or to dwell among the wild beasts of the desert or the forest, but anybody who wants to live within society should earn his living by his own work, or run the risk of being considered a parasite, an exploiter of the wealth (i.e. the labour) of others, and a thief.

10(i). *Labour* is the fundamental basis of dignity and human rights, for it is only by means of his own free, intelligent work that man becomes a creator in his turn, wins from the surrounding world and his own animal nature his humanity and rights, and creates the world of civilization. As for the shame which clung to the idea of labour both in the ancient world and under feudalism, and which survives in large measure today, despite the daily lip-service paid to its dignity, this witless contempt has two sources.

The first is a conviction characteristic of the ancients, but still claiming any amount of secret sympathizers, which holds that in order to give some section of human society the wherewithal to humanize itself through science, the arts, learning and the rule of law, another and naturally more numerous section must be destined for labour and slavery. This basic principle of ancient civilization was the cause of its downfall. The city, corrupted and disjointed by the privileged idleness of its citizens, and undermined by the imperceptibly slow but constant inroads of the disinherited world of the slaves—moralized in spite of their condition, and maintaining their pristine strength through the salutary effects even of forced labour—fell beneath the on-slaught of those barbarian peoples to which the majority of these slaves belonged by birth.

Christianity, that religion of slaves, destroyed the ancient disorder only so as to create a new one. The privilege of divine grace and election, founded upon the inequality which is the natural outcome of the right of conquest, again divided human society into two camps—rabble and nobility, serfs and lords—by assigning to the latter the noble trades of arms and government and leaving the serfs with nothing but their labour, which was both debased and reviled. The same cause necessarily produced the same effects: the aristocratic world, enfeebled and demoralized by the privilege of idleness, fell in 1789 under the assault of the serfs, workers rising in united, powerful rebellion. The freedom of labour, and its rehabilita-tion under the law, was now proclaimed. But only under the law, for the living fact of labour still remains discredited and subjected.

Now that the first source of subjection, the dogma of the political inequality of men, has been eliminated by the Great Revolution, the current contempt for labour has to be ascribed to the second source, which is none other than the *separation* which has grown up and holds true to this day *between intel-lectual and manual labour*, and which, by reproducing the same old inequality under a new guise, is once again splitting the social world into two camps: the *minority, privileged* henceforth not by the law but by its capital, and the *majority, forced into labour*, no longer by the iniquity of legal privilege but by hunger.

Today, in fact, the dignity of labour is already acknowledged in theory, and public opinion accepts that it is shameful to live without working, except that work as a whole is now divided into categories, one of them thoroughly intellectual and ranked as exclusively noble, embracing the arts and sciences and their applications in industry, ideas, concepts, invention, calcula-tion, government and the general or subordinate management of the labour force, the other consisting of nothing more than manual exertion reduced to a purely mechanical action, devoid of mind and intelligence. By this economic and social law of the division of labour, what happens is that those whose capital makes them privileged, including those whose individual abilities give them the least entitlement, grab the former and leave the latter to the people. The result is three great evils: the first afflicts the privileged by capital; the second the popular masses; the third, arising out of the first two, the production of wealth and the well-being, justice and intellectual and moral growth of society as a whole.

The evil which afflicts the privileged classes is this, that by claiming the lion's share in the allocation of social functions, they play an increasingly shabby part in the intellectual and moral world. It is quite true that a certain amount of leisure is absolutely necessary to the development of the mind and the arts and sciences, but this leisure has to be earned, it has to follow the healthy tiredness of daily labour, it has to be a just leisure, its potential depending solely on the energy, ability and good will of the individual, equally available to all, whereas privileged leisure, far from reinforcing the mind, enfeebles, demoralizes and chokes it. All history shows that with a few exceptions the classes privileged in terms of wealth and lineage have always been the least productive in terms of the mind, and the greatest discoveries in science, the arts and industry have generally been the work of men who had to earn their living by hard work in their youth.

The structure of human nature is such that the potential for evil unerringly gives rise to the substance and the morality of the individual is much more dependent on his living conditions and the environment he inhabits than on his own will. In this as in every other context, the law of social solidarity is inexorable, so that in order to improve individual morality it is not so much conscience as the nature of social life which has to be tackled, and there is no other moralizing factor, either for society or the individual, than liberty within the utmost equality. Take the truest democrat and set him on any kind of throne, and if he does not come down at once he is certain to become a scoundrel. If a man born into the aristocracy is luckless enough not to learn to despise and abominate his descent and be ashamed of aristocracy, he will necessarily become both a bad man and a vain one, sighing for the past, sterile in the present and passionately set against the future. Likewise the bourgeois, the darling of capital and of privileged leisure, will turn that leisure to idleness, corruption and debauchery, or else will wield it as a terrible weapon for the further enslavement of the working classes and eventually provoke against himself a revolution even more terrible than that of 1793.

The evil which afflicts the common man is easier still to diagnose. He works for others, and his labour, bereft of liberty, leisure and intelligence and debased by their absence, degrades, crushes and kills him. He is compelled to work for others because, born as he is into hardship, deprivation of all rational upbringing and education and moral enslavement at the hands of religious interests, he sees himself propelled into life defenceless, disowned and lacking both personal initiative and personal thinking. Hunger forces him from his tenderest infancy to scrape his wretched living. He has to sell his physical strength, his labour, under the harshest conditions, without either the mental attributes or the material occasion to ask any better. Reduced to desperation by hardship, sometimes he rebels, but lacking the unity and power which come from thought, ill-prepared, more often than not betrayed and sold out by his leaders, seldom knowing where to lay the blame for the hardships he suffers and usually aiming in the wrong direction, he has — until now, at any rate — usually bungled his rebellions and relapsed into his perennial enslavement, exhausted by sterile struggle. That enslavement will endure just as long as capital stands aside from the collective action of the labour force in order to exploit it, and as long as the education which would be shared by all in a well-organized society continues to prop up the vested interests of a privileged class by restricting the spiritual element of labour to that class and leaving the people nothing but the exertion of brute force, conditioned and perpetually condemned to the execution of ideas which are not their own.

Through this unjust and fatal separation, the labour of the people becomes a purely mechanical task, no different from that of a beast of burden: it is discredited, despised and in the event disinherited of all rights. From the political, intellectual and moral standpoint, the outcome is immensely destructive to society. The minority which enjoys its monopolies and its learning is afflicted both in heart and mind by the very effect of its privilege, to the point of becoming learnedly asinine, for there is nothing so pernicious and sterile as licensed, privileged intelligence. On the other hand the people, totally devoid of knowledge, crushed by daily mechanical labour more calculated to deaden than develop their natural intelligence, and seeing no glimmer of deliverance, mill about aimlessly in their condemned cell, and because they always have strength of numbers on their side constitute a permanent threat to the very existence of society.

The unequal line drawn between intellectual and manual labour must therefore be removed. The economic output of society is itself considerably impaired, because mind cut off from physical activity weakens, withers and fades, whereas the physical vigour of humanity cut off from intelligence is brutalized, and in this state of artificial divorce neither produces the half of what could and should be produced once they are restored by a new social synthesis to form an indivisible productive process. When the thinker works and the worker thinks, free, intelligent labour will emerge as humanity's highest aspiration, the basis of its dignity and law and the embodiment of its human power on earth—and humanity will be instituted.

10(*k*).* *Intelligent free labour will necessarily be associated labour.* Everybody will be free to associate or not to associate in labour, but there can be no doubt that with the exception of works of imagination, whose nature requires the inner concentration of the individual mind, in all those industrial and even scientific and artistic enterprises whose nature admits of associated labour, such association will be generally preferred for the simple reason that it would miraculously increase the productive energies of each associate member of a productive association, who will earn a great deal more in less time and with far less trouble. Once the free productive associations stop being slaves and become their own masters and the owners of the necessary capital, once they include all the specialist minds required by each enterprise as members

* There is no sub-entry (*j*) in the original text—EDITOR.

co-operating side by side with the labour force, and once they amalgamate among themselves—still freely, in accordance with their needs and natures—then sooner or later they will expand beyond national frontiers. They will form one vast economic federation, with a parliament informed by precise, detailed statistics on a world scale, such as are not yet possible today, and will both offer and demand to control, decide and distribute the output of world industry among the various countries, so that there will no longer, or hardly ever, be commercial or industrial crises, enforced stagnation, disasters and waste of energy and capital. Human labour, emancipating each and every man, will regenerate the world.

10(l). *The land, with all its natural resources, belongs to all, but will be held only by those who work it.*

10(m). Woman, *differing from man* but *not inferior to him, intelligent, industrious and free like him, is declared his equal both in rights and in all political and social functions and duties.*

10(n). Abolition not of the natural but of the *legal* family, based on civil law and ownership. Religious and civil marriage are replaced by *free marriage.* Two *adult* individuals of opposite sex have the right to unite and separate in accordance with their desires and mutual interests and the promptings of their hearts, nor does society have any right either to prevent their union or to hold them to it against their will. Once the right of succession is abolished and society guarantees the upbringing of all its children, every reason previously advanced for the political and civil backing given to marital indissolubility disappears, and the union of the sexes reverts to the complete liberty which, here as elsewhere, is always the *sine qua non* of genuine morality. In free marriage, man and woman must enjoy equal measure of liberty. Neither violence, passion nor the rights freely granted in the past may excuse any infringement by one party of the other's liberty, and any such infringement shall be considered criminal.

10(o). From the moment of conception until her child is born, a woman is entitled to a social subvention paid not for her benefit but for her child's. Any mother wishing to feed and rear her children will also receive all the costs of their maintenance and care from society.

10(p). Parents will have the right to keep their children at their side and to attend to their upbringing, under the guardianship and supreme supervision of society, which will always retain the right and duty to part children from their parents whenever the latter may be in a position to demoralize or even hamper their children's development, either by example or by brutal, inhuman precepts or treatment.

10(*q*). Children belong neither to their parents nor to society but to themselves and their future liberty. From infancy to coming of age they are only potentially free, and must therefore find themselves under the aegis of *authority*. It is true that their parents are their natural protectors, but *the legal and ultimate protector is society*, which has the right and duty to tend them because its own future depends on the intellectual and moral guidance they receive. Society can only give liberty to adults provided it supervises the upbringing of minors.

10(*r*). *School must take the place of church*, with the immense difference that the religious education provided by the latter has no other purpose than to perpetuate the rule of human ignorance or so-called divine authority, whereas school upbringing and education will have no other purpose than the true emancipation of the children upon reaching the age of majority, and will consist of nothing less than their progressive initiation into liberty by the threefold development of their physical and mental powers and their will. Reason, truth, justice, human respect, awareness of personal dignity (inseparable from the human dignity of another), love of liberty for one's own sake and for others', belief in work as the basis and condition of all rights; contempt for unreason, falsehood, injustice, cowardice, slavery and idleness — these must be the keystones of public education. First it must shape men, then specialists and citizens, and, in step with the children's growth, authority must naturally make more and more room for liberty, so that by the time the adolescent has come of age and become lawfully emancipated he will have forgotten how his infancy was controlled and guided by something other than liberty. Human respect, the seed of liberty, must be present even in the harshest and most absolute behaviour of authority. This is the touchstone of all moral education: inculcate that respect in children, and you create men.

After completing their primary and secondary education the children will be advised, informed, but not coerced, by their superiors with a view to choosing some higher or specialist school, according to their abilities and inclinations. At the same time, each will apply himself to the theoretical and practical study of that branch of industry which most attracts him, and whatever sums he earns by working during his apprenticeship will be made available when he comes of age.

10(*s*). As soon as he comes of age, the adolescent will be declared a free citizen and absolute master of his actions. In exchange for the care it has exercised during his infancy, society will ask for three things: that he remain *free*, that he *live by his own labour*, and that he *respect the liberty of others*. And because the crimes and vices by which present-day society is afflicted are the sole outcome of defective social organization, we may be sure that given a form of organization and up-bringing based on reason, justice, liberty, human respect and complete equality, good will become the rule and evil a morbid exception, ever decreasing under the all-powerful influence of moralized public opinion.

10(*t*). The old, the disabled and the sick will be cared for and respected, enjoy all public and social rights, and be generously maintained at the common expense ...

12. *Revolutionary policy.*

It is our profound conviction that since all national liberties are interdependent the individual revolutions of each country should also be interdependent, and that in the Europe of the future and in the whole civilized world there will no longer be *revolutions* but only *universal revolution*, just as *European and world reaction* are one and indivisible; that consequently all individual interests and national vanities, ambitions, jealousies and antagonisms must now give way to the *sole, common and universal interest of revolution, which will uphold the liberty and independence of each nation through the solidarity of all.* We believe that the Holy Alliance of worldwide counter-revolution and the conspiracy of kings, clergy, aristocracy and bourgeois feudalism, shored up by enormous budgets, standing armies and a formidable bureaucracy, armed with all the terrible resources that modern centralization provides, accustomed and inured to action, and with the means of planning and executing any course of action under the cloak of legality, constitute a vast, menacing and crushing force, and that in order to combat that force, confront it with an equally powerful movement and defeat and destroy it, nothing less than *the simultaneous revolutionary alliance and action of all the peoples of the civilized world* are required. *No single popular revolution could withstand* this worldwide reaction. It would be folly, and consequently not only a mistake in its own terms but a betrayal, a crime against all other nations. From now on, every popular uprising must be performed not on its own behalf but for the sake of the whole world. Yet in order for a nation to revolt on behalf and in the name of the whole world, it must have a world programme, broad, deep, true, in other words human enough to embrace the interests of the world and to electrify the passions of the entire popular masses of Europe, regardless of nationality. *The programme can be none other than that of democratic and social revolution.*

12(*a*). *The aim of democratic and social revolution* can be summarized under two headings.

Politically, it is the abolition of historic rights, the right of conquest and the law of diplomacy. It is the complete emancipation of individuals and associations from the yoke of divine and human authority, the absolute destruction of all compulsory unions and amalgamations of communes into provinces, provinces and conquered lands into the State, and lastly the radical dissolution of the centralist, custodial, authoritarian State, with all its military, bureaucratic, administrative, judicial and civil institutions. In other words, the *restoration of liberty to all — individuals, collective bodies, associations, communes, provinces, regions and nations alike — and mutual safeguard of that liberty through federation.*

Socially, it is *the confirmation of political equality through economic equality*. It is *equality* — not natural but social — *for every individual at the start of his or her career*, which means equality of maintenance, upbringing and education for every child until the age of majority.

Organization of the International Revolutionary Brotherhood

1. The International Revolutionary Brotherhood will be constituted into two different organizations:

I. *The international family* proper;
II. *The national families*;

the latter to be organized throughout so as always to remain subordinate to the absolute control of the *international family*.

I. *The international family*

2. Solely consisting of *honorary and active international brothers*, this is our great revolutionary undertaking. Its success will therefore mainly depend upon correct selection of the international brothers.

A. Requisite qualities for membership of the international family

3. Apart from the indispensable qualities which make up the character of the honest, reliable revolutionary — good faith, courage, caution, discretion, constancy, steadfastness, resolution, boundless dedication, absence of personal vanity and ambition, intelligence, experience — the candidate must also have adopted all the fundamental principles of our *revolutionary catechism* in heart, mind and spirit.

3.(*a*). *He must be an atheist*. On behalf of the earth and of mankind, he must join us in laying claim to everything which religions have hauled off into the heavens and bestowed upon their gods: truth, liberty, happiness, justice, goodness. He must recognize that *morality* is totally independent of theology and divine metaphysics and has no other source than the collective conscience of man.

3(*b*). *He must, like ourselves, be the adversary of the principle of authority* and loathe all its applications and consequences in the intellectual and moral as well as in the political, economic and social spheres.

3(*c*). *Above all, he must love liberty and justice* and acknowledge as we do that any political and social organization based on the denial or even the limitation of this absolute principle of liberty must inevitably give rise to inequity and disorder, and that the sole rational, equitable social organization compatible with human dignity and happiness will be that which takes liberty as its basis, soul, primary law and supreme goal.

3(*d*). He must understand that there is no liberty without

equality, and that the realization of the utmost liberty in the most perfect equality, in fact and in law, politically, economically and socially, is justice.

3(*e*). *He must be a federalist*, like ourselves, both inside and outside his native country. He must understand that the advent of liberty is incompatible with the existence of *States*. He must therefore desire the overthrow of all States and at the same time of all religious, political and social institutions, such as official Churches, standing armies, centralized ministries, bureaucracy, governments, unitary parliaments and State universities and banks, as well as aristocratic and bourgeois monopolies. All this, so that a free human society may arise upon the ruins, no longer organized, as it is today, from high to low and from centre to circumference by means of enforced unity and concentration, but starting with the free individual, the free association and the autonomous commune, from low to high and from circumference to centre, by means of free federation.

3(*f*). He must adopt the following principle, both in theory and practice, and in the full scope of its consequences: *All individuals, associations, communes, provinces, regions and nations have the absolute right to dispose of their own fate, associate or not associate, ally with whomever they please and break off alliances without the slightest regard for so-called historic rights or for their neighbours' convenience.* And he must be thoroughly convinced that only when they are moulded by the supreme power of their own mutual attractions and innate, natural necessities, consecrated by liberty, will these new federations of communes, provinces, regions and nations become truly strong, fertile and indissoluble.

3(*g*). *He must therefore renounce the so-called principle of nationality* —an equivocal principle full of hypocrisy and pitfalls, fit only for the historic, self-seeking State—*for the far greater, far simpler and sole legitimate principle of liberty,* whereby every individual or collective body has the right to be itself, and no one has the right to impose his own costume, customs, language, opinions and laws upon it; each man must be absolutely free in his own home. This is what any honest national law amounts to. Anything which goes further does not confirm true national liberty, but denies the liberty of another nation.

The candidate must therefore loathe, as we do, *all those narrow, absurd, liberticidal and consequently criminal notions of greatness, ambition and national glory,* which are fit only for monarchies and oligarchies, or, as today, for the higher bourgeoisie, because they help to deceive the people and to set them at loggerheads so as to further enslave them.

3(*h*). Henceforth patriotism must play a secondary role in his heart and give place to the love of justice and liberty, and if his own country has the misfortune to lose touch with these he must not hesitate if need be to side against it—which he will do at no great personal cost if he is truly convinced, as he must be, that for no country is there any other road to prosperity and political greatness than that of justice and liberty.

3(*i*). Lastly, he must be convinced that, far from being at odds with those of every other country, his own country's prosperity and fortune are in fact dependent upon them for their proper realization, that between the destinies of all nations there is an ultimate, all-powerful solidarity, and that by gradually transforming the narrow and usually inequitable sentiment of patriotism into a broader, more generous and rational love of mankind, that solidarity will eventually create the universal worldwide federation of nations.

3(*j*). *He must be a socialist* in the full sense given to this term by our revolutionary catechism, and, with us, must acknowledge as legitimate and just, desire with all his heart and be ready to devote all his energies to *the triumph of a social organization in which every human individual born into this world, man and woman alike, shall find equal provision for his or her maintenance, upbringing and education in childhood and adolescence, and on coming of age shall find the further—meaning equal political, economic and social—facilities for the creation of his own well-being by using the various strengths and aptitudes with which nature has endowed him and which equal education for all has developed in him.*

3(*k*). He must understand that just as the heredity of evil which alas! is only too indisputable as a natural phenomenon, is everywhere rejected by the principle of justice, so in the same way and by the same logic the heredity of good must be rejected. That since the dead no longer exist, they cannot impose their will upon the living. In other words, that *economic, social and political equality for all at the very outset—the absolute condition of the liberty of all—is incompatible with hereditary ownership and with the law of succession.*

3(*l*). He must be convinced that, since labour is the sole producer of social wealth, whoever enjoys it without working is an exploiter of the work of others, a thief, and that since labour is the fundamental basis of human dignity, the unique means by which man truly wins and creates his liberty, *all political and social rights must in future belong only to those who work.*

3(*m*). He must recognize that the land—nature's free gift to all—cannot and must not be any man's property. But that its fruits, in so far as they are the produce of labour, should revert only to those who work it with their hands.

3(*n*). He must be convinced, as we are, that woman, different from man but not inferior to him, intelligent, industrious and free like man himself, must be declared his *equal* in all political and social rights. That in a free society, religious and civil marriage must be replaced by free marriage, and that the maintenance, upbringing and education of all children must be equally available to all, at society's expense, with no requirement for society to separate them (although protecting them against stupidity, negligence or parental maltreatment), since children belong neither to society nor their parents but to their future liberty. The custodial authority of society must have no other goal or mission in this connection than to train its children for liberty by means of a rational, manly upbringing, based solely upon justice, human respect and belief in labour.

4. *He must be a revolutionary.* He must understand that such a complete and radical transformation of society, which must necessarily involve the downfall of all privilege, monopoly and constituted power, will naturally not occur by peaceful means. That for the same reason it will be opposed by the rich and powerful, and supported, in every land, only by the people, together with that intelligent and genuinely noble section of youth whose open-hearted convictions and burning aspirations lead it to embrace the cause of the people despite being born into the privileged classes.

5. He must understand that the sole and final purpose of this revolution is the true political, economic and social emancipation of the people, and that while it may be assisted and largely

organized by the above-mentioned section of youth, in the long run it will only come through the people. That history has completely exhausted all other religious, national and political questions, and that only one question remains outstanding today, subsuming all the rest and uniquely capable of mobilizing the people—*the social question*. That any so-called revolution—whether it resembles the recent Polish insurrection, or the doctrine which Mazzini now preaches, whether it is exclusively political, constitutional, monarchist or even republican, like the last abortive move of the Spanish progressives—any such revolution, working as it does apart from the people, and consequently unable to succeed without drawing upon some privileged class and representing the interests of the latter, will necessarily work against the people and will be a retrograde, harmful, counter-revolutionary movement.

6. He will therefore despise any secondary movement whose immediate, direct aim is other than the political and social emancipation of the working classes, in other words the people, and will see it either as a fatal error or a shabby trick. Hostile to all compromise and conciliation—henceforward impossible—and to any false coalition with those whose interests make them the natural enemies of the people, *he must see that the only salvation for his own country and for the entire world lies in social revolution.*

7. He must also understand that this revolution, being essentially cosmopolitan, like justice and liberty themselves, will only be able to triumph by sweeping like a universal holocaust across the flimsy barriers of nations and bringing all States tumbling in its wake, embracing first the whole of Europe, and then the world. *He must understand that the social revolution will necessarily become a European and worldwide revolution.*

8. That the world will inevitably split into two camps, that of the new life and of the old privileges, and that between these two opposing camps, created as in the time of the wars of religion not by national sympathies but by community of ideas and interests, a war of extermination is bound to erupt, with no quarter and no respite. That in the very interest of its own security and self-preservation the social revolution—contrary in its whole essence to that hypocritical policy of non-intervention, which is fit only for the moribund and the

impotent — cannot live and thrive except by growing, and will not lay down the sword until it has destroyed all States and all the old religious, political and economic institutions both in Europe and throughout the civilized world.

9. That this will not be a war of conquest, but of emancipation — sometimes enforced, perhaps, but salutary all the same — because its purpose and outcome will be nothing more nor less than the destruction of States and their secular roots, which have always been the basis of all slavery, with the blessing of religion.

10. That even in the most apparently hostile countries, once the social revolution breaks out at one point it will find keen and tenacious allies in the popular masses, who will be unable to do other than rally to its banner as soon as they understand and come in contact with its activities and purpose. That it will consequently be necessary to choose the most fertile soil for its beginning, where it has only to withstand the first assault of reaction before expanding to overwhelm the frenzies of its enemies, federalizing all the lands it has absorbed and welding them into a single indomitable revolutionary alliance.

11. That the elements of social revolution are already widespread in practically all the countries of Europe, and that their fusion into an effective force is purely a matter of mediation and concentration. *That this must be the task of the dedicated revolutionaries of every land, gathered at once into both public and private association* with the twofold object of broadening the revolutionary front and at the same time paving the way for simultaneous concerted action in all countries in which action proves initially possible, through secret agreement among the wisest revolutionaries of those countries.

12. Understanding is not enough. Our candidate must also contain within himself the *revolutionary spirit*, and must love liberty and justice to the point of seriously wishing to contribute to their triumph by his own efforts and making it his duty to sacrifice his repose, his well-being, vanity, personal ambition and often his personal interests to them.

13. He must be convinced that there is no better way to serve them than by sharing our efforts, and must realize that by taking his place in our ranks he will be contracting the same

solemn commitment towards ourselves that all of us likewise contract towards him. He must have familiarized himself with our revolutionary catechism and all our rules and laws, and must swear always to observe them with scrupulous fidelity.

14. He must understand that an association whose purpose is revolution must necessarily form itself into a *secret society*, and that in the interest of the cause it serves, as well as of effective action and the security of each of its members, any secret society must be subject to *rigorous discipline*, which in any case amounts to nothing more nor less than the expression and direct outcome of the reciprocal commitment contracted by each of its members towards the others, so that it is both an honour and a duty for each to submit to it.

15. Whatever the differences in ability among the international brothers, we shall never tolerate any but this one master: our principle, and this single will: our laws, which we have all helped to create or at any rate equally approved by our free consent. Although we respect a man's past services, and appreciate the contributions which some might make through their wealth, others through their knowledge and others through their high rank and public, literary, political or social influence, far from paying court to them on these grounds we tend instead to see them as motives for distrust. All such men are capable of introducing either their customs, their pretensions to authority or the inheritance of their past into our ranks, and we can accept none of these, looking ever forward, never back, and acknowledging no deserts or rights except in the man who serves our association most actively and most resolutely.

16. The candidate will understand that he can join this association only in order to serve it, and that it will therefore have the right to expect some kind of positive usefulness from each of its members, so that its absence, duly proved and attested, will result in expulsion.

17. Upon entering our ranks, the new brother must solemnly undertake to make this society his primary duty and to give second place to his duty towards each member of this society — his brother. From now onward, these two duties must take pride of place, if not in his heart, then at least in his will, over all others ...

V ON FEDERALISM AND SOCIALISM

These two extracts come from *Fédéralisme, socialisme et anti-théologisme*, published in *Œuvres*, vol. I (Paris, 1895), pp. 14–21 and 36–59. They are here translated from the French by Steven Cox.

I. *Federalism*

We are glad to be able to state that this principle has been unanimously hailed by the Geneva Congress. Switzerland herself, practising federalism so successfully today, has adhered to it without reservation and accepted it in all its implications. Unfortunately, the principle has been very badly formulated in the resolutions of the Congress, and is mentioned only indirectly, first in connection with the League which we are to establish, and later with reference to the journal which we are to publish under the title of *The United States of Europe*, whereas it is our own view that it ought to have taken pride of place in our statement of principles.

This is a very anxious omission, and one which we must make haste to remedy. In accordance with the unanimous feelings of the Congress, we must proclaim:

1. That in order to achieve the triumph of liberty, justice and peace in the international relations of Europe, and to render civil war impossible among the various peoples which make up the European family, only a single course lies open: to constitute *the United States of Europe*.

2. That the formation of these States of Europe can never come about between the States as constituted at present, in view of the monstrous disparity which exists between their various powers.

3. That the example of the now defunct German Confederation conclusively proved that a confederation of monarchies is a mockery, incapable of ensuring either the peace or the liberty of the people.

4. That not even if it called itself a republic could any centralized, bureaucratic and by the same token militarist State enter seriously and genuinely into an international

94

federation. By virtue of its constitution, which will always be an explicit or implicit denial of domestic liberty, it would necessarily imply a declaration of permanent war and a threat to the existence of neighbouring countries. Founded essentially upon an original act of violence, conquest, which in private life is known as breaking and entering—an act blessed by some kind of Church, hallowed by time and transformed *ipso facto* into an historic right—and taking its stand upon this holy consecration as if upon some supreme, exclusive law, every centralist State automatically constitutes an absolute denial of the rights of every other State, and never recognizes them in the treaties it concludes with them except at the dictates of political self-interest or impotence.

5. That all the supporters of the League should therefore bend all their energies towards the reconstruction of their various countries, in order to replace the old organization founded throughout upon violence and the principle of authority by a new organization based solely upon the interests, needs and inclinations of the populace, and owning no principle other than that of the free federation of individuals into communes, communes into provinces,*

* The illustrious Italian patriot Joseph Mazzini, whose republican ideal is none other than the French republic of 1793, recast in the poetic tradition of Dante and the ambitious memory of Rome as lord of the world, then revised and corrected from the standpoint of a new, half-rational, half-mystical theology—this eminent patriot, an ambitious, passionate and always blinkered spirit, despite all his efforts to raise himself to the heights of international justice, who has always put his country's power and greatness before her well-being and liberty—Mazzini, then, has always been bitterly opposed to provincial autonomy, which would be bound to unsettle the austere uniformity of his great Italian State. He argues that communal autonomy will be an adequate counterbalance to the almighty powers of his solidly constituted republic. He is mistaken: no single commune would be capable of withstanding the pressure of that formidable centralization; it would only be crushed. In order not to succumb, it would therefore have to federate with all the neighbouring communes with a view to common resistance—in other words, it would have to form an autonomous province with them. Furthermore, if the provinces are not autonomous they will have to be ruled by State officials. There is no middle path between rigorously consistent federalism and bureaucratic government. It follows, then, that the republic envisaged by Mazzini would be a bureaucratic and consequently militarist State, founded with a view to external power, not international justice and domestic liberty. In 1793, during the Reign of Terror, the French communes were recognized as

provinces into nations, and the latter into the United States, first of Europe, then of the whole world.

6. Consequently, absolute rejection of everything which comes within the compass of the historic right of States; all questions relating to natural, political, strategic and commercial frontiers must in future be treated as ancient history and sternly rejected by all supporters of the League.

7. Recognition of the absolute right of all nations, great or small, all peoples, weak or strong, and all communes to complete autonomy, provided that their domestic constitution does not endanger the autonomy and liberty of neighbouring lands.

8. Just because a region has formed part of a State, even by voluntary accession, it by no means follows that it incurs any obligation to remain tied to it for ever. No obligation in perpetuity is acceptable to human justice—the only justice which can obtain among us—and we shall never acknowledge any rights or duties except those based on liberty. The right of free union and equally free secession comes first and foremost among all political rights; without it, confederation would be nothing but centralization in disguise.

9. It follows from all the preceding statements that the League must deliberately proscribe any alliance of any national section of European democracy with the monarchic States, even if the purpose of such an alliance were to regain the independence or liberty of an oppressed country. This kind of alliance could only give rise to disappointments, and would also be a betrayal of revolution.

10. On the other hand, precisely because it is the League of Peace, and because it is convinced that peace can only be achieved and established upon the closest, fullest solidarity of the people in justice and liberty, the League must loudly proclaim its sympathy for any national insurrection against any kind of oppression from an external or native source, provided that any such insurrection acts in the name of our principles and in the economic as well as the social interest

---

autonomous, but this did not prevent them from being crushed by the revolutionary despotism of the Convention or rather by that of the Commune of Paris, inherited in due course by Napoleon.

of the popular masses, but not with the ambition of founding a powerful State.

11. The League will wage total war against everything which comes under the heading of State glory, greatness and power. As a counter to those false and malicious idols which have seen the sacrifice of millions of human victims, we shall raise high the glories of human intelligence manifested in science, and of universal prosperity based upon work, justice and liberty.

12. The League will recognize *nationality* as a natural phenomenon, with the incontrovertible right to free existence and development, but not as a principle, since every principle must be universal in application, whereas nationality is an exclusive, separatist phenomenon. This so-called *principle of nationality* as advocated in our own time by the governments of France, Russia and Prussia and even by many German, Polish, Italian and Hungarian patriots is nothing but a decoy offered by the forces of reaction to the spirit of revolution. It is basically aristocratic, even to the point of discrediting the dialects of illiterate populations and inherently denying the liberty of provinces and the real autonomy of communes, and is not supported in any land by the popular masses, whose real interests it systematically sacrifices to the so-called public good, which always turns out to be that of the privileged classes. Nationality as a principle expresses nothing but the pretended historic rights and ambitions of states; as a right, therefore, it can never be recognized by the League as anything but a natural corollary of the overriding principle of liberty, ceasing to be a right from the moment when it stands against or even apart from liberty.

13. The irresistible tendency of mankind is towards unity, but unity becomes fatal and destructive of the intelligence, dignity and welfare of individuals and peoples whenever it comes into being to the exclusion of liberty, either by violence or under the authority of any kind of theological, metaphysical, political or even economic idea. The patriotism which strives for unity to the exclusion of liberty is an evil patriotism, always fatal to the true popular interests of the land it claims to exalt and serve, often the unwitting friend of reaction and the enemy of revolution, meaning the

4

emancipation of nations and human beings. The League can acknowledge only one unity — unity which is freely constituted by the federation of autonomous parts into a whole so that the latter, ceasing to be the negation of individual rights and interests, a graveyard for the compulsory burial of all local welfare, instead becomes the confirmation and fountain-head of all autonomy and welfare. Therefore the League will roundly condemn any religious, political, economic and social organization not thoroughly imbued with that great principle of liberty without which there is no intelligence, no justice, no prosperity and no humanity.

II. *Socialism*

After proclaiming the right and duty of every human being to become a man, the French Revolution finally gave rise to Babouvism. Babeuf, who was among the last of the pure, forceful citizens whom the Revolution created and dispatched in such large numbers, and who had the good fortune to include men like Buonarroti among his friends, fused the political traditions of the ancient motherland and the thoroughly modern ideas of social revolution into one remarkable concept. Seeing the Revolution declining for want of a radical and very likely impossible change in the economic organization of society, and loyal to the spirit of that Revolution, which had reached the point of replacing all individual initiative with the overriding power of the State, he conceived a political and social system by whose terms the republic, the expression of the collective will of the citizenry, would confiscate all private property, administer it in the general interest, divide upbringing, education, means of livelihood and pleasures into equal shares for all, and require physical or mental labour from every citizen, without exception, according to the strength and capacity of each. Babeuf failed in his conspiracy, and was guillotined together with several of his companions. But his ideal of a socialist republic did not die with him. It was taken up by his friend Buonarroti, the greatest conspirator this century has seen, and handed down by him as a sacred trust to new generations. Thanks to the secret societies he founded in Belgium and France, communist ideas took root in the popular imagination. Between 1830 and 1848 they found able interpreters in Cabet and M. Louis Blanc, who definitively established *revolutionary socialism*. Another socialist current, flowing from the same revolutionary source and converging on the same goal, but by quite different means, is what we shall term *doctrinaire socialism*, created by two eminent men, Saint-Simon and Fourier. Saint-Simonism was annotated, expanded, transformed and established as a quasi-practical system—a kind of Church—by Père Enfantin, together with many friends, most of whom have today become financiers and statesmen, singularly devoted to the Empire. Fourierism found its advocate in *La Démocratie pacifique*, edited up to December 2nd by M. Victor Considérant.

The merit of these two socialist systems, differing as they do in many respects, lies mainly in their thoroughgoing, scientific, rigorous critique of the present-day organization of society, whose grotesque contradictions they have boldly laid bare, and then in the important function of having vigorously attacked and shaken Christianity in the name of the rehabilitation of matter and of the human passions slandered and yet so expertly practised by Christian priests. It was the intention of the Saint-Simonians to replace Christianity by a new religion, based on the mystic worship of the flesh, with a new hierarchy of priests, new exploiters of the common herd by right of genius, ability and talent. The far more (one might even say more sincerely) democratic Fourierists envisaged their phalansteries as ruled and administered by leaders elected by universal suffrage, believing that each would find his function and level of his own accord, as his passions dictated. The errors of the Saint-Simonians are too glaring to need dwelling upon. The twofold error of the Fourierists was, first, the honest belief that by dint of persuasion and pacifist propaganda alone they could succeed in touching the hearts of the wealthy so deeply that they would eventually turn up at the phalanstery gates of their own accord to deposit their surplus wealth; second, the assumption that it was theoretically and *a priori* possible to build a social paradise in which all of future humanity could recline. They had not realized that while we may well define the great principles of its future development we must leave the practical expression of those principles to the experience of the future.

As a rule, laying down the law has been the common enthusiasm of all socialists prior to 1848, with a single exception. Cabet, Louis Blanc, the Fourierists and Saint-Simonians all delighted in indoctrinating and organizing the future, all were more or less *authoritarian*.

But then came Proudhon, son of a peasant, and both practically and instinctively a hundred times more revolutionary than all these doctrinaire and bourgeois socialists. To destroy all their systems, he armed himself with a critique as profound and penetrating as it was ruthless. Contrasting liberty and authority, in answer to these State socialists he boldly declared himself an anarchist, and in the teeth of their deism or pantheism he had the courage simply to call himself an atheist, or rather, with Auguste Comte, a *positivist*.

His own socialism, based on individual and collective liberty and upon the spontaneous action of free associations, obeying no other laws than the general laws of social economy discovered or yet to be discovered by science, excluding all governmental regimentation and State protection and subordinating politics to the economic, intellectual and moral interests of society, was subsequently and logically to culminate in federalism.

This was the state of social science prior to 1848. The polemics of socialist journals, leaflets and pamphlets brought a spate of new ideas into the midst of the working classes. Saturation point was reached, and when the revolution of 1848 broke out socialism emerged as a real force.

Socialism, we have said, was the last offspring of the great revolution, but before that birth it had given rise to a more immediate heir, its eldest son, the darling of the Robespierres and Saint-Justs. That heir was *pure republicanism*, without any socialist content, revived out of antiquity and deriving its inspiration from the heroic traditions of the great citizens of Greece and Rome. Much less humanitarian than socialism, it is hardly aware of man and acknowledges only the citizen, so that whereas socialism seeks to found a *republic of men*, it seeks only a *republic of citizens*, even if—as in the constitutions which came as the necessary sequel to that of 1793, from the moment when, after a brief hesitation, the latter came to the point of deliberately ignoring the social question—even if the *active citizens*, to use an expression of the Constituent Assembly, must base their civic privilege on exploiting the labour of the *passive citizens*. While the political republican is not, or is not supposed to be, self-seeking, he is supposed to seek the interests of the motherland, ranking it in his free heart above himself and above all individuals, all the nations of the world and the whole of humanity. Consequently he will always be deaf to international justice, will give his country the verdict in all disputes with others—right or wrong—and will wish it always to be dominant and always to trample foreign countries beneath its power and glory. He will inevitably drift into conquest, despite the centuries of experience which show that military triumphs are bound to lead to Caesarism. The socialist republican loathes State grandeur, power and military glory, and prefers liberty and welfare. A federalist at home, he favours international federalism, firstly out of a sense of justice, next because he is convinced that economic and social revolution, breaking the artificial and deadening bounds of the State, can only occur (at least in part) by means of the joint action of most if not all the nations which constitute the civilized world of today, and that sooner or later all of them must rally to this cause.

The exclusively political republican is a stoic; he claims no rights, only duties; or else, as in Mazzini's republic, he acknowledges one right alone—that of dedicating and sacrificing himself to the motherland, living only to serve her, and joyfully dying for her, as in the words of the song which is M. Alexandre Dumas's free gift to the Girondins—'Mourir pour la patrie, c'est le sort le plus beau, le plus digne d'envie.' The socialist, on the other hand, takes his stand on his positive right to life and all its pleasures, both intellectual, moral and physical. He loves life, and intends to enjoy it to the full. Since his convictions are part of himself, and his duties to society are of a piece with his rights, in order to remain faithful to both he will be capable of living by justice, like Proudhon, and dying if need be, like Babeuf, but he will never assert that the life of mankind should be self-sacrifice or that death is the sweetest fate. Liberty is merely a word for the political republican; it is the liberty to be a voluntary slave, a devoted victim of the State; being ready to sacrifice his own, he will readily sacrifice that of others. Political republicanism therefore inevitably culminates in despotism. To the socialist republican, liberty is everything, goes hand in hand with welfare, and produces humanity for all through the humanity of each individual; he sees the State as nothing more than a tool, the servant of his own welfare and of every man's liberty. The socialist is distinguished from the bourgeois by *justice*, and claims only the real fruit of his own labour. He is distinguished from the exclusive republican by his *frank and human selfishness*, living candidly and unsententiously for himself, and knowing that by doing so *in accordance with justice* he serves the whole of society and that by serving it he is going about his proper business. The republican is rigid, and his patriotism—like the priest's religion—often makes him cruel. The socialist is natural, moderately patriotic, yet always very humane. In other words, there is a gulf between the republican socialist and the political republican: one, like a *semi-religious relic*, belongs to the past; the other, *positivist or atheist*, to the future.

This antagonism came into the open in 1848. From the very outset of the revolution the two were utterly at odds: their ideas and instincts pulled them in diametrically opposite directions. The whole period between February and June was taken up with wrangles which, by spreading civil war in the camp of the revolutionaries and paralysing their forces, were bound to benefit the new and formidable coalition of the whole gamut of reaction, united by fear and combined from then on into a single party. They thought they had won a victory, yet they had pushed their beloved republic into the abyss. General Cavaignac showed the flag against the revolution and was the forerunner of Napoleon III. Everybody then understood this—if not the French themselves, everybody else at least—for this fatal defeat of the Paris workers by the republicans was hailed as a great triumph by all the courts of Europe, and the officers of the Prussian guard, generals in the forefront, fell over themselves to send a message of fraternal congratulations to General Cavaignac.

Panic-stricken by the red bogey, the European bourgeoisie let itself relapse into absolute servility. Captious and liberal by nature, it is not enamoured of military rule, but opted for it in the presence of the looming threat of popular emancipation.

Having sacrificed its dignity along with all its glorious conquests of the eighteenth and early nineteenth centuries, it believed that it had at least purchased the peace and quiet necessary to the success of its commercial and industrial transaction. 'We are sacrificing our liberty to you,' it seemed to say to the military forces which rose again on the ruins of that third revolution. 'In return, leave us in peace to exploit the labour of the popular masses and protect us against their aspirations, which may seem legitimate in theory but are detestable from the standpoint of our own interests.' They promised everything, and even kept their word. Why then is the bourgeoisie—the entire bourgeoisie of Europe—generally discontented today?

It had reckoned without the high cost of military rule, which paralyses, unsettles and ruins nations by the very fact of its internal organization, and whose inevitable consequence, obedient to an inherent logic which has never failed, is *war*. Dynastic wars, wars of honour, wars of conquest or of natural frontiers, balance-of-power wars, destruction and permanent ingestion of State by State, rivers of human blood, burning countryside and ruined towns, whole provinces laid waste—and all to satiate the ambitions of princes and their favourites, to enrich them, to keep their peoples busy and disciplined, and to write another page in history.

Now the bourgeoisie understands, and that is why it is dissatisfied with the regime it toiled so hard to create. It is weary of it, but what could take its place?

Constitutional monarchy has had its day, and besides it has never been enormously prosperous on the continent of Europe. Even England, that historic cradle of modern constitutionalism, now under assault by the rise of democracy, is shaken, is tottering, and will soon be in no condition to stem the rising tide of popular feeling and demands.

The republic? But what republic? Purely political, or democratic and social? Are the masses still socialists? Yes, more than ever.

The casualty of June 1848 was not socialism in general but *State socialism*, prescriptive, authoritarian socialism, of the kind which believed and hoped that full satisfaction of the needs and legitimate aspirations of the working classes was to be provided by the State, and that this same State, armed with supreme power, wanted and was capable of inaugurating a new social order. So it was not socialism that succumbed in June, but rather the State which declared itself bankrupt with respect to socialism, and finding itself unable to pay its contracted debt attempted to discharge its responsibility in the easiest way by murdering its debtor. It did not manage to kill socialism, but it did succeed in killing the faith which socialism had invested in it, while annihilating all theories of authoritarian or doctrinaire socialism, some of which, like Cabet's 'Icaria' and M. Louis Blanc's 'Organization of labour', had advised the people to rely on the State for everything, while the rest had exhibited their inanity by a series of ludicrous experiments. Even Proudhon's bank, which might have prospered in happier times, was crushed by the censure and general hostility of the bourgeoisie, and succumbed.

Socialism lost this first battle for quite a simple reason: it was rich in instinct and in negative theoretical ideas which justified its case against privilege a thousand times over; but it was still totally devoid of the positive and practical ideas which would have been necessary to build a new system—that of popular justice—on the ruins of the bourgeois world. The workers who fought for the emancipation of the people in June were united by instinct, not ideas—and the vague ideas they did possess made a tower of Babel, a chaos, from which nothing could emerge. This was the principal cause of their defeat. Should we on this account be doubtful of the future and the present-day strength of socialism? Christianity set itself the task of founding the reign of justice in heaven, and took several centuries to triumph in Europe. Need we, then, be surprised that socialism, which has set itself a task of a quite different order of difficulty—that of implementing the reign of justice on earth—has failed to triumph in the course of a few years?

Is there any need, gentlemen, to prove that socialism is not dead? To find out, we have only to look at what is happening all over Europe today. Behind the diplomatic cancans and the clamour of war which has filled Europe since 1852, has any country faced a serious question that was not the social question? It is the great unknown whose coming is sensed by all the world, which makes each man tremble, but which no man dares speak of ... But it speaks for itself, and ever louder—the working men's co-operative associations, banks of mutual aid and workers' credit, trade unions, the international league of workers of every land,[5] all that rising tide of workers in England, France, Belgium, Germany, Italy and Switzerland, do these not prove that they have not abandoned their goal or lost faith in their coming emancipation, and that at the same time they have realized that to bring their time of freedom closer they cannot afford to depend on States or on the more or less hypocritical assistance of privileged classes, but on themselves and on their utterly spontaneous independent associations?

In most European countries this movement is a stranger to politics at first sight, and still maintains an exclusively economic and so to speak private character. But in England it has already taken a decisive stand on the fiery ground of politics, organized into a formidable Reform League, and gained a resounding victory over the politically organized privilege of the aristocracy and the higher bourgeoisie. With altogether English patience and practicality, the Reform League has drafted a plan of campaign, refuses to be deterred, and lets no obstacle frighten or halt it. 'Inside ten years at most,' they declare, 'allowing for the greatest hindrances, we shall have universal suffrage, and then ... ', then they will make the social revolution!

Moving unobtrusively, by way of private economic associations, socialism has already reached such a high degree of influence both in France and Germany that Napoleon III on the one hand and Graf von Bismarck on the other are beginning to angle for alliance with it ... In Italy and Spain, after the pathetic failure of every political party, and considering the dreadful hardships in which both are involved, all other questions will soon be buried beneath the economic and social question. In Russia and Poland, is there basically any other question? That is what has just shattered the last hopes of the old, aristocratic, historic Poland. That is what threatens and will bring about the collapse of that dread Empire of All the Russias, already tottering on its foundations. Even in

America, has socialism not come into the open with the proposal of an eminent Boston senator, Mr Charles Sumner, to
distribute land among the freed slaves of the southern States?

So you see, gentlemen, socialism is everywhere, and in spite
of its June defeat it has worked underground, slowly infiltrated
the depths of political life in every land, and has reached the
point of making its presence everywhere felt as the latent
power of the century. Another few years and it will emerge as
an active, formidable power.

With very few exceptions, and sometimes without even
knowing the word itself, all the peoples of Europe are socialists
today; they recognize no banner but that of their coming
economic emancipation, and would relinquish a thousand
causes rather than this one. Consequently it is only through
socialism that they can be drawn into the political arena in the
proper way.

Is this not enough, gentlemen, to suggest that we cannot
afford to overlook socialism in our programme, and that we
cannot hold aloof from it without blasting all our work with
impotence? Through our programme, in which we declare
ourselves federalist republicans, we have proved ourselves
revolutionary enough to alienate a sizeable section of the
bourgeoisie, that section which speculates against the hardships and misfortunes of the people and takes advantage even
of the great catastrophes which assail nations today more than
ever. Setting aside this active, restless, scheming, speculative
section of the bourgeoisie, we are left with the majority of
quiet, industrious bourgeois, who do cause some harm, but
more from necessity than inclination, and who would ask
nothing better than to be rid of that fatal necessity, which
sets them permanently at odds with the working populace and
ruins them at the same time. It has to be said that the lesser
bourgeoisie and minor trade and industry are now beginning
to suffer almost as much as the working classes, and if the process goes on at the same rate this respectable bourgeois
majority could easily find its economic situation merging with
that of the proletariat. Large-scale trade and industry and
especially wholesale shady speculation are crushing and
consuming them and squeezing them out. Their position is
thus becoming more and more revolutionary, and ideas which

have been reactionary for too long are having to be revised in the light of painful lessons. The intelligent are beginning to realize that the one hope for the honest bourgeois is alliance with the people—and that the social question affects him as much and *in the same way* as it does the people.

This progressive alteration in the thinking of the European petty bourgeoisie is a reassuring and undeniable factor. But make no mistake: the initiative of future developments will belong not to them but to the people—in the West, to the factory and urban workers; among ourselves, in Russia, Poland and most of the Slav lands, to the peasantry. The petty bourgeois have become too fearful, too timid and too sceptical to take any decisive step on their own account; they will let themselves be led, certainly, but they will not lead, because not only are they short of ideas but they lack faith and passion. The passion which shatters barriers and creates new worlds dwells only in the people. Therefore it is to the people that the initiative of the new movement will unquestionably belong! Yet we would disregard them! and we would make no mention of the socialism which is the new religion of the people!

But it is said that socialism looks ready to conclude an alliance with Caesarism. First, this is slander—it is Caesarism, on the contrary, which spies the threatening dawn of socialist power and is trying to enlist its sympathies and exploit them to its own ends. But is this not yet another reason for us to become involved, so as to be able to prevent such a monstrous alliance, whose outcome would undoubtedly be the greatest conceivable threat to the liberty of the world?

Quite apart from these practical considerations, we should also be involved because socialism is *justice*. By justice we do not mean the kind which is provided by legal codes and Roman jurisprudence, based to a great extent on violent acts, established by force, consecrated by time and the blessings of every Church, Christian and pagan alike, and accepted in those terms as absolute principles, of which the others are just logical extensions.* We mean the justice which is based

* In this connection, the science of law offers a perfect analogy with theology: both of these sciences lend equal acceptance, the one to a real but iniquitous fact—appropriation by force, conquest—the other to an illusory and absurd fact—divine revelation seen as an absolute

solely on human conscience, is found in all men, even in children, and which translates simply as *equity*.

This justice, which is so universal and yet which — thanks to the intervention of force and religious influences — has never prevailed in the political, judicial or economic spheres, must be the foundation of a new world. Without it, no liberty, no republic, no prosperity, no peace! It must therefore preside over all our deliberations, so that we may collaborate effectively in the establishment of peace.

This justice compels us to take up the cause of the people who to this day are so appallingly ill-treated, and together with political liberty, to work for economic and social emancipation on their behalf.

We are not advocating some specific socialist system, gentlemen. What we ask of you is a new proclamation of this great principle of the French Revolution: that every man should have the material and moral means to develop his full humanity, a principle voiced, we believe, by the following problem:

How to organize society in such a way that every man and woman who comes into the world may find approximately equal provision for the development of his or her various faculties and for their exercise through labour; how to organize a society which, by making it impossible for one man to exploit the work of another, allows each to share in the enjoyment of social wealth — which in fact is produced only by labour — only to the extent that he has contributed his own to its production.

The complete resolution of this problem will probably be the task of centuries. But history has posed it, and we cannot in future disregard it without condemning ourselves to complete impotence.

We hasten to add that we firmly reject any attempt at social organization so alien to the utmost liberty of individuals and associations as to require the establishment of any kind of regulatory authority, and that in the name of that liberty which we acknowledge as the one foundation and one legitimate creator of order we shall always resist anything having

principle. Whether they base themselves on absurdity or iniquity, both have recourse to the most rigorous logic in order to erect here a theological, there a judicial system.

the slightest resemblance to State communism or socialism.

The one thing that the State can and must do, in our opinion, is gradually to modify the right of inheritance so as to achieve its complete abolition as soon as possible. Being purely a creation of the State, and one of the essential conditions of the very existence of the authoritarian and divine State, the right of inheritance can and should be abolished by liberty within the State—which amounts to saying that the State itself must dissolve into a society freely organized on the basis of justice. We claim that this right will necessarily have to be abolished because as long as *inheritance* lasts, there will be *hereditary* economic inequality—not the natural inequality of individuals, but the artificial inequality of classes—which will necessarily continue to be expressed in hereditary inequality of the development and cultivation of intelligence and will remain the source and sanction of all political and social inequality. Equality for all, from birth until entry into adult life, as far as such equality depends on the economic and political organization of society, in order for every individual—natural differences apart—to be the true offspring of their own efforts: this is the problem of justice. We argue that the public trust for the upbringing and education of both sexes, including their maintenance from birth until coming of age, should be the sole heir of the dead. Speaking as Slavs and Russians, we would add that among ourselves it is a general social tenet, based on the traditional instincts of the populace, that the land belongs to all, and should be held only by those who work it with their hands.

We are convinced, gentlemen, that this principle is a just one, and an essential, inevitable condition of any serious social reform, and therefore that Western Europe cannot fail to accept and acknowledge it, in spite of all the difficulties arising out of its realization in certain lands, such as France, for example, where the majority of peasants already enjoy ownership of the land but where most of these same peasants will soon reach the point of owning nothing, as a result of the land-division which is the inevitable consequence of the politico-economic system at present prevailing in that country. We make no proposal in this matter, just as in general we refrain from any proposals on specific problems of social science and policy, being convinced that all these questions must receive serious, thorough discussion in our journal. Today, therefore, we go no further than to propose the issue of the following declaration:

> *Convinced that the significant realization of liberty, justice and peace in the world will be impossible as long as the vast majority of the population remains dispossessed of all wealth, deprived of education and condemned to political and social futility and* de facto *if not* de jure *slavery by hardship as well as by the necessity to work without pause, producing all the wealth the world takes pride in today and keeping only so small a share that it barely suffices to provide tomorrow's bread;*

> *Convinced that for all those peoples so terribly dealt with by the centuries the question of bread is that of intellectual emancipation, liberty and humanity;*

> *That liberty without socialism is privilege and injustice, and that socialism without liberty is slavery and brutality;*

> *The League boldly proclaims the need for radical social and economic reform aimed at the deliverance of popular labour from the yoke of capital and the landowners, based on the strictest justice, not judicial, theological or metaphysical but simply human, on positivist science and the most absolute liberty.*

> *It also resolves that its Journal will open its columns wide to all serious debate of social and economic questions, as long as it is sincerely inspired by desire for the broadest popular emancipation, both in economic terms and from the political and intellectual standpoint.*

VI GOD AND THE STATE

The following pages were written in February–March 1871 and are part of a long manuscript of 340 pages of which only the first part was published, in July 1871, under the title *L'Empire knouto-germanique*; lack of financial means prevented the publication of the second part, which was to appear only posthumously in 1908. In 1882 Élisée Redus and Carlo Cafiero published an extract from this manuscript, printed in a somewhat revised version, under the title *Dieu et l'État*; the first correct text in French is in vol. III of the *Œuvres* (Paris, 1908). The present text is taken from the first correct English edition, published in 1910 by Freedom Press, London, pp. 1–22; the translation is based on that made by Benjamin R. Tucker, published in Boston, Mass., 1883. The most recent edition was published in 1970, with an Introduction by Paul Avrich (New York: Dover Publications).

Who are right, the idealists or the materialists? The question once stated in this way, hesitation becomes impossible. Undoubtedly the idealists are wrong and the materialists right. Yes, facts are before ideas; yes, the ideal, as Proudhon said, is but a flower, whose root lies in the material conditions of existence. Yes, the whole history of humanity, intellectual and moral, political and social, is but a reflection of its economic history.

All branches of modern science, of true and disinterested science, concur in proclaiming this grand truth, fundamental and decisive: the social world, properly speaking, the human world — in short, humanity — is nothing other than the last and supreme development — at least on our planet and as far as we know — the highest manifestation of animality. But as every development necessarily implies a negation, that of its base or point of departure, humanity is at the same time and essentially the deliberate and gradual negation of the animal element in man; and it is precisely this negation, as rational as it is natural, and rational only because natural — at once historical and logical, as inevitable as the development and realization of all the natural laws in the world — that constitutes and creates the ideal, the world of intellectual and moral convictions, ideas.

Yes, our first ancestors, our Adams and our Eves, were, if not gorillas, very near relatives of gorillas, omnivorous, intelligent and ferocious beasts, endowed in a higher degree than the animals of any other species with two precious faculties — *the power to think* and *the desire to rebel.*

These two faculties, combining their progressive action in history, represent the essential factor, the negative power in the positive development of human animality, and create consequently all that constitutes humanity in man.

The Bible, which is a very interesting and here and there very profound book when considered as one of the oldest surviving manifestations of human wisdom and fancy, expresses this truth very naively in its myth of original sin. Jehovah, who of all the good gods adored by men was certainly the most jealous, the most vain, the most ferocious, the most unjust, the most bloodthirsty, the most despotic and the most hostile to human dignity and liberty — Jehovah had just created Adam and Eve, to satisfy we know not what caprice; no doubt to while away his time, which must weigh heavy on his hands in his eternal egoistic solitude, or that he might have some new slaves. He generously placed at their disposal the whole earth, with all its fruits and animals, and set but a single limit to this complete enjoyment. He expressly forbade them from touching the fruit of the tree of knowledge. He wished, therefore, that man, destitute of all understanding of himself, should remain an eternal beast, ever on all fours before the eternal God, his creator and his master. But here steps in Satan, the eternal rebel, the first freethinker and the emancipator of worlds. He makes man ashamed of his bestial ignorance and obedience; he emancipates him, stamps upon his brow the seal of liberty and humanity, in urging him to disobey and eat of the fruit of knowledge.

We know what followed. The good God, whose foresight, which is one of the divine faculties, should have warned him of what would happen, flew into a terrible and ridiculous rage; he cursed Satan, man, and the world created by himself, striking himself so to speak in his own creation, as children do when they get angry; and, not content with smiting our ancestors themselves, he cursed them in all the generations to come, innocent of the crime committed by their forefathers. Our Catholic and Protestant theologians look upon that as very profound and very just, precisely because it is monstrously iniquitous and absurd. Then, remembering that he was not only a God of vengeance and wrath but also a God of love, after having tormented the existence of a few milliards of poor human beings and condemned them to an eternal hell, he took pity on the rest, and, to save them and reconcile his eternal and divine love with his eternal and divine anger, always greedy for victims and blood, he sent into the world, as an expiatory victim, his only son, that he might be killed by men. That is called the mystery of the Redemption, the basis of all the Christian religions. Still, if the divine Saviour had saved the human world! But no; in the paradise promised by Christ, as we know, such being the formal announcement, the elect will number very few. The rest, the immense majority of the generations present and to come, will burn eternally in hell. In the meantime, to console us, God, ever just, ever good, hands over the earth to the government of the Napoleon IIIs, of the William Is, of the Ferdinands of Austria, and of the Alexanders of all the Russias.

Such are the absurd tales that are told and the monstrous doctrines that are taught, in the full light of the nineteenth century, in all the popular schools of Europe, at the express commands of the governments. They call this civilizing people! Is it not plain that all these governments are systematic poisoners, interested stupefiers of the popular masses?

I have wandered from my subject, because anger gets hold of me whenever I think of the base and criminal means which they employ to keep the nations in perpetual slavery, undoubtedly that they may be the better able to fleece them. Of what consequence are the crimes of all the Tropmanns in the world compared with this crime of treason against humanity committed daily, in broad day, over the whole surface of the civilized world, by those who dare to call themselves the guardians and the fathers of the people? I return to the myth of original sin.

God admitted that Satan was right; he recognized that the devil did not deceive Adam and Eve in promising them knowledge and liberty as a reward for the act of disobedience which he had induced them to commit; for, immediately they had eaten of the forbidden fruit, God himself said (see the Bible), 'Behold, the man is become as one of the gods, to know good and evil; prevent him, therefore, from eating of the fruit of eternal life, lest he become immortal like Ourselves.'

Let us disregard now the fabulous portion of this myth and consider its true meaning, which is very clear. Man has emancipated himself; he has separated himself from animality and constituted himself a man; he has begun his distinctively human history and development by an act of disobedience and science — that is, by *rebellion* and by *thought*.

Three elements or, if you like, three fundamental principles constitute the essential conditions of all human development, collective or individual, in history: (1) *human animality*; (2) *thought*; and (3) *rebellion*. To the first properly corresponds *social and private economy*; to the second, *science*; to the third, *liberty*.

Idealists of all schools, aristocrats and *bourgeois*, theologians and metaphysicians, politicians and moralists, religionists, philosophers or poets, not forgetting the liberal economists — unbounded worshippers of the ideal, as we know — are much offended when told that man, with his magnificent intelligence, his sublime ideas and his boundless aspirations, is, like all else existing in the world, nothing but matter, only a product of *vile matter*.

We may answer that the matter of which materialists speak, matter spontaneously and eternally mobile, active, productive, matter chemically or organically determined and manifested by the properties or forces, mechanical, physical, animal, and intelligent, which necessarily belong to it — that this matter has nothing in common with the *vile matter* of the idealists. The latter, a product of their false abstraction, is indeed a stupid, inanimate, immobile thing, incapable of giving birth to the smallest product, a *caput mortuum*, an *ugly* fancy in contrast to the *beautiful* fancy which they call *God*; as the opposite of this supreme Being, matter, their matter, stripped by them of all that constitutes its real nature, necessarily represents supreme nothingness. They have taken away from matter intelligence, life, all its determining qualities, active relations or forces, motion itself, without which matter would not even have weight, leaving it nothing but impenetrability and absolute immobility in space; they have attributed all these natural forces, properties and manifestations to the imaginary being created by their abstract fancy; then, interchanging *roles*, they have called this product of their imagination, this phantom, this God who is nothing, 'supreme Being', and, as a necessary consequence, have declared that the real Being, matter, the world, is nothing. After which they gravely tell us that this matter is incapable of producing anything, not even of setting itself in motion, and consequently must have been created by their God.

I [have elsewhere] exposed the truly revolting absurdities to which one is inevitably led by this imagination of a God, let him be considered as a personal being, the creator and orga-nizer of worlds; or even as impersonal, a kind of divine soul spread over the whole universe and constituting thus its eternal principle; or let him be an idea, infinite and divine, always present and active in the world, and always manifested by the totality of material and definite beings. Here I shall deal with one point only.

The gradual development of the material world, as well as of organic animal life and of the historically progressive intelli-gence of man, individually or socially, is perfectly conceivable. It is a wholly natural movement from the simple to the com-plex, from the lower to the higher, from the inferior to the superior; a movement in conformity with all our daily ex-periences, and consequently in conformity also with our natural logic, with the distinctive laws of our mind, which being formed and developed only by the aid of these same ex-periences, is, so to speak, but the mental, cerebral reproduction or reflected summary thereof.

The system of the idealists is quite the contrary of this. It is the reversal of all human experiences and of that universal and common good sense which is the essential condition of all human understanding, and which, in rising from the simple and unanimously recognized truth that twice two are four to the sublimest and most complex scientific considerations — admitting, moreover, nothing that has not stood the severest tests of experience or observation of things and facts — becomes the only serious basis of human knowledge.

Very far from pursuing the natural order from the lower to the higher, from the inferior to the superior, and from the relatively simple to the more complex; instead of wisely and rationally accompanying the progressive and real movement from the world called inorganic to the world organic, vegetable, animal, and then distinctively human — from chemical matter or chemical being to living matter or living being, and from living being to thinking being — the idealists, obsessed, blinded, and pushed on by the divine phantom which they have inherited from theology, take precisely the opposite course. They go from the higher to the lower, from the superior to the inferior, from the complex to the simple. They begin with God, either as a person or as divine substance or idea, and the first step that they take is a terrible fall from the sublime heights of the eternal ideal into the mire of the material world; from absolute perfection into absolute imperfection; from thought to being, or rather, from supreme being to Nothing. When, how, and why the divine Being, eternal, infinite, absolutely perfect, probably weary of himself, decided upon this desperate *salto mortale* is something which no idealist, no theologian, no metaphysician, no poet, has ever been able to understand himself or explain to the profane. All religions, past and present, and all the systems of transcendental philosophy hinge on this unique and iniquitous mystery.* Holy men, inspired lawgivers, prophets, messiahs, have searched it for life, and found only torment and death. Like the ancient sphinx, it has devoured them, because they could not explain it. Great philosophers, from Heraclitus and Plato down to Descartes, Spinoza, Leibnitz, Kant, Fichte, Schelling, and Hegel, not to mention the Indian philosophers, have written heaps of volumes and built systems as ingenious as sublime,

* I call it 'iniquitous' because ... this mystery has been and still continues to be the consecration of all the horrors which have been and are being committed in the world; I call it unique, because all the other theological and metaphysical absurdities which debase the human mind are but its necessary consequences.

in which they have said by the way many beautiful and grand things and discovered immortal truths, but they have left this mystery, the principal object of their transcendental investigations, as unfathomable as before. The gigantic efforts of the most wonderful geniuses that the world has known, and who, one after another, for at least thirty centuries, have undertaken anew this labour of Sisyphus, have resulted only in rendering this mystery still more incomprehensible. Is it to be hoped that it will be unveiled to us by the routine speculations of some pedantic disciple of an artificially warmed-over metaphysics at a time when all living and serious spirits have abandoned that ambiguous science born of a compromise — historically explicable no doubt — between the unreason of faith and sound scientific reason?

It is evident that this terrible mystery is inexplicable — that is, absurd, because only the absurd admits of no explanation. It is evident that whoever finds it essential to his happiness and life must renounce his reason, and return, if he can, to naive, blind, stupid faith, to repeat with Tertullian and all sincere believers these words, which sum up the very quintessence of theology: *Credo quia absurdum.* Then all discussion ceases, and nothing remains but the triumphant stupidity of faith. But immediately there arises another question: *How comes an intelligent and well-informed man ever to feel the need of believing in this mystery?*

Nothing is more natural than that the belief in God, the creator, regulator, judge, master, curser, saviour, and benefactor of the world, should still prevail among the people, especially in the rural districts, where it is more widespread than among the proletariat of the cities. The people, unfortunately, are still very ignorant, and are kept in ignorance by the systematic efforts of all the governments, who consider this ignorance, not without good reason, as one of the essential conditions of their own power. Weighted down by their daily labour, deprived of leisure, of intellectual intercourse, of reading, in short of all the means and a good portion of the stimulants that develop thought in men, the people generally accept religious traditions without criticisms and in a lump. These traditions surround them from infancy in all the situations of life, and artificially sustained in their minds by a multitude of official poisoners of all sorts, priests and laymen, are transformed therein into a sort of mental and moral habit, too often more powerful even than their natural good sense.

There is another reason which explains and in some sort justifies the absurd beliefs of the people — namely, the wretched situation to which they find themselves fatally condemned by the economic organization of society in the most civilized countries of Europe. Reduced, intellectually and morally as well as materially, to the minimum of human existence, confined in their life like a prisoner in his prison, without horizon, without outlet, without even a future if we believe the economists, the people would have the singularly narrow souls and blunted instincts of the bourgeois if they did not feel a desire to escape; but of escape there are but three methods — two chimerical and a third real. The first two are the dram-shop and the church, debauchery of the body or debauchery of the mind; the third is social revolution. Hence I conclude this last will be much more potent than all the theological propagandism of the freethinkers to destroy to their last vestige the religious beliefs and dissolute habits of the people, beliefs and habits much more intimately connected than is generally supposed. In substituting for the at once illusory and brutal enjoyments of bodily and spiritual licentiousness the enjoyments, as refined as they are real, of humanity developed in each and all, the social revolution alone will have the power to close at the same time all the dram-shops and all the churches.

Till then the people, taken as a whole, will believe; and, if they have no reason to believe, they will have at least a right.

There is a class of people who, if they do not believe, must at least make a semblance of believing. This class, comprising all the tormentors, all the oppressors and all the exploiters of humanity: priests, monarchs, statesmen, soldiers, public and private financiers, officials of all sorts, policemen, gendarmes, jailers and executioners, monopolists, capitalists, tax-leeches, contractors and landlords, lawyers, economists, politicians of all shades, down to the smallest vendor of sweetmeats, all will repeat in unison those words of Voltaire:

'If God did not exist, it would be necessary to invent him.' For, you understand, 'the people must have a religion.' That is the safety-valve.

There exists, finally, a somewhat numerous class of honest but timid souls who, too intelligent to take the Christian dogmas seriously, reject them in detail, but have neither the courage nor the strength nor the necessary resolution to summarily renounce them altogether. They abandon to your criticism all the special absurdities of religion, they turn up their noses at all the miracles, but they cling desperately to the principal absurdity, the source of all the others, to the miracle that explains and justifies all the other miracles, the existence of God. Their God is not the vigorous and powerful Being, the brutally positive God of theology. It is a nebulous, diaphanous, illusory Being that vanishes into nothing at the first attempt to grasp it; it is a mirage, an *ignis fatuus* that neither warms nor illuminates. And yet they hold fast to it, and believe that, were it to disappear, all would disappear with it. They are uncertain, sickly souls, who have lost their reckoning in the present civilization, belonging to neither the present nor the future, pale phantoms eternally suspended between heaven and earth, and occupying exactly the same position between the politics of the bourgeois and the socialism of the pro-letariat. They have neither the power nor the wish nor the determination to follow out their thought, and they waste their time and pains in constantly endeavouring to reconcile the irreconcilable. In public life these are known as bourgeois socialists.

With them, or against them, discussion is out of the question. They are too puny.

But there are a few illustrious men of whom no one will dare to speak without respect, and whose vigorous health, strength of mind, and good intention no one will dream of calling in question. I need only cite the names of Mazzini, Michelet, Quinet, John Stuart Mill.* Generous and strong souls, great hearts, great minds, great writers, and the first the heroic and revolutionary regenerator of a great nation, they are all

* Mr Stuart Mill is perhaps the only one whose serious idealism may be fairly doubted, and that for two reasons: first, that, if not absolutely the disciple, he is a passionate admirer, an adherent of the positive philosophy of Auguste Comte, a philosophy which, in spite of its numerous reservations, is really atheistic; second, that Mr Stuart Mill is English, and in England to proclaim one's self an atheist is to ostracise one's self, even at this late day.

apostles of idealism and bitter despisers and adversaries of materialism, and consequently of Socialism also, in philosophy as well as in politics.

Against them, then, we must discuss this question.

First, let it be remarked that not one of the illustrious men I have just named nor any other idealistic thinker of any consequence in our day has given any attention to the logical side of this question properly speaking. Not one has tried to settle philosophically the possibility of the divine *salto mortale* from the pure and eternal regions of spirit into the mire of the material world. Have they feared to approach this irreconcilable contradiction and despaired of solving it after the failures of the greatest geniuses of history, or have they looked upon it as already sufficiently well settled? That is their secret. The fact is that they have neglected the theoretical demonstration of the existence of a God, and have developed only its practical motives and consequences. They have treated it as a fact universally accepted, and, as such, no longer susceptible of any doubt whatever, for sole proof thereof limiting themselves to the establishment of the antiquity and this very universality of the belief in God.

This imposing unanimity, in the eyes of many illustrious men and writers—to quote only the most famous of them who eloquently expressed it, Joseph de Maistre and the great Italian patriot, Guiseppe Mazzini—is of more value than all the demonstrations of science; and if the reasoning of a small number of logical and even very powerful, but isolated, thinkers is against it, so much the worse, they say, for these thinkers and their logic, for universal consent, the general and primitive adoption of an idea, has always been considered the most triumphant testimony to its truth. The sentiment of the whole world, a conviction that is found and maintained always and everywhere, cannot be mistaken; it must have its root in a necessity absolutely inherent in the very nature of man. And since it has been established that all peoples, past and present, have believed and still believe in the existence of God, it is clear that those who have the misfortune to doubt it, whatever the logic that led them to this doubt, are abnormal exceptions, monsters.

Thus, then, the *antiquity* and *universality* of a belief should be regarded, contrary to all science and all logic, as sufficient and unimpeachable proof of its truth. Why?

Until the days of Copernicus and Galileo everybody believed that the sun revolved about the earth. Was not everybody mistaken? What is more ancient and more universal than slavery? Cannibalism perhaps. From the origin of historic society down to the present day there has been always and everywhere exploitation of the compulsory labour of the masses — slaves, serfs or wage-workers — by some dominant minority; oppression of the people by the Church and by the State. Must it be concluded that this exploitation and this oppression are necessities absolutely inherent in the very existence of human society? These are examples which show that the argument of the champions of God proves nothing.

Nothing, in fact, is as universal or as ancient as the iniquitous and absurd; truth and justice, on the contrary, are the least universal, the youngest features in the development of human society. In this fact, too, lies the explanation of a constant historical phenomenon — namely, the persecution of which those who first proclaim the truth have been and continue to be the objects at the hands of the official, privileged, and interested representatives of 'universal' and 'ancient' beliefs, and often also at the hands of the same popular masses who, after having tortured them, always end by adopting their ideas and rendering them victorious.

To us materialists and Revolutionary Socialists, there is nothing astonishing or terrifying in this historical phenomenon. Strong in our conscience, in our love of truth at all hazards, in that passion for logic which of itself alone constitutes a great power and outside of which there is no thought; strong in our passion for justice and in our unshakable faith in the triumph of humanity over all theoretical and practical bestialities; strong, finally, in the mutual confidence and support given each other by the few who share our convictions — we resign ourselves to all the consequences of this historical phenomenon, in which we see the manifestation of a social law as natural, as necessary and as invariable as all the other laws which govern the world.

This law is a logical, inevitable consequence of the *animal origin* of human society; for in face of all the scientific, physiological, psychological, and historical proofs accumulated at the present day, as well as in face of the exploits of the Germans conquering France, which now furnish so striking a demonstration thereof, it is no longer possible to really doubt this origin. But from the moment that this animal origin of man is accepted, all is explained. History then appears to us as the revolutionary negation, now slow, apathetic, sluggish, now passionate and powerful, of the past. It consists precisely in the progressive negation of the primitive animality of man by the development of his humanity. Man, a wild beast, cousin of the gorilla, has emerged from the profound darkness of animal instinct into the light of the mind, which explains in a wholly natural way all his past mistakes and partially consoles us for his present errors. He has gone out from animal slavery, and, passing through divine slavery, a temporary condition between his animality and his humanity, he is now marching on to the conquest and realization of human liberty. Whence it results that the antiquity of a belief, of an idea, far from proving anything in its favour, ought, on the contrary, to lead us to suspect it. For behind us is our animality and before us our humanity; human light, the only thing that can warm and enlighten us, the only thing that can emancipate us, give us dignity, freedom, and happiness, and realize fraternity among us, is never at the beginning, but, relatively to the epoch in which we live, always at the end of history. Let us, then, never look back, let us look ever forward; for forward is our sunlight, forward our salvation. If it is justifiable, and even useful and necessary, to turn back to study our past, it is only in order to establish what we have been and what we must no longer be, what we have believed and thought and what we must no longer believe or think, what we have done and what we must do nevermore.

So much for *antiquity*. As for the *universality* of an error, it proves but one thing — the similarity, if not the perfect identity, of human nature in all ages and under all skies. And, since it is established that all peoples, at all periods of their life, have believed and still believe in God, we must simply conclude that the divine idea, an outcome of ourselves, is an error historically necessary in the development of humanity, and ask why and how it was produced in history and why an immense majority of the human race still accept it as a truth.

Until we shall account to ourselves for the manner in which the idea of a supernatural or divine world was developed and had to be developed in the historical evolution of the human conscience, all our scientific conviction of its absurdity will be in vain; until then we shall never succeed in destroying it in the opinion of the majority, because we shall never be able to attack it in the very depths of the human being where it had birth. Condemned to a fruitless struggle, without issue and without end, we should for ever have to content ourselves with fighting it solely on the surface, in its innumerable manifestations, whose absurdity will be scarcely beaten down by the blows of common sense before it will reappear in a new form no less nonsensical. While the root of all the absurdities that torment the world, belief in God, remains intact, it will never fail to bring forth new offspring. Thus, at the present time, in certain sections of the highest society, Spiritualism tends to establish itself upon the ruins of Christianity.

It is not only in the interest of the masses, it is in that of the health of our own minds, that we should strive to understand the historic genesis, the succession of causes which developed and produced the idea of God in the consciousness of men. In vain shall we call and believe ourselves Atheists, until we comprehend these causes, for, until then, we shall always suffer ourselves to be more or less governed by the clamours of this universal conscience whose secret we have not discovered; and, considering the natural weakness of even the strongest individual against the all-powerful influence of the social surroundings that trammel him, we are always in danger of relapsing sooner or later, in one way or another, into the abyss of religious absurdity. Examples of these shameful conversions are frequent in society today.

I have stated the chief practical reason of the power still exercised today over the masses by religious beliefs. These mystical tendencies do not signify in man so much an aberration of mind as a deep discontent at heart. They are the instinctive and passionate protest of the human being against the narrownesses, the platitudes, the sorrows, and the shames of a wretched existence. For this malady, I have already said, there is but one remedy—Social Revolution.

I have endeavoured to show [elsewhere] the causes responsible for the birth and historical development of religious
hallucinations in the human conscience. Here it is my purpose
to treat this question of the existence of a God, or of the divine
origin of the world and of man, solely from the standpoint of its
moral and social utility, and I shall say only a few words, to
better explain my thought, regarding the theoretical grounds
of this belief.

All religions, with their gods, their demigods and their
prophets, their messiahs and their saints, were created by the
credulous fancy of men who had not attained the full development and full possession of their faculties. Consequently, the
religious heaven is nothing but a mirage in which man, exalted
by ignorance and faith, discovers his own image, but enlarged
and reversed—that is, *divinized*. The history of religions, of the
birth, grandeur and decline of the gods who have succeeded
one another in human belief, is nothing, therefore, but the
development of the collective intelligence and conscience of
mankind. As fast as they discovered, in the course of their
historically progressive advance, either in themselves or in
external nature, a power, a quality, or even any great defect
whatever, they attributed them to their gods, after having
exaggerated and enlarged them beyond measure, after the
manner of children, by an act of their religious fancy. Thanks
to this modesty and pious generosity of believing and credulous
men, heaven has grown rich with the spoils of the earth, and,
by a necessary consequence, the richer heaven became, the
more wretched became humanity and the earth. God once
installed, he was naturally proclaimed the cause, reason,
arbiter, and absolute disposer of all things: the world thence-
forth was nothing, God was all; and man, his real creator, after
having unknowingly extracted him from the void, bowed
down before him, worshipped him, and avowed himself his
creature and his slave.

Christianity is precisely the religion *par excellence*, because it
exhibits and manifests, to the fullest extent, the very nature and
essence of every religious system, which is *the impoverishment,
enslavement, and annihilation of humanity for the benefit of divinity*.

God being everything, the real world and man are nothing.
God being truth, justice, goodness, beauty, power and life,

man is falsehood, iniquity, evil, ugliness, impotence and death. God being master, man is the slave. Incapable of finding justice, truth and eternal life by his own effort, he can attain them only through a divine revelation. But whoever says revelation says revealers, messiahs, prophets, priests and legislators inspired by God himself; and these, once recognized as the representatives of divinity on earth, as the holy instructors of humanity, chosen by God himself to direct it in the path of salvation, necessarily exercise absolute power. All men owe them passive and unlimited obedience; for against the divine reason there is no human reason, and against the justice of God no terrestrial justice holds. Slaves of God, men must also be slaves of Church and State, *in so far as the State is consecrated by the Church.* This truth Christianity, better than all other religions that exist or have existed, understood, not excepting even the old Oriental religions, which included only distinct and privileged nations, while Christianity aspires to embrace entire humanity; and this truth Roman Catholicism, alone among all the Christian sects, has proclaimed and realized with rigorous logic. That is why Christianity is the absolute religion, the final religion; why the Apostolic and Roman Church is the only consistent, legitimate, and divine Church.

With all due respect, then, to the metaphysicians and religious idealists, philosophers, politicians or poets: *The idea of God implies the abdication of human reason and justice; it is the most decisive negation of human liberty, and necessarily ends in the enslavement of mankind, both in theory and practice.*

Unless, then, we desire the enslavement and degradation of mankind, as the Jesuits desire it, as the *mômiers*, pietists or Protestant Methodists desire it, we may not, must not make the slightest concession either to the God of theology or to the God of metaphysics. He who, in this mystical alphabet, begins with A will inevitably end with Z; he who desires to worship God must harbour no childish illusions about the matter, but bravely renounce his liberty and humanity.

If God is, man is a slave; now, man can and must be free; then, God does not exist.

I defy anyone whomsoever to avoid this circle; now, therefore, let all choose.

*

Is it necessary to point out to what extent and in what manner religions debase and corrupt the people? They destroy their reason, the principal instrument of human emancipation, and reduce them to imbecility, the essential condition of their slavery. They dishonour human labour, and make it a sign and source of servitude. They kill the idea and sentiment of human justice, ever tipping the balance to the side of triumphant knaves, privileged objects of divine indulgence. They kill human pride and dignity, protecting only the cringing and humble. They stifle in the heart of nations every feeling of human fraternity, filling it with divine cruelty instead.

All religions are cruel, all founded on blood; for all rest principally on the idea of sacrifice—that is, on the perpetual immolation of humanity to the insatiable vengeance of divinity. In this bloody mystery man is always the victim, and the priest —a man also, but a man privileged by grace—is the divine executioner. That explains why the priests of all religions, the best, the most humane, the gentlest, almost always have at the bottom of their hearts—and, if not in their hearts, in their imaginations, in their minds (and we know the fearful influence of either on the hearts of men)—something cruel and sanguinary.

None know all this better than our illustrious contemporary idealists. They are learned men, who know history by heart; and, as they are at the same time living men, great souls penetrated with a sincere and profound love for the welfare of humanity, they have cursed and branded all these misdeeds, all these crimes of religion with an eloquence unparalleled. They reject with indignation all solidarity with the God of positive religions and with his representatives, past, present and on earth.

The God whom they adore, or whom they think they adore, is distinguished from the real gods of history precisely in this— that he is not at all a positive god, defined in any way whatever, theologically or even metaphysically. He is neither the supreme Being of Robespierre and J. J. Rousseau, nor the pantheistic god of Spinoza, nor even the at once immanent, transcendental and very equivocal god of Hegel. They take good care not to give him any positive definition whatever, feeling very strongly that any definition would subject him to the dissolving power of criticism. They will not say whether he is a personal or impersonal god, whether he created or did not create the world; they will not even speak of his divine providence. All that might compromise him. They content themselves with saying 'God' and nothing more. But, then, what is their God? Not even an idea; it is an aspiration.

It is the generic name of all that seems grand, good, beautiful, noble, human to them. But why, then, do they not say 'Man'. Ah! because King William of Prussia and Napoleon III and all their compeers are likewise men; which bothers them very much. Real humanity presents a mixture of all that is most sublime and beautiful with all that is vilest and most monstrous in the world. How do they get over this? Why, they call one *divine* and the other *bestial*, representing divinity and animality as two poles, between which they place humanity. They either will not or cannot understand that these three terms are really but one, and that to separate them is to destroy them.

They are not strong on logic, and one might say that they despise it. That is what distinguishes them from the pan-theistical and deistical metaphysicians, and gives their ideas the character of a practical idealism, drawing its inspiration much less from the severe development of a thought than from the experiences, I might almost say the emotions, historical and collective as well as individual, of life. This gives their propaganda an appearance of wealth and vital power, but an appearance only; for life itself becomes sterile when paralysed by a logical contradiction.

This contradiction lies here: they wish God, and they wish humanity. They persist in connecting two terms which, once separated, can come together again only to destroy each other. They say in a single breath: 'God and the liberty of man,' 'God and the dignity, justice, equality, fraternity, prosperity of men' — regardless of the fatal logic by virtue of which, if God exists, all these things are condemned to non-existence. For, if God is, he is necessarily the eternal, supreme, absolute master, and, if such a master exists, man is a slave; now, if he is a slave, neither justice nor equality nor fraternity nor prosperity is possible for him. In vain, flying in the face of good sense and all the teachings of history, do they represent their God as animated by the tenderest love of human liberty; a master, whoever he may be and however liberal he may desire to show himself, remains none the less always a master. His existence necessarily implies the slavery of all that is beneath him. Therefore, if God existed, only in one way could he serve human liberty—by ceasing to exist.

A jealous lover of human liberty, and deeming it the absolute condition of all that we admire and respect in humanity, I reverse the phrase of Voltaire, and say that *if God really existed, it would be necessary to abolish him.*

The severe logic that dictates these words is far too evident to require a development of this argument. And it seems to me impossible that the illustrious men, whose names so celebrated and so justly respected I have cited, should not have been struck by it themselves, and should not have perceived the contradiction in which they involve themselves in speaking of God and human liberty at once. To have disregarded it, they must have considered this inconsistency or logical licence *practically* necessary to humanity's well-being.

Perhaps, too, while speaking of *liberty* as something very respectable and very dear in their eyes, they give the term a meaning quite different from the conception entertained by us, materialists and Revolutionary Socialists. Indeed, they never speak of it without immediately adding another word, *authority*—a word and a thing which we detest with all our hearts.

What is authority? Is it the inevitable power of the natural laws which manifest themselves in the necessary concatenation and succession of phenomena in the physical and social worlds? Indeed, against these laws revolt is not only forbidden—it is even impossible. We may misunderstand them or not know them at all, but we cannot disobey them; because they constitute the basis and fundamental conditions of our existence; they envelop us, penetrate us, regulate all our movements, thoughts and acts; even when we believe that we disobey them, we only show their omnipotence.

Yes, we are absolutely the slaves of these laws. But in such slavery there is no humiliation, or, rather, it is not slavery at all. For slavery supposes an external master, a legislator outside of him whom he commands, while these laws are not outside of us; they are inherent in us; they constitute our being, our whole being, physically, intellectually and morally: we live, we breathe, we act, we think, we wish only through these laws. Without them we are nothing, *we are not*. Whence, then, could we derive the power and the wish to rebel against them?

In his relation to natural laws but one liberty is possible to man—that of recognizing and applying them on an ever-extending scale in conformity with the object of collective and individual emancipation or humanization which he pursues. These laws, once recognized, exercise an authority which is never disputed by the mass of men. One must, for instance, be at bottom either a fool or a theologian or at least a meta-physician, jurist or bourgeois economist to rebel against the law by which twice two make four. One must have faith to imagine that fire will not burn nor water drown, except, indeed, recourse be had to some subterfuge founded in its turn on some other natural law. But these revolts, or, rather, these attempts at or foolish fancies of an impossible revolt, are decidedly the exception; for, in general, it may be said that the mass of men, in their daily lives, acknowledge the government of common sense—that is, of the sum of the natural laws generally recognized—in an almost absolute fashion.

The great misfortune is that a large number of natural laws, already established as such by science, remain unknown to the popular masses, thanks to the watchfulness of these tutelary governments that exist, as we know, only for the good of the people. There is another difficulty—namely, that the major portion of the natural laws connected with the development of human society, which are quite as necessary, invariable, fatal, as the laws that govern the physical world, have not been duly established and recognized by science itself.

Once they shall have been recognized by science, and then, from science, by means of an extensive system of popular educa-tion and instruction, shall have passed into the consciousness of all, the question of liberty will be entirely solved. The stubbornest authorities must admit that then there will be no need either of political organization or direction or legislation, three things which, whether they emanate from the will of the sovereign or from the vote of a parliament elected by universal suffrage, and even should they conform to the system of natural laws—which has never been the case and never will be the case—are always equally fatal and hostile to the liberty of the masses from the very fact that they impose upon them a system of external and therefore despotic laws.

The liberty of man consists solely in this: that he obeys natural laws because he has *himself* recognized them as such, and not because they have been externally imposed upon him by any extrinsic will whatever, divine or human, collective or individual.

Suppose a learned academy, composed of the most illustrious representatives of science; suppose this academy charged with legislation for and the organization of society, and that, inspired only by the purest love of truth, it frames none but laws in absolute harmony with the latest discoveries of science. Well, I maintain, for my part, that such legislation and such organization would be a monstrosity, and that for two reasons: first, that human science is always and necessarily imperfect and that, comparing what it has discovered with what remains to be discovered, we may say that it is still in its cradle. So that were we to try to force the practical life of men, collective as well as individual, into strict and exclusive conformity with the latest data of science, we should condemn society as well as individuals to suffer martyrdom on a bed of Procrustes, which would soon end by dislocating and stifling them, life ever remaining an infinitely greater thing than science.

The second reason is this: a society which should obey legislation emanating from a scientific academy, not because it understood itself the rational character of this legislation (in which case the existence of the academy would become useless), but because this legislation, emanating from the academy, was imposed in the name of a science which it venerated without comprehending—such a society would be a society, not of men, but of brutes. It would be a second edition of those missions in Paraguay which submitted so long to the government of the Jesuits. It would surely and rapidly descend to the lowest stage of idiocy.

But there is still a third reason which would render such a government impossible—namely that a scientific academy invested with a sovereignty, so to speak, absolute, even if it were composed of the most illustrious men, would infallibly and soon end in its own moral and intellectual corruption. Even today, with the few privileges allowed them, such is the history of all academies. The greatest scientific genius, from the moment that he becomes an academician, an officially licensed *savant*, inevitably lapses into sluggishness. He loses his spontaneity, his revolutionary hardihood, and that troublesome and savage energy characteristic of the grandest geniuses, ever called to destroy old tottering worlds and lay the foundations of new. He undoubtedly gains in politeness, in utilitarian and practical wisdom, what he loses in power of thought. In a word, he becomes corrupted.

It is the characteristic of privilege and of every privileged position to kill the mind and heart of men. The privileged man, whether politically or economically, is a man depraved in mind and heart. That is a social law which admits of no exception, and is as applicable to entire nations as to classes, corporations and individuals. It is the law of equality, the supreme condition of liberty and humanity. The principal object of this treatise is precisely to demonstrate this truth in all the manifestations of human life.

A scientific body to which had been confided the government of society would soon end by devoting itself no longer to science at all, but to quite another affair; and that affair, as in the case of all established powers, would be its own eternal perpetuation by rendering the society confided to its care ever more stupid and consequently more in need of its government and direction.

But that which is true of scientific academies is also true of all constituent and legislative assemblies, even those chosen by universal suffrage. In the latter case they may renew their composition, it is true, but this does not prevent the formation in a few years' time of a body of politicians, privileged in fact though not in law, who, devoting themselves exclusively to the direction of the public affairs of a country, finally form a sort of political aristocracy or oligarchy. Witness the United States of America and Switzerland.

Consequently, no external legislation and no authority — one, for that matter, being inseparable from the other, and both tending to the servitude of society and the degradation of the legislators themselves.

Does it follow that I reject all authority? Far from me such a thought. In the matter of boots, I refer to the authority of the bootmaker; concerning houses, canals, or railroads, I consult that of the architect or engineer. For such or such special knowledge I apply to such or such a *savant*. But I allow neither the bootmaker nor the architect nor the *savant* to impose his authority upon me. I listen to them freely and with all the respect merited by their intelligence, their character, their knowledge, reserving always my incontestable right of criticism and censure. I do not content myself with consulting a single authority in any special branch; I consult several; I compare their opinions, and choose that which seems to me the soundest. But I recognize no infallible authority, even in special questions; consequently, whatever respect I may have for the honesty and the sincerity of such or such an individual, I have no absolute faith in any person. Such a faith would be fatal to my reason, to my liberty, and even to the success of my undertakings; it would immediately transform me into a stupid slave, an instrument of the will and interests of others.

If I bow before the authority of the specialists and avow my readiness to follow, to a certain extent and as long as may seem to me necessary, their indications and even their directions, it is because their authority is imposed upon me by no one, neither by men nor by God. Otherwise I would repel them with horror, and bid the devil take their counsels, their directions, and their services, certain that they would make me pay, by the loss of my liberty and self-respect, for such scraps of truth, wrapped in a multitude of lies, as they might give me.

I bow before the authority of special men because it is imposed upon me by my own reason. I am conscious of my inability to grasp, in all its details and positive developments, any very large portion of human knowledge. The greatest intelligence would not be equal to a comprehension of the whole. Thence results, for science as well as for industry, the necessity of the division and association of labour. I receive and I give—such is human life. Each directs and is directed in his turn. Therefore there is no fixed and constant authority, but a continual exchange of mutual, temporary, and, above all, voluntary authority and subordination.

This same reason forbids me, then, to recognize a fixed, constant, and universal authority, because there is no universal man, no man capable of grasping in that wealth of detail, without which the application of science to life is impossible, all the sciences, all the branches of social life. And if such universality could ever be realized in a single man, and if he wished to take advantage thereof to impose his authority upon us, it would be necessary to drive this man out of society, because his authority would inevitably reduce all the others to slavery and imbecility. I do not think that society ought to maltreat men of genius as it has done hitherto; but neither do I think it should indulge them too far, still less accord them any privileges or exclusive rights whatsoever; and that for three reasons: first, because it would often mistake a charlatan for a man of genius; second, because, through such a system of privileges, it might transform into a charlatan even a real man of genius, demoralize him, and degrade him; and, finally, because it would establish a master over itself.

To sum up. We recognize, then, the absolute authority of science, because the sole object of science is the mental reproduction, as well-considered and systematic as possible, of the natural laws inherent in the material, intellectual, and moral life of both the physical and the social worlds, these two worlds constituting, in fact, but one and the same natural world. Outside of this solely legitimate authority, legitimate because rational and in harmony with human liberty, we declare all other authorities false, arbitrary and fatal.

We recognize the absolute authority of science, but we reject the infallibility and universality of the *savant*. In our church— if I may be permitted to use for a moment an expression which I so detest: Church and State are my two *bêtes noires*—in our church, as in the Protestant church, we have a chief, an invisible Christ, science; and, like the Protestants, more logical even than the Protestants, we will suffer neither pope, nor council, nor conclaves of infallible cardinals, nor bishops, nor even priests. Our Christ differs from the Protestant and Christian Christ in this—that the latter is a personal being, ours impersonal; the Christian Christ, already completed in an eternal past, presents himself as a perfect being, while the completion and perfection of our Christ, science, are ever in the future: which is equivalent to saying that they will never be realized. Therefore, in recognizing *absolute science* as the only absolute authority, we in no way compromise our liberty.

I mean by the words 'absolute science' the truly universal science which would reproduce ideally, to its fullest extent and in all its infinite detail, the universe, the system or co-ordination of all the natural laws manifested by the incessant development of the world. It is evident that such a science, the sublime object of all the efforts of the human mind, will never be fully and absolutely realized. Our Christ, then, will remain eternally unfinished, which must considerably take down the pride of his licensed representatives among us. Against that God the Son in whose name they assume to impose upon us their insolent and pedantic authority, we appeal to God the Father, who is the real world, real life, of which he (the Son) is only a too imperfect expression, whilst we real beings, living, working, struggling, loving, aspiring, enjoying, and suffering, are its immediate representatives.

But, while rejecting the absolute, universal, and infallible authority of men of science, we willingly bow before the respectable, although relative, quite temporary, and very restricted authority of the representatives of special sciences, asking nothing better than to consult them by turns, and very grateful for such precious information as they may extend to us, on condition of their willingness to receive from us on occasions when, and concerning matters about which, we are more learned than they. In general, we ask nothing better than to see men endowed with great knowledge, great experience, great minds, and, above all, great hearts, exercise over us a natural and legitimate influence, freely accepted, and never imposed in the name of any official authority whatsoever, celestial or terrestrial. We accept all natural authorities and all influences of fact, but none of right; for every authority or every influence of right, officially imposed as such, becoming directly an oppression and a falsehood, would inevitably impose upon us, as I believe I have sufficiently shown, slavery and absurdity.

In a word, we reject all legislation, all authority, and all privileged, licensed, official, and legal influence, even though arising from universal suffrage, convinced that it can turn only to the advantage of a dominant minority of exploiters against the interests of the immense majority in subjection to them.

This is the sense in which we are really Anarchists.

VII STATE AND SOCIETY

The first of these three extracts is from *Fédéralisme, socialisme et anti-théologisme*, published in *Œuvres*, vol. I (Paris, 1895), pp. 139–45. The other two texts are from *L'Empire knouto-germanique* (see p. 139); they are to be found in *Œuvres*, vol I, pp. 264–89 and vol. III (Paris, 1908), pp. 211–15. They are here translated from the French by Steven Cox.

I

Man is not only the most individual being on earth, but also the most *social*. Jean-Jacques Rousseau was sorely mistaken in his belief that primitive society was established by a free contract, effected by savages. But Jean-Jacques Rousseau is not alone in his assertion. The majority of modern jurists and publicists, whether of the Kantian or any other individualist, liberal school, accept neither the society of the theologian, based upon divine right, nor the society depicted by the Hegelian school as the more or less mystical embodiment of objective Morality, nor the primitively animal society of the naturalists. Willy-nilly, and for want of any other foundation, they take the *tacit contract* as their point of departure. A tacit contract—a wordless and consequently a thoughtless and unintentional contract—what terrible nonsense! An absurd and, worse, a pernicious fiction! A shameful deceit, pre-supposing that while I was in no condition either to decide, think or speak, and let myself be fleeced without a murmur, I could have agreed to eternal enslavement for myself and all my descendants!

The implications of the *social contract* are in fact fatal, because they culminate in the absolute domination of the State. And yet the principle seems extremely liberal at first sight. Before arranging their contract, individuals are assumed to have enjoyed absolute liberty, because this theory holds that only man in his natural, wild state is totally free. We have expressed our opinion of this natural liberty, which is nothing but the absolute dependence of the ape-man in his permanent struggle with the external world. But supposing that he really is free to begin with, why then does he band himself into society? And back comes the answer—in order to ensure his safety against all the possible inroads of that same external world, including any other associated or unassociated men who do not belong to this nascent society.

So here we have primitive men, each one totally free in his own right, and enjoying his freedom only as long as he does not come into contact with another and remains immersed in absolute individual isolation. The liberty of one does not require the liberty of the other. On the contrary, since each individual's liberty is sufficient in itself, each man's liberty necessarily involves denial of every other man's, and when all these liberties encounter one another they are bound to be mutually limited and diminished and to contradict and destroy one another ...

In order not to utterly destroy one another, they form an explicit or tacit *contract* by which they relinquish a part of themselves so as to safeguard the rest. This contract becomes the basis of society, or rather of the State, for it must be noted that there is no room in this theory for society, only for the State, or rather that society is totally absorbed by the State.

Society is the natural medium of the human collectivity, regardless of contracts. It progresses slowly, through the momentum imparted by individual initiatives, not through the mind and will of the legislator. There may be many unarticulated laws that rule it, but these are natural laws, inherent in the social body just as physical laws are inherent in the material. Most of these laws remain unknown to this day, and yet they have governed human society from its inception, irrespective of the thoughts and intentions of the men who have composed it. It follows that they are not to be confused with the judicial and political laws proclaimed by some legislative authority, which are assumed by the system under investigation to be the logical conclusion of the first contract deliberately entered into by men.

The State is not a direct product of nature; it does not, like Society, precede the awakening of thought in man, and later on we shall attempt to show how *it is created by the religious conscience in the midst of natural society.* According to the liberal propagandists, the first State was created by the free, deliberate decision of men; according to the absolutists, it is a divine creation. In either case it dominates society and tends to absorb it altogether.

In the second case, this absorption is self-explanatory: a divine institution is bound to absorb any natural organization. The odd thing is that the individualist school with its free contract arrives at the same conclusion. And in fact this school sets out by denying the very existence of a natural society prior to the contract, since such a society would presuppose natural contact among individuals and consequently *reciprocal limitation of their liberties*, which would run counter to the absolute liberty which everybody is theoretically assumed to have enjoyed before the conclusion of the contract, and which would amount to nothing more or less than the contract itself, existing as a natural fact prior even to the free contract. So according to this system human society begins only with the conclusion of the contract. Then what is society? It is the pure and logical application of the contract with all its legislative and practical apparatus and consequences—it is the State.

Let us look closer. What does it represent? The sum of all its members' denials of individual liberty, or of the sacrifices made by all its members in renouncing a portion of their liberty for the common welfare. We have seen that according to the individualist theory each man's liberty is the boundary or natural denial of everybody else's: so, this absolute limitation, this denial of each man's liberty in the name of the liberty of all, or of the common law—it is the State. Therefore individual liberty ends where the State begins, and vice versa.

The reply will be that the State represents the public safety or common interest of all, and that it only removes part of a man's liberty in order to preserve the remainder. But while that remainder may, if you will, be security, it is never liberty. Liberty is indivisible: no part can be removed without killing the whole. By a natural, necessary and irresistible process, all my liberty is concentrated precisely in the fragment you remove, however tiny. This is the story of Bluebeard's wife, who had a whole palace at her disposal, with absolute freedom to go anywhere and see and touch anything, except for one paltry little room which the sovereign will of her terrible husband forbade her to enter on pain of death. So her soul withdrew from all the splendours of the palace and focused wholly on this paltry little room. She opened it. And she was right to open it, because the action was necessary to her liberty, flagrantly violated by the prohibition. It is also the story of Adam and Eve: forbidding them to taste the fruit of the tree of knowledge, for no other reason than because he required it, was an act of sheer despotism on the part of the good Lord, and if our first parents had obeyed, the whole human race would still be weltering in the most humiliating slavery. Instead, their disobedience emancipated and rescued it. Mythologically speaking, it was the first step towards human liberty.

But perhaps it will be said that the State, the democratic State, based on free suffrage among all its citizens, could not be a denial of their liberty. And why not? This will wholly depend on the functions and power which the citizens leave to the State. A republican State based on universal suffrage can be very despotic, even more despotic than a monarchic State, because under the pretext of representing the will of all it will bear down on the will and free impulse of each of its members with all the weight of its collective power.

II

The doctrinaire liberals turn out to be no less fanatical partisans of the absolute right of the State than the monarchist and Jacobin absolutists.

Their worship of the State in spite of everything, even when it may seem to be so contrary to their liberal doctrine, has two kinds of explanation. First, *practical*: it is in the interests of their class, since the vast majority of doctrinaire liberals belong to the bourgeoisie. This numerous, respectable class would ask nothing better than to award itself the right or rather the privilege of utter anarchy; its whole social economy, the real base of its political existence, is well known for having no other law than the kind of anarchy expressed in the famous phrase *Laissez faire et laissez passer*. But it loves that anarchy only for its own advantage, and strictly on condition that the masses, 'too ignorant to enjoy it without abusing it', remain subject to the harshest State discipline. For if the masses were to weary of working for others and rebel, the entire political and social existence of the bourgeoisie would collapse. Which explains why whenever the working masses stir we see the most upstanding bourgeois liberals revert at once to rabid support of State dominance. And since agitation among the popular masses is now becoming a growing, chronic evil, we see the liberal bourgeois converting to the cult of absolute power even in the freest countries.

As well as this practical reason, there is another quite *theoretical* reason which likewise compels even the most genuine liberals to keep harking back to worship of the State. They are, and are called, liberals because they take the freedom of the individual as the basis and starting-point of their theory, and it is precisely because they set out from this premise that they are bound to arrive at recognition of absolute State power.

From their standpoint, the freedom of the individual is not a creation, an historical product of society. They claim that it is previous to any society, and that every man bears it from birth onwards, together with his immortal soul, as a divine gift. It follows that only outside society is man complete and in some sense absolute in himself. Being himself free prior to and apart from society, he necessarily forms the latter by a voluntary action and by a kind of instinctive and tacit or deliberate and formal contract. In other words, according to this theory it is not individuals who are created by society but the other way about, as a result of some external necessity such as work and war.

What emerges from this theory is that society proper does not exist; it utterly ignores natural human society, the real starting-point of all human civilization and the only medium in which the personality and liberty of man can really be born and grow. All it acknowledges is, at one extreme, the individual, a being who exists in himself and is free in himself, and at the other that conventional society arbitrarily formed by these individuals and based on a formal or tacit contract—the State. (Liberals are well aware that no historic State has ever been based on a contract, and that they have all been founded by violence and conquest. But they need this fiction of the free contract as the basis of the State, so they grasp at it without further ado.)

The human individuals whose conventionally united aggregate forms the State are shown up by this theory as quite peculiar creatures, bulging with contradictions. Each equipped with an immortal soul and inborn liberty or free will, on the one hand they are infinite, absolute beings and as such complete in themselves, self-sufficient and with no need for anyone else — at a pinch, not even God, because being immortal and infinite they are gods themselves. On the other hand, they are very crassly material beings, weak, imperfect, limited and absolutely dependent on the external nature which holds and enfolds them and eventually carries them away. Seen from the former viewpoint, they have so little need for society that it seems something of an impediment to the plenitude of their being, their perfect liberty. Thus, ever since the dawn of Christianity there have been austere, holy men who have taken the immortality and salvation of their souls seriously, broken their social ties, shunned all human contact and sought perfection, virtue and God in the wilderness. Quite rationally and logically, they have considered society as a source of corruption and the utter isolation of the soul as the earnest of all the virtues. If they ever left their solitude it was never from need but from generosity and Christian charity towards those who, continuing to fester in the social sphere, had need of their advice, prayers and guidance. It was always to save others, never to save and perfect themselves — in fact they were running the risk of losing their souls by returning to the society which they had fled in horror as the forcing-ground of all corruption, and once acquitted of their holy mission they hurried back to their wilderness, there to purify themselves once again in ceaseless contemplation of their individual being and solitary soul, in the presence of God alone.

It is an example which ought to be followed by all who still believe in the immortality of the soul, inborn liberty or free will, if they really want to save their souls and train them properly for eternal life. I repeat that the anchorite saints who achieved complete imbecility through isolation were being perfectly logical. Once grant that the soul is immortal, infinite in essence, free and *sui generis*, then it should be sufficient in itself. Only fleeting, limited, finite beings can mutually fulfil one another; the infinite cannot be fulfilled—on the contrary, when it encounters another, which is not itself, it feels hemmed in and has to escape, to exclude everything which is not itself. At a pinch, I have said, the immortal soul should even be able to do without God. A being which is infinite in itself cannot acknowledge another equal being at its own level, let alone one which is higher and superior. Any being as infinite as itself and other than itself would impose a limit on it and would therefore make it a determinate, finite being. In recognizing a being as infinite— like itself but separate from itself—the immortal soul is necessarily recognizing itself as finite. For infinity is infinity only when it is all-embracing and leaves nothing outside itself. More important, an infinite being cannot and must not recognize an infinite being which is superior to itself. The infinite does not allow for anything relative or comparative; the idea of a superior and an inferior infinity is therefore an absurdity. And God is that absurdity. The theology whose privilege it is to be absurd, and which believes in things precisely because they are absurd, has promoted the superior, absolute infinity of God above the immortal and consequently infinite souls of men. But it has created the compensatory fiction of Satan, the image of an infinite being rebelling against the existence of an absolute infinity, against God. And just as Satan rebelled against the superior infinity of God, so the anchorite saints of Christendom, too humble to rebel against God, turned against the equal infinity of man, against society.

Reasonably enough, they asserted that they did not need to be saved, and that since a strange fatality dictated that they were infinities, the society of God and the contemplation of their own selves in the presence of that absolute infinity was enough for them.

And I say again that theirs is an example to be followed by all believers in the immortality of the soul. From their point of view, society has nothing to offer except certain damnation. After all, what does it give to men? First, material wealth, which can only be produced in sufficient quantity by collective labour. But surely a believer in the life eternal is supposed to despise this wealth? Did Jesus Christ not tell his disciples, 'Lay not up treasures on this earth, for where your treasure is, there shall your heart be also,' and 'It is easier for a camel to pass through the eye of the needle than for a rich man to enter the kingdom of Heaven'? (I often wonder how those rich, pious Protestants in England, America, Germany and Switzerland must feel when they read those lines, which apply so directly and so unpleasantly to their own selves.)

Jesus Christ is right: there is no possible compromise between coveting material wealth and the salvation of immortal souls. And in that case, given a genuine belief in the immortality of the soul, is it not advisable to give up the comforts and luxuries of society and live on roots like the anchorites for the sake of an eternity of salvation, rather than lose one's chance for the sake of a few dozen years' material enjoyment? It is a simple sum, and the solution is so obvious that we are driven to the conclusion that all those pious wealthy bourgeois, bankers, industrialists and merchants doing such thriving trade by the same old methods, and for ever paying lip-service to the Gospel, do not really expect their souls to be immortal, and are generously leaving that privilege to the proletariat, humbly keeping their own hands on the worthless material goods they lay up on this earth.

What else does society offer, apart from material wealth? Carnal, human, earthly affection, civilization and culture — vast enough from the transitory, earthbound point of view, but insignificant compared with eternity, immortality and God, in whose sight the greatest human wisdom is but folly.

There is a legend of the Eastern Church which tells how two anchorite saints voluntarily marooned themselves on a desert island for some decades, avoiding even each other and spending night and day in prayer and meditation. The time came when they had lost even the use of words, and were left with only three or four out of all their old vocabulary, which made no sense when put together, but nevertheless expressed their souls' sublime yearnings towards God. They lived on raw roots, like herbivores. From the human standpoint these two were fools or lunatics, but from the viewpoint of the divine, of belief in the immortality of the soul, they proved themselves much more profound in their calculations than a Galileo or a Newton by sacrificing a few decades of earthly wealth and worldly wisdom to win eternal beatitude and divine wisdom.

So it is obvious that, as a being equipped with a divine soul and the infinity and liberty inherent in that soul, man is eminently anti-social. And had he always been wise, had he always been so exclusively preoccupied with his own eternity and had the sense to despise all the wealth, affection and vanities of this world, he would never have relinquished this state of innocence or holy imbecility and would never have organized himself into society. In other words, Adam and Eve would never have tasted the fruit of the tree of knowledge and we should all have lived like animals in that terrestrial paradise which God gave them for a dwelling. But from the moment when men wanted to know, to civilize and humanize themselves, think, speak and enjoy material wealth, they had no choice but to leave their solitude and form themselves into society. For to the extent that their *inner* selves are infinite, immortal and free, their *outer* selves are limited, mortal, weak and dependent upon the external world.

Seen from the viewpoint of their earthly, that is, their non-fictional, real existence, the mass of mankind presents such a degrading spectacle and seems so woefully devoid of initiative, will-power and sense that it really takes great capacity for self-deception to locate an immortal soul among them, or even the merest hint of free will. To us, they appear as utterly and inexorably determined beings — determined above all by external nature, the configuration of the soil and all the material conditions of their existence, but also determined by the unending political, religious and social pressures, the customs, habits and laws and the whole world of prejudices or thoughts slowly developed in the course of centuries which they encounter when they enter social life and whose products and instruments they may be, but never their creators. Even from a relative, let alone an absolute viewpoint, there is hardly one man in a thousand of whom it could be said that his wants and thoughts are his own. Both among the *ignorant masses* and the civilized and privileged classes, the vast majority of human individuals want and think only what the surrounding world wants and thinks: they probably believe that their minds are their own, but they are tied to the servile, routine regurgitation of the thoughts and wishes of others, with utterly imperceptible, empty modifications. Servility and routine, those bottomless wells of the commonplace, together with the absence of scepticism and initiative in the individual mind and will, are the main causes of the distressingly slow historic development of humanity. For materialists and realists like ourselves, who believe neither in the hereafter nor in free will, this sluggishness, painful though it is, appears as a natural factor. Emerging from the simian state, it is only with great difficulty that man achieves awareness of his humanity and realization of his liberty. At the beginning he is capable neither of awareness nor of liberty; he is born a wild beast and a slave, and his progressive humanization and emancipation come only in the context of society, which is necessarily prior to the birth of thought, word and will, and only through the collective pressure of every member of that society, past and present. Consequently society is the basis and natural starting-point of man's human existence, and it follows that he only realizes his individual liberty or personality by integration with all the individuals around him and by virtue of the collective power of society, without which there can be no doubt that of all the wild beasts on the face of the earth he would for ever remain the most stupid and the most wretched. According to the materialist theory, the only natural, logical theory, instead of diminishing and constricting the freedom of the individual, society creates it. Society is the root and branch, liberty the fruit. Therefore in every era man must find his liberty not at the beginning but at the end of history, and it may be said that the real and total emancipation of every human individual is the true great objective and ultimate goal of history.

Anything else is idealism. According to this theory, man starts out as a free immortal being and ends in slavery. As a free immortal, infinite and self-sufficient, he has no need of society, which implies that if he then submits to society it can only be as a result of some kind of failure, or else because he forgets and loses the awareness of his immortality and liberty. A paradoxical creature, inwardly infinite and spiritual but outwardly dependent, ineffective and material, he is forced to enter into association not for his soul's requirements but for his body's protection. So society only comes about through a kind of sacrifice of the interests and independence of the soul to the despicable call of the body. It is a true fall and enthralment for the inwardly free and immortal individual, and involves him in what is at the least a partial abdication of his original liberty.

We are familiar with the sacrimental saying which expresses this fall and this sacrifice, this first fatal step into human slavery, in the jargon of every supporter of the State and of judicial law. By his entry into any society the individual —who enjoys complete liberty in the state of nature, prior to becoming a member of that society—offers up a portion of this liberty so that society will vouchsafe him the rest. Anybody who asks for an explanation is usually presented with a further saying: '*The liberty of each human being should have no limits other than that of every other.*'

At first glance, this seems utterly fair, does it not? And yet this theory holds the germ of the whole theory of despotism. In agreement with the basic thinking of every idealist school, and contrary to all the actual facts, the human individual emerges as a completely free being only as long as he holds aloof from society, which means that the latter, seen and interpreted in judicial and political terms—as State, in fact—is the negation of liberty. This is the end-product of idealism, and is quite opposed to the deductions of materialism, which hold, in agreement with the pattern of the real world, that the freedom of the individual is a function of man in society, a necessary consequence of the collective development of mankind.

The materialist, realist and collectivist definition of liberty flatly contradicts the idealists. It is as follows: man does not become man, nor does he achieve awareness or realization of his humanity, other than in society and in the collective movement of the whole of society; he only shakes off the yoke of external nature through collective or social labour, the one force capable of transforming the earth's surface into an environment favourable to the growth of humanity; and without this material emancipation there can be no intellectual and moral emancipation for anyone. No one can shake off the yoke of his own nature, subordinate the instincts and drives of his body to the guidance of his ever-developing mind, except through upbringing and education. Yet these are eminently, in fact exclusively, social phenomena, for without society man would eternally have remained a wild beast or a saint—there being little difference between the two. Lastly, man in isolation can have no awareness of his liberty. Being free for man means being acknowledged, considered and treated as such by another man, and by all the men around him. Liberty is therefore a feature not of isolation but of interaction, not of exclusion but rather of connection, for the liberty of any individual is nothing more or less than the reflection of his humanity and his human rights in the awareness of all free men—his brothers, his equals.

I can only call myself free and feel free in the presence and in terms of other men. In the presence of a lesser animal, I am neither free nor a man, because no animal is capable of conceiving and therefore also of acknowledging my humanity. I myself am human and free only to the extent that I acknowledge the humanity and liberty of all my fellows. It is only by respecting their human character that I respect my own. When a cannibal treats his prisoner like an animal, he himself is not a man but an animal. A slavemaster is not a man but a master. By ignoring his slave's humanity he ignores his own. The whole of ancient society demonstrates that the Greeks and Romans did not feel free as human beings and in terms of human rights; they thought themselves privileged as Greeks or Romans, in terms of their own society, and only as long as it continued to be independent and unconquered and in fact to conquer other countries, through the special protection of their national Gods, so that when they themselves were conquered they felt no surprise and no right or duty to rebel if they themselves relapsed into slavery.

It is greatly to the credit of Christianity that it proclaimed the humanity of all human beings, women included, and the equality of all men in the sight of God. But how was this message proclaimed? It applied to heaven and the life to come, not to earth and the real life of the present. In any case this equality in the hereafter is still a falsehood, since the number of the elect is extremely small, we know. Theologians of the most diversified Christian sects are unanimous on this point. Thus the so-called Christian equality leads to the most flagrant privilege, whereby a few thousand are selected by divine grace out of the millions of the damned. In any case, even if it were to apply to everybody, this equality in the sight of God would only be the equal insignificance and servitude of all men under one supreme master. Is it not the basis of Christian worship and the prime condition of salvation to renounce human dignity and to despise that dignity in the presence of divine greatness? A Christian is therefore not a man in this respect, since he has no awareness of humanity; when he does not respect human dignity in himself, he cannot respect it in others, and when he does not respect it in others, he cannot respect it in himself. A Christian can be prophet, saint, priest, king, general, minister, civil servant, spokesman for authority, policeman, executioner, aristocrat, bourgeois exploiter or wage-slave, oppressor or oppressed, torturer or tortured, but he has no right to call himself a man, because man is not truly man until he respects and loves the humanity and liberty of all, and his own liberty and humanity are respected, loved, upheld and created by all.

I am only properly free when all the men and women about me are equally free. Far from being a limitation or denial of my liberty, the liberty of another is its necessary condition and confirmation. I only become truly free through the liberty of others, so that the more I am surrounded by free men, and the deeper and wider this freedom grows, the further my own extends. It is the servitude of men which erects a barrier against my liberty, or rather—and this amounts to the same thing—it is their bestiality which is a denial of my liberty because once again I cannot truly call myself free until my liberty, in other words my dignity as a man, and my human right, which consists in not obeying any other man and behaving only in accordance with my own convictions, are reflected in the equally free awareness of all men and return to me confirmed by the assent of all the world. When my personal liberty is thus confirmed by the liberty of all, it extends to infinity.

We see that liberty as conceived by the materialists is a very positive, complex and, above all, an eminently social matter, which can only be realized by means of society and through the strictest equality and solidarity of each and everybody. We can distinguish three aspects of its development, the first being eminently positive and social; it is the full development and full enjoyment of all human faculties and powers in every man, through upbringing, scientific education and material prosperity, which cannot be provided for all without the collective physical and intellectual labour of society as a whole.

The second aspect of liberty is negative. It consists in the *rebellion* of the human individual against all authority, whether divine or human, collective or individual.

This rebellion is first of all directed against the supreme phantom of theology, against God. It is obvious that as long as we have a master in heaven we shall be slaves on earth. Our reason and will-power will be equally nullified. As long as we believe that we owe absolute obedience—and no other kind is possible in the sight of God—we are bound to submit, passively and uncritically, to the divine authority of his spokesmen and his elect: Messiahs, prophets, divinely in-spired legislators, emperors, kings and all their dignitaries and ministers, the representatives and devoted servants of the two great institutions which inflict themselves upon ourselves as God's instruments for the guidance of men. Those institutions are *Church* and *State*: all temporal or human authority derives directly from spiritual or divine authority. But authority is denial of liberty, therefore God, or rather the fiction of God, is the sanction and the intellectual and moral source of all slavery on earth, and men's liberty will not be complete until it has utterly eradicated the pernicious fiction of a heavenly master.

It follows that another aspect of liberty is the rebellion of every man against the tyranny of men, the individual and social authority embodied and legalized by the State. But we must make ourselves very clear at this point, and to do so we must begin by making a precise distinction between the official and therefore tyrannical authority of the State-organized society and the influence and natural effect of non-official, natural society upon each of its members.

Rebellion against this natural influence of society is a great deal harder for the individual than rebellion against the official, organized society of the State, although it may often be just as essential. Social tyranny is often overwhelming and deadly, but it does not exhibit the character of imperative violence, of legalized, formal despotism, which distinguishes State authority. It is not applied like some law which forces the individual to comply on pain of incurring legal punishment. Its effect is gentler, more insinuating and imperceptible, but correspondingly more powerful than that of State authority. It exerts its domination by means of conventions, morals and a multitude of sentiments, prejudices and habits, in the material as well as in the mental sphere, and constitutes what we call public opinion. It envelops man from the moment of his birth, transfuses and permeates him and forms the very basis of his own individual existence, so that every man is its more or less unsuspecting accomplice against himself. It follows that in order to rebel against this natural influence exerted by society man must at least partially rebel against himself, for with all his material, intellectual and moral learnings and aspirations, he himself is only a product of society. Hence the immense power which society exercises over men.

From the viewpoint of absolute morality—that is, from the viewpoint of human respect, and I shall explain what I mean by this phrase presently—this power may be just as much beneficial as harmful. It is beneficial when it contributes to the development of knowledge, material prosperity, liberty, equality and brotherly solidarity, harmful when it has the opposite tendencies. A man born into a society of brutes remains a near-brute, with very few exceptions; born into a society ruled by priests, he becomes an idiot, a cretin; born into a band of thieves, he is liable to become a thief; born into the bourgeoisie, he will be an exploiter of other men's labour; and if he has the misfortune to be born into the society of demigods who rule this earth—nobles, princes, kings' sons—he will, to the extent of his abilities, resources and power, be a despiser and enslaver of humanity, a tyrant. In all these cases, if the individual is to humanize himself he is bound to rebel against his native society.

But I repeat that rebellion by the individual against society requires an altogether more difficult step than his rebellion against the State. The State is a historical, transitory institution, a temporary form of society, like its elder brother the Church, but it lacks the inexorable, changeless character of society which exists prior to all the developments of mankind and partakes of the universality of natural laws and phenomena to constitute the very basis of human existence. Ever since he took his first step towards humanity and started to be a human being—a talking and more or less thinking creature—man has been born into society like the ant into the nest, the bee into the hive. Far from choosing it, he is produced by it, and he is just as subject to the natural laws which preside over its necessary growth as he is to all other natural laws. Society precedes the human individual and at the same time it survives him, like nature itself; like nature, it is eternal, or rather, having been born on earth, it will endure as long as our earth endures. Radical rebellion against society would therefore be as impossible as rebellion against nature, since human society is, after all, nothing but the last great manifestation or creation of nature on earth. An individual who tried to call society—that is, nature in general and his own nature in particular—in question would be cutting himself off from all the conditions of a real existence and launching out into nothingness, utter vacuity, deathly abstraction—into God. So there is just as little point in asking whether society is good or evil as in asking whether nature, the universal, material, real, unique, supreme and absolute entity, is good or evil; it is more than all this; it is a vast, positive, primitive fact, prior to all awareness, ideation or intellectual and moral values, it is the very foundation, the world in which what we call good and evil later and inevitably develop.

The state is another matter, and I have no hesitation in saying that the State is evil, but an historically necessary evil, as necessary in the past as its utter extinction will eventually become in the future, as necessary as the primitive bestiality and theological divagations of mankind. The State is not society, but one of its historical forms, at once brutish and abstract. Historically, it was born out of the marriage of violence, rapine and plunder—in other words of war and conquest—with the successive Gods created by the theological imagination of nations. From its beginning it has been the divine mainstay of brute force and rampant injustice. Even in the most democratic lands, such as the U.S.A. and Switzerland, it is the prevailing [sanction] of minority privilege and the practical subjugation of the vast majority.

It is much easier to rebel against the State, because there is something in the very nature of the State which provokes rebellion. The State is authority, force on display, infatuation with power. It does not insinuate and does not seek to persuade, and whenever it makes the attempt it does so clumsily, for its nature is not to convert but to coerce and impose, however much it strives to conceal its function as the legal violator of man's will and the permanent denial of his liberty. So even while commanding the good it frustrates and despoils it, precisely because it does command, and every command provokes and kindles the legitimate rebelliousness of liberty; and because from the viewpoint of real, non-divine human morality and of true respect and liberty, good becomes evil once it is made subject to command. The liberty, morality and human dignity of man consist in his doing good not because he is compelled but because he conceives, desires and loves it.

Society, however, does not make its pressure felt in a formal, official, authoritarian manner, but naturally, and it is for this very reason that its effect on the individual is incomparably more powerful than the State's. It creates and moulds all the individuals who are born and develop within it. From the cradle to the grave, it slowly instils them with all its material, intellectual and moral essence; we may say that it incarnates itself in every man.

III

Do you want to prevent men from ever oppressing other men? Arrange matters such that they never have the opportunity. Do you want them to respect the liberty, rights and human character of their fellow men? Arrange matters such that they are compelled to respect them—*compelled not by the will or oppression of other men, nor by the repression of the State and legislation, which are necessarily represented and implemented by men* and would make them slaves in their turn, *but by the actual organization of the social environment, so constituted that while leaving each man to enjoy the utmost possible liberty it gives no one the power to set himself above others or to dominate them, except through the natural influence of his own intellectual or moral qualities,* which must never be allowed either to convert itself into a right or to be backed by any kind of political institution.

The same tendency underlies all political institutions, even those which are the most democratic, are founded upon the broadest application of universal suffrage, and commence, as they often do at the outset, by giving power to the worthiest, most liberal men, the ones most dedicated to the common good and most capable of serving it. *Precisely because their inevitable effect is to transform the natural and, as such, quite legitimate influence of these men into a right,* their final outcome is always to produce a dual demoralization and dual evil.

First of all, their immediate and direct effect is to transform really free *men* into allegedly free *citizens* who may even continue to maintain the fatuous delusion that they are every man's equal, but who are in fact *compelled to obey the representatives of the law from now onward*—to obey men. And even if these men really are their equals from the economic and social point of view, nevertheless in political terms they are leaders, and under the pretext of the public welfare and the popular will, expressed not even by unanimous acclaim but by majority vote, all citizens owe them *passive obedience,* within the limits determined by law, to be sure, yet everyday experience shows how elastic these limits are for the man in command, and how unbending for the citizen wishing to claim the right of legal disobedience.

My own view is that as long as citizens obey the official representatives of the law and the leaders imposed upon them by the State, even when these leaders may have been sanctioned by universal suffrage, they are slaves.

What is liberty? What is slavery? Does man's liberty consist in rebellion against all laws? *No,* in so far as these are natural economic and social laws, not imposed from above but inherent in the things, relationships and situations whose natural growth they express. Yes, in so far as they are political and juridical laws, imposed by men upon men, whether by right of superior strength, violently, or in the name of some religious or metaphysical doctrine, hypocritically, or by virtue of that fiction, that democratic lie known as universal suffrage.

It is impossible for man to rebel against the laws of nature, for the simple reason that he himself is nature's product and exists only by virtue of its laws. Rebellion would therefore be an act of absurdity on his own part, a rebellion against himself, a true suicide. And even when man makes up his mind to destroy himself, even when he carries out his decision, he is still acting in accordance with those natural laws from which nothing could detach him—not thought or will, despair or any other passion, not even life or death. He himself is nothing except nature; his most sublime or monstrous feelings, the most perverted, selfish or heroic resolves of his will, the most abstract, theological or lunatic of his thoughts, all are nothing more or less than nature. Nature enfolds and saturates him, it constitutes his entire existence; how can he ever take leave of nature?

It is remarkable that he could ever have conceived the idea of taking leave of nature. Since such a separation is so utterly impossible, how could man even dream of it? Where could such a monstrous dream originate?—Where but in *theology*, the science of Nothingness, and later in *metaphysics*, the science of the impossible reconciliation of Nothingness with reality.

Theology ought not to be confused with religion, or the theological spirit with religious feeling. Religion arises out of animal life. It is the direct expression of the absolute dependence binding all the things and creatures of this world to the Great All, to Nature, to the infinite Totality of real things and real creatures.

VIII ON SCIENCE AND AUTHORITY

The first of these two extracts is from *L'Empire knouto-germanique* (see p. 139), published in *Œuvres*, vol. III (Paris, 1908), pp. 314–22, and is here translated from the French by Steven Cox. The second is taken from the English translation of *Dieu et l'État*, pp. 38–43 (see p. 111).

I

What is scientific method? It is the realist method at its highest. It proceeds from the details to the whole, and from the confirmation and study of facts to their understanding, to ideas, which are no other than faithful accounts of the successive, related connections and mutual interaction and causality which really exist among real things and phenomena; its logic is none other than the logic of things. Since positivist science always succeeds theology and metaphysics in the historical development of the human mind, man always comes to science predisposed and considerably corrupted by an abstract kind of education, and projects on to it any number of abstract ideas developed out of theology or metaphysics. These will be matters of blind faith to the former and objects of transcendental speculation and more or less ingenious word-play to the latter, whose explanations and demonstrations explain and demonstrate nothing whatsoever, because they have no frame of experimental reference and because metaphysics has no guarantee for the very existence of its subject-matter other than the assurances and categorical mandates of theology.

Man, the erstwhile theologian and metaphysician, but weary both of theology and metaphysics because of their sterile outcome in theory as well as their injurious consequences in practice, naturally imports all these ideas into science, but treats them not as fixed principles which must therefore serve as points of departure, but as questions to be resolved by science. He has come to science just because he has begun to be doubtful, and he doubts because long experience of the theology and metaphysics which created these ideas has shown him that neither offers any worthwhile guarantee of the validity of its creations. What he doubts and rejects above all are not so much these creations and ideas as the ways and means by which theology and metaphysics engendered them. He rejects the revelatory system of the theologians and *belief in the absurd because it is absurd*,* and he will no longer put up with the despotism of priests and the fires of the Inquisition. He rejects metaphysics for the most part precisely because of its uncritical acceptance or illusory, facile critique of the fundamental ideas of theology — its account of the Universe, of God, and of soul or spirit as separable from matter — and because by constructing its systems upon these assumptions and taking the absurd as its point of departure, it has always and necessarily culminated in the absurd. So what man is seeking above all as he emerges from theology and metaphysics is a genuinely scientific method, whose primary effect is to give him complete certainty of the reality of the objects of his reasoning.

But man has no other way of ascertaining the concrete reality of a thing, phenomenon or fact except by really confronting, registering and acknowledging it in its proper integrity, unadulterated by fantasy, supposition and spiritual ingredients. Experience thus becomes the basis of science — but not the experience of any single man. No man, however intelligent, inquisitive and gifted he may be in every respect, can have seen and confronted everything, or tested everything in person. If each man's science had to be confined to his own personal experience there would be as many sciences as there are men, and each science would die with each man. There would be no science.

The basis of science therefore is the collective experience not only of all contemporaries but also of all preceding generations. But it accepts no evidence without examination. Before accepting the evidence of a contemporary, or of a man who is no longer alive, assuming that I am anxious not to be deceived I must first ask myself about the character and nature as well as the mental cast of that man, *about his method*. I must first of all be confident that he is or was an honest man,

* *Credo quia absurdum* (Tertullian).

hostile to falsehood and seeking the truth with enthusiasm and good faith; that he was neither day-dreamer, poet, metaphysician, theologian, jurist nor politician (with a consequent vested interest in political deception); and that these qualifications are borne out by his contemporaries. There are men, for example, who are very intelligent and enlightened, have no prejudices or day-dreams, in other words have the realist mentality, but who are too lazy to take the trouble to establish the existence and true nature of facts, and therefore suppose and invent them. This is how statistics are produced in Russia. These men's evidence is obviously worthless. There are other men, equally intelligent and too honest to lie and to make unverified assertions, but with minds swayed by metaphysics, religion or one or another version of idealism. Their evidence must likewise be rejected, at least where it touches upon matters related to their own obsessions, because their eagles always turn out to be sparrows. But if a man combines a good realistic mind, developed and properly trained by science, with the further advantage of being a painstaking seeker after the reality of things, then his evidence becomes invaluable.

And yet I must still refuse to accept it uncritically, and my criticism will consist of comparing what he tells me with the evidence of my personal experience. Where there is no conflict, I have no reason to reject it, and I accept it as further confirmation of my own findings, but where we disagree, am I to reject his findings without asking myself which of us is correct? Not at all. I know by experience that my own experience of things may be at fault. I therefore compare his data with my own, and subject them to further observation and experiment. If necessary I appeal to the verdict and experience of a third or any number of other reliable scientific observers, and I arrive, sometimes not without great difficulty and the modification of my or his own data, at a common conclusion. But what is a man's experience? It is the evidence of his senses, guided by his intelligence. For myself, I accept nothing that I have not materially confronted, seen, heard or if necessary touched with my fingers. It is the only way to be certain of the reality of a thing. And the only evidence I trust comes from those who proceed in exactly the same way.

It follows from all this that science is based first and foremost on the correlation of a mass of past and present individual experience, constantly subjected to rigorous mutual examination. No more democratic basis is imaginable. It is primary and decisive, and any human knowledge which does not ultimately depend on it must be dismissed as being devoid of any certainty or scientific value. Yet science cannot remain at this level, which provides nothing but a vast accumulation of widely varying facts, duly established by any number of personal observations and experiments. Science proper begins with the understanding of things, phenomena and facts. Understanding something *whose reality has first been duly verified*, a step which the theologians and metaphysicians always overlook, means using the same empirical method used to establish its existence in order to discover, distinguish and demonstrate all its properties and all its direct or indirect links with all other existing things, which involves determining the various ways in which it impinges on everything other than itself. To understand a phenomenon or fact means discovering and establishing its successive phases of real development, recognizing its *natural law*.

The confirmation of these properties and natural laws has a single source — concrete observations and experiments performed by some person, or by several people together. But however considerable their number and their scholarship, science only accepts their evidence on this essential condition, that when they announce their findings they must also provide an extremely detailed, precise account of their methods and their observations and experiments, so that interested parties can reproduce these observations and experiments for themselves, using the same methods. It is only after new findings have been checked in this manner by different investigators that they are generally admitted into the body of definite scientific knowledge. And it often happens that further observation and experiments performed by different methods and from different points of view will reverse or greatly alter the original findings. Nothing is more alien to science than faith, and criticism is never silenced. As representative of the great principle of rebellion, it is the stern, incorruptible guardian of scientific truth.

By this means, the work of centuries has gradually established a system of universally accepted truths. Once this
system has been established, and always provided that it is
accompanied by the most detailed account of methods,
observations and experiments, together with the history of the
investigations and developments which have contributed to its
acceptance, so that it remains open to cross-checking and new
critical approaches, it now becomes the second basis of science.
It serves as a starting-point for further investigations, which
necessarily develop and enrich it with new methods.

The world, in spite of the infinite diversity of beings which
compose it, is one and the same. The human spirit which
fastens upon it and tries to recognize and understand is equally
indivisible, in spite of the innumerable quantity of past and
present human beings who represent it. This identity is
exhibited in the inarguable fact that whatever a man's background, nature, race, rank and degree of intellectual and
moral development—even when he digresses and talks
nonsense—if he thinks at all, his thought always develops in
accordance with the same laws, and this is what constitutes the
great unity of the human race. Consequently science, which is
nothing more or less than the human spirit's knowledge and
understanding of the world, must also be one.

II

The mission of science is, by observation of the general relations of passing and real facts, to establish the general laws
inherent in the development of the phenomena of the physical
and social world; it fixes, so to speak, the unchangeable
landmarks of humanity's progressive march by indicating the
general conditions which it is necessary to rigorously observe
and always fatal to ignore or forget. In a word, science is the
compass of life; but it is not life. Science is unchangeable,
impersonal, general, abstract, insensible, like the laws of which
it is but the ideal reproduction, reflected or mental—that is
cerebral (using this word to remind us that science itself is but
a material product of a material organ, the *brain*). Life is
wholly fugitive and temporary, but also wholly palpitating
with reality and individuality, sensibility, sufferings, joys,
aspirations, needs, and passions. It alone spontaneously

creates real things and beings. Science creates nothing; it establishes and recognizes only the creations of life. And every time that scientific men, emerging from their abstract world, mingle with living creation in the real world, all that they propose or create is poor, ridiculously abstract, bloodless and lifeless, still-born, like the *homunculus* created by Wagner, the pedantic disciple of the immortal Doctor Faust. It follows that the only mission of science is to enlighten life, not to govern it.

The government of science and of men of science, even be they Positivists, disciples of Auguste Comte, or, again, disciples of the *doctrinaire* school of German Communism, cannot fail to be impotent, ridiculous, inhuman, cruel, oppressive, exploiting, maleficent. We may say of men of science, *as such*, what I have said of theologians and metaphysicians: they have neither sense nor heart for individual and living beings. We cannot even blame them for this, for it is the natural consequence of their profession. In so far as they are men of science, they have to deal with and can take interest in nothing except generalities ...

Though we may be well-nigh certain that a *savant* would not dare to treat a man today as he treats a rabbit, it remains always to be feared that the *savants* as a body, if not interfered with, may submit living men to scientific experiments, undoubtedly less cruel but none the less disagreeable to their victims. If they cannot perform experiments upon the bodies of individuals, they will ask nothing better than to perform them on the social body, and that is what must be absolutely prevented.

In their existing organization, monopolizing science and remaining thus outside of social life, the *savants* form a separate cast, in many respects analogous to the priesthood. Scientific abstraction is their God, living and real individuals are their victims, and they are the consecrated and licensed sacrificers.

Science cannot go outside of the sphere of abstractions. In this respect it is infinitely inferior to art, which, in its turn, is peculiarly concerned also with general types and general situations, but which incarnates them by an artifice of its own in forms which, if they are not living in the sense of real life, none the less excite in our imagination the memory and sentiment of life; art in a certain sense individualizes the types and situations which it conceives; by means of the individualities without flesh and bone, and consequently permanent and immortal, which it has the power to create, it recalls to our minds the living, real individualities which appear and disappear under our eyes. Art, then, is as it were the return of abstraction to life; science, on the contrary, is the perpetual immolation of life, fugitive, temporary but real, on the altar of eternal abstractions.

Science is as incapable of grasping the individuality of a man as that of a rabbit, being equally indifferent to both. Not that it is ignorant of the principle of individuality: it conceives it perfectly as a principle, but not as a fact. It knows very well that all the animal species, including the human species, have no real existence outside of an indefinite number of individuals, born and dying to make room for new individuals equally fugitive. It knows that in rising from the animal species to the superior species the principle of individuality becomes more pronounced; the individuals appear freer and more complete. It knows that man, the last and most perfect animal of earth, presents the most complete and most remarkable individuality, because of his power to conceive, concrete, personify, as it were, in his social and private existence, the universal law. It knows, finally, when it is not vitiated by theological or metaphysical, political or judicial *doctrinairism*, or even by a narrow scientific pride, when it is not deaf to the instincts and spontaneous aspirations of life — it knows (and this is its last word) that respect for man is the supreme law of Humanity, and that the great, the real object of history, its only legitimate object, is the humanization and emancipation, the real liberty, the prosperity and happiness of each individual living in society. For, if we would not fall back into the liberticidal fiction of the public welfare represented by the State, a fiction always founded on the systematic sacrifice of the people, we must clearly recognize that collective liberty and prosperity exist only so far as they represent the sum of individual liberties and prosperities.

Science knows all these things, but it does not and cannot go beyond them. Abstraction being its very nature, it can well enough conceive the principle of real and living individuality, but it can have no dealings with real and living individuals; it

6

concerns itself with individuals in general, but not with Peter or James, not with such or such a one, who, so far as it is concerned, do not, cannot, have any existence. Its individuals, I repeat, are only abstractions.

Now, history is made, not by abstract individuals, but by acting, living and passing individuals. Abstractions advance only when borne forward by real men. For these beings made not in idea only, but in reality of flesh and blood, science has no heart: it considers them at most as *material for intellectual and social development*. What does it care for the particular conditions and chance fate of Peter or James? It would make itself ridiculous, it would abdicate, it would annihilate itself, if it wished to concern itself with them otherwise than as examples in support of its eternal theories. And it would be ridiculous to wish it to do so, for its mission lies not there. It cannot grasp the concrete; it can move only in abstractions. Its mission is to busy itself with the situation and the *general* conditions of the existence and development, either of the human species in general, or of such a race, such a people, such a class or category of individuals; the *general* causes of their prosperity, their decline, and the best *general* methods of securing their progress in all ways. Provided it accomplishes this task broadly and rationally, it will do its whole duty, and it would be really unjust to expect more of it.

But it would be equally ridiculous, it would be disastrous to entrust it with a mission which it is incapable of fulfilling. Since its own nature forces it to ignore the existence of Peter and James, it must never be permitted, nor must anybody be permitted in its name, to govern Peter and James. For it were capable of treating them almost as it treats rabbits. Or rather, it would continue to ignore them; but its licensed representatives, men not at all abstract, but on the contrary in very active life and having very substantial interests, yielding to the pernicious influence which privilege inevitably exercises upon men, would finally fleece other men in the name of science, just as they have been fleeced hitherto by priests, politicians of all shades and lawyers, in the name of God, of the State, of judicial Right.

What I preach then is, to a certain extent, the *revolt of life against science*, or rather against the *government of science*, not to destroy science — that would be high treason to humanity — but to remand it to its place so that it can never leave it again. Until now all human history has been only a perpetual and bloody immolation of millions of poor human beings in honour of some pitiless abstraction — God, country, power of State, national honour, historical rights, judicial rights, political liberty, public welfare. Such has been up to today the natural, spontaneous and inevitable movement of human societies. We cannot undo it; we must submit to it so far as the past is concerned, as we submit to all natural fatalities. We must believe that that was the only possible way to educate the human race. For we must not deceive ourselves: even in attributing the larger part to the Machiavellian wiles of the governing classes, we have to recognize that no minority would have been powerful enough to impose all these horrible sacrifices upon the masses if there had not been in the masses themselves a dizzy spontaneous movement which pushed them on to continual self-sacrifice, now to one, now to another of these devouring abstractions, the vampires of history, ever nourished upon human blood.

We readily understand that this is very gratifying to the theologians, politicians, and jurists. Priests of these abstractions, they live only by the continual immolation of the popular masses. Nor is it more surprising that metaphysics, too, should give its consent. Its only mission is to justify and rationalize as far as possible the iniquitous and absurd. But that positive science itself should have shown the same tendencies is a fact which we must deplore while we establish it. That it has done so is due to two reasons: in the first place, because, constituted outside of life, it is represented by a privileged body; and in the second place, because thus far it has posited itself as an absolute and final object of all human development. By a judicious criticism, which it can and finally will be forced to pass upon itself, it would understand, on the contrary, that it is only a means for the realization of a much higher object — that of the complete humanization of the *real* situation of all the *real* individuals who are born, who live, and who die, on earth.

The immense advantages of positive science over theology, metaphysics, politics, and judicial right consists in this — that, in place of the false and fatal abstractions set up by these doctrines, it posits true abstractions which express the general nature and logic of things, their general relations, and the general laws of their development. This separates it profoundly from all preceding doctrines, and will assure it for ever a great position in society: it will constitute in a certain sense society's collective consciousness. But there is one aspect in which it resembles all these doctrines: its only possible object being abstractions, it is forced by its very nature to ignore real men, outside of whom the truest abstractions have no existence. To remedy this radical defect positive science will have to proceed by a different method from that followed by the doctrines of the past. The latter have taken advantage of the ignorance of the masses to sacrifice them with delight to their abstractions, which, by the way, are always very lucrative to those who represent them in flesh and bone. Positive science, recognizing its absolute inability to conceive real individuals and interest itself in their lot, must definitely and absolutely renounce all claim to the government of societies; for if it should meddle therein, it would only sacrifice continually the living men whom it ignores to the abstractions which constitute the sole object of its legitimate preoccupations.

The true science of history, for instance, does not yet exist; scarcely do we begin today to catch a glimpse of its extremely complicated conditions. But suppose it were definitely developed; what could it give us? It would exhibit a faithful and rational picture of the natural development of the general conditions — material and ideal, economical, political and social, religious, philosophical, aesthetic, and scientific — of the societies which have a history. But this universal picture of human civilization, however detailed it might be, would never show anything beyond general and consequently *abstract* estimates. The milliards of individuals who have furnished the *living and suffering materials* of this history at once triumphant and dismal — triumphant by its general results, dismal by the immense hecatomb of human victims 'crushed under its car' — those milliards of obscure individuals without whom none of the great abstract results of history would have been obtained — and who, bear in mind, have never benefited by any of these results — will find no place, not even the slightest, in our annals. They have lived and been sacrificed, crushed for the good of abstract humanity, that is all.

Shall we blame the science of history? That would be unjust and ridiculous. Individuals cannot be grasped by thought, by reflection, or even by human speech, which is capable of expressing abstractions only; they cannot be grasped in the present day any more than in the past. Therefore social science itself, the science of the future, will necessarily continue to ignore them. All that we have a right to demand of it is that it shall point us with faithful and sure hand to the *general causes of individual suffering*—among these causes it will not forget the immolation and subordination (still too frequent, alas!) of living individuals to abstract generalities—at the same time showing us the *general conditions necessary to the real emancipation of the individuals living in society*. That is its mission; those are its limits, beyond which the action of social science can be only impotent and fatal. Beyond those limits begin the *doctrinaire* and governmental pretensions of its licensed representatives, its priests. It is time to have done with all popes and priests; we want them no longer, even if they call themselves Social Democrats.

IX FOUR ANARCHIST PROGRAMMES

The first of these programmes was written by Bakunin in 1868 for his secret society, the 'Fraternité internationale'; it was published as an appendix to the pamphlet by Engels and Lafargue, *L'Alliance de la Démocratique socialiste et l'Association internationale des Travailleurs. Rapports et documents publiés par ordre du Congrès international de la Haye* (London, 1873), pp. 126–32. The second programme, published in the same document, pp. 125–6, is that of the secret Alliance, founded together with the public organization in 1868 (see p. 21). The programme of this public Alliance appears here as the third text; it is taken from the appendix to the *Mémoire présenté par la Fédération jurassienne de l'Association internationale des Travailleurs à toutes les fédérations de l'Internationale* (Sonvillier, 1873), pp. 39–40. The fourth text was written by Bakunin on August 14th–15th, 1872, as a programme for the Slav Section of Zurich, founded on July 7th and affiliated to the Jura Federation; the ideas expressed here are essentially those accepted by the 'anti-authoritarian' federations of the International after the Conference of London. It was published in *Archives Bakounine*, vol. III, 'Étatisme et anarchie, 1873' (Leiden, 1967), pp. 180–81. The first three programmes are here translated from the French by Steven Cox; and the fourth is translated from the Russian by Olive Stevens.

I. *Programme and Purpose of the Revolutionary Organization of International Brothers*

1. The principles of this organization are the same as those in the programme of the International Alliance of Socialist Democracy. They are further clarified, with reference to the questions of woman, the religious and juridical family and the State, in the *Russian social democratic* programme.

The central bureau expects to produce a fuller theoretical and practical amplification in the near future.

2. The association of international brothers advocates universal revolution — social, philosophic, economic and

political at once—so that of all the present order of things, based on property, exploitation, domination and the principle of religious, metaphysical, bourgeois doctrinaire and even Jacobin revolutionary authority, not one stone shall remain standing on another, first in Europe and then in the rest of the world. To the cry of 'peace to the workers, liberty to all the oppressed and death to rulers, exploiters and overseers of all kinds', we intend to destroy all States and all Churches, together with all their institutions and all their religious, judicial, financial, police and university, economic and social laws, so that all those millions of poor human beings now hoodwinked, enslaved, tormented and exploited shall be delivered from all their official and officious guides and benefactors and breathe at last in total freedom as associations and individuals.

3. Convinced that individual and social evil stems far less from individuals than from the organization of things and from social position, we shall act humanely as much out of a sense of justice as from any calculation of utility, and we shall ruthlessly destroy positions and things so as to be able to spare human beings without endangering the Revolution. We deny *free will* and society's alleged right of punishment. In the broadest, most humane sense, justice itself is only an idea, which might be termed negative and transitional: it raises the social question, but does not elucidate it, doing no more than indicating the one possible path towards human emancipation —the humanization of society through liberty in equality. The positive solution can only be given by the increasingly rational organization of society. This long-awaited solution, our common ideal ... is the liberty, morality, fellowship and welfare of all men through the solidarity of all—the brother-hood of mankind.

Every human individual is the involuntary product of a natural and social environment within which he is born and grows and which continues to influence him. The three major causes of all human immorality are: inequality—political as well as economic and social; ignorance, its natural outcome; and their necessary consequence—*slavery*.

Since the organization of society is always the sole cause of the crimes men commit, it is obviously both hypocritical and absurd to punish criminals, since all punishment presupposes guilt, and criminals are never guilty. The theory of guilt and punishment grew out of theology—the marriage of absurdity with religious hypocrisy.

The only right which can be accorded to society in its present state of transition is the natural right of *murdering* the criminals it has itself produced, in the interests of its own defence, not the right of trying and condemning them. This right will not even be a right in the strict sense of the word; instead it will be a natural fact, painful but inevitable, the emblem and product of the impotence and stupidity of present-day society, and the more society can avoid its exercise the closer it will be to its real emancipation. All revolutionaries, the oppressed and the suffering victims of the prevailing organization of society, whose hearts are naturally bursting with revenge and hatred, should remind themselves that kings, oppressors and exploiters of all kinds are as guilty as the criminals emerging from the popular masses: they are evil-doers, but they are not guilty, since they too, like ordinary criminals, are the involuntary products of the present organization of society. It ought not to be surprising if the people slaughter many of them in the first flush of rebellion—it may be an inevitable misfortune, as futile as the havoc created by a storm.

But this natural occurrence will be neither moral nor even useful. History is full of lessons in this connection: the terrible guillotine of 1793, which could hardly be accused of being idle or dilatory, did not succeed in wiping out the French aristocracy. Though not wiped out, this class was at least thoroughly shaken, not by the guillotine but by the confiscation and sale of its possessions. And in general it may be said that political butchery has never killed off any party, but has in the main proved powerless against the privileged classes, since power stems far less from men than from the positions made available to privileged men by the organization of things, in other words *the institution of the State* and its by-product as well as its natural basis, *individual ownership*.

In order to launch a radical revolution, it is therefore necessary to attack positions and things and to destroy property and the State, but there will be no need to destroy men and to condemn ourselves to the inevitable reaction which is unfailingly produced in every society by the slaughter of men.

Yet in order to earn the right to take a humane attitude towards men, it will be necessary to be ruthless with positions and things; it will be necessary to destroy everything, and first and foremost property and its bedfellow, *the State*. This is the whole secret of revolution.

It is not surprising that the Jacobins and Blanquists, who became socialists more out of necessity than conviction, for whom socialism is a means, not the end, of Revolution, and whose goal is dictatorship, which means State centralization, with its necessary, inevitable outcome of the reconstitution of property—it is only natural, we say, that having no intention of waging radical revolution against things they should long for bloody revolution against men. But the inevitable result of this bloody revolution based on the construction of a highly centralized revolutionary State will be military dictatorship under a new master, as we shall prove at length below. Thus the triumph of the Jacobins or the Blanquists would be the death of Revolution.

4. We are the natural enemies of those revolutionaries— future dictators, regimenters and custodians of revolution— who, even before today's monarchic, aristocratic and bourgeois States are destroyed, are already longing to create new revolutionary States just as centralist and despotic as those we already know—who are so habituated to the order created from above by authority and so horrified by what they see as disorder (which is in fact nothing but the frank and natural expression of popular life) that even before revolution has produced some good healthy disorder they are already wondering how to halt and muzzle it, by the intervention of some authority which would be revolutionary in name only, but in practice would be nothing more than a new reaction whose effect would be once again to condemn the popular masses to rule by decree and to obedience, stagnation and death, in other words to enslavement and exploitation at the hands of a new quasi-revolutionary aristocracy.

5. What we understand by revolution is unleashing what are known as dangerous passions and destroying what the same jargon refers to as 'public order'.

We do not fear anarchy, but invoke it, convinced as we are that anarchy, meaning the full affirmation of unfettered popular life, must inaugurate liberty, equality, justice, the new order and the clash between Revolution and Reaction. This new life—popular revolution—will probably not be slow to organize, but it will create its revolutionary organization from the bottom upwards and from the circumference inwards, in accordance with the principle of liberty, and not from the top downwards and from the centre outwards, as is the way of all authority—for it makes precious little difference to us whether authority dubs itself Church, Monarchy, constitutional State or even revolutionary dictatorship. We loathe and reject them all alike as never-ending sources of exploitation and despotism.

6. As we see it, the revolution must set out from the first radically and totally to destroy the State and all State institutions. The natural and necessary consequences of this destruction will be: (*a*) State bankruptcy; (*b*) cessation of State intervention in the payment of private debts, leaving every debtor to pay or not to pay as he sees fit; (*c*) cessation of all tax payments and all raising of taxation, direct or indirect; (*d*) dissolution of the army, magistracy, bureaucracy, police and priesthood; (*e*) abolition of official justice, suspension of everything judicially known as right, and the exercise of those rights. Consequently the abolition and incineration of all title-deeds, wills, bills of sale and gift, legal papers—in other words all legal and civil red tape. The fact of revolution replaces the law created and guaranteed by the State; (*f*) confiscation of all productive capital and means of production on behalf of workers' associations, who are to put them to collective use; (*g*) confiscation of all Church and State property, together with individual holdings of precious metals, on behalf of the federative Alliance of all working men's associations—the Alliance which will constitute the Commune.

In return for goods confiscated, the Commune will provide the bare necessities to the expropriated individuals, who will then be able to earn more by their own labour if they can and will. (*h*) The Commune will be organized by the standing federation of the Barricades and by the creation of a Revolutionary Communal Council composed of one or two delegates from each barricade, one to each street or district, vested with plenary but accountable and removable mandates. The Communal Council thus created will have the power to choose executive committees from among its membership, one for each branch of the revolutionary administration of the Commune. (*i*) The insurgent, communally organized capital to declare that having destroyed the authoritarian, custodial State—as it had every right to do, having been its slave, like all other localities—it renounces all rights or rather all claims to govern and interfere with the provinces. (*k*)* Appeal to all provinces, communes and associations, inviting them to follow the example given by the capital by first *reorganizing* on revolutionary lines and then sending their representatives to an agreed meeting-place, these too vested with similar mandates to constitute the federation of insurgent associations, communes and provinces in the name of the same principles and to organize a revolutionary force capable of defeating reaction. Revolutionary propagandists, not official revolutionary envoys with some official insignia, to be dispatched to all provinces and communes, and particularly among the peasants, who can never become revolutionaries on principle or by any kind of dictatorial decree, but only under the influence of the revolutionary fact itself, meaning the inevitable outcome of the complete cessation of the judicial and official life of the State inside each commune. Abolition of the national State, in the sense that every foreign land, province, commune or single individual that rebels in the name of the same principles will be received into the revolutionary federation regardless of the actual frontiers of States and their membership of different political or national systems, while any native provinces, communes, associations and individuals siding with reaction shall be debarred. So it is the very fact of the expansion and organization of the revolution for the purpose of self-defence among the insurgent areas that will bring about the triumph of the revolution, based on the abolition of frontiers and the downfall of States.

7. There can no longer be any successful political or national revolution unless the political revolution is transformed into social revolution, and unless national revolution,

* There is no sub-entry (*j*) in the original text—EDITOR.

precisely because of its radically socialist, anti-State character, becomes universal revolution.

8. Since revolution everywhere must be created by the people, and supreme control must always belong to the people organized into a free federation of agricultural and industrial associations, the new revolutionary State, organized from the bottom upwards by means of revolutionary delegation and embracing all insurgent areas in the name of the same principles, irrespective of old frontiers and national differences, will set out to administer public services, not to rule over peoples. It will constitute the *new motherland, the Alliance of Universal Revolution* against the alliance of all the reactions.

9. This organization rules out any idea of dictatorship and custodial control. But for the very establishment of the revolutionary alliance and the triumph of revolution over reaction, *the unity of revolutionary thought and action must find an agent* in the thick of the popular anarchy which will constitute the very life and all the energy of the revolution. That agent must be *the secret universal association of international brothers*.

10. This association stems from the conviction that revolutions are never made by individuals or even by secret societies. They come about of themselves, produced by the force of things, the tide of events and facts. They ferment for a long time in the depths of the instinctive consciousness of the popular masses — then they explode, often triggered by apparently trivial causes. All that a well-organized secret society can do is first to assist the birth of the revolution by sowing ideas corresponding to the instincts of the masses, then to organize, not the army of the revolution — the army must always be the people — but a kind of revolutionary general staff made up of devoted, hardworking and intelligent men, and above all of sincere friends of the people, without ambition or vanity, and capable of acting as intermediaries between the revolutionary idea and the popular instinct.

11. Therefore there should be no vast number of these individuals. A hundred powerfully and seriously allied revolutionaries are enough for the international organization of the whole of Europe. Two or three hundred revolutionaries are enough for the largest country's organization.

II. *Programme of the International Socialist Alliance*

1. The International Alliance has been founded with the aim of helping to organize and accelerate the universal Revolution on the basis of the principles proclaimed in our programme.

2. In accordance with these principles, the aim of the revolution can be none other than: (*a*) Demolition of all religious, monarchic, aristocratic and bourgeois authorities and powers in Europe. Consequently, destruction of all present-day States together with all their political, judicial, bureaucratic and financial institutions. (*b*) Reconstitution of a new society on the strict basis of freely associated labour, taking collective ownership, equality and justice as starting-points.

3. The Revolution as we conceive it, or rather as the pressure of events naturally posits it today, bears an essentially international, or universal, character. In view of the threatening coalition of all the vested interests and reactionary powers in Europe, with access to all the formidable apparatus provided by experience and organization, and in view of the deep schism now in force everywhere between the bourgeoisie and the workers, no national revolution could succeed without spreading out to all other nations immediately, and it could never cross frontiers and take on this universal character if it did not contain all the elements of this universality, in other words if it were not an avowedly socialist revolution, destroying the State and creating liberty through equality and justice. The one force now capable of moving, electrifying and uplifting the great, the only true power of the century — the workers — is the real and complete emancipation of labour, on the ruins of all institutions that protect hereditary ownership and capital.

4. Since the coming Revolution can only be universal, the Alliance, or to be candid the conspiracy, which is to prepare, organize and hasten it must also be universal.

5. The Alliance will pursue a dual objective: (*a*) It will do its best to disseminate truthful ideas about politics, social economy and all philosophical questions among the popular masses in all lands. It will wage active propaganda through

journals, pamphlets and books, as well as by founding public associations. (b) It will seek to enlist all the intelligent, energetic, discreet men of good will who are sympathetic to our ideas, both in Europe and as far as possible in America, in order to form an invisible network of dedicated revolutionaries, strengthened by the fact of alliance.

III. *Programme of the Alliance*

1. The *Alliance* stands for atheism, the abolition of cults and the replacement of faith by science, and divine by human justice.

2. Above all, it stands for the final and total abolition of classes and the political, economic and social equalization of individuals of either sex, and, to this end, it demands above all the abolition of the right of inheritance, so that every man's possessions may in future be commensurate to his output, and so that in pursuance of the decision reached by the last working men's Congress in Brussels, the land, the in-instruments of work and all other capital may become the collective property of the whole of society and be utilized only by the workers, in other words by the agricultural and industrial associations.[6]

3. It stands for equality of the means of development for all children of both sexes from the cradle onward—maintenance, upbringing and education to all levels of science, industry and the arts—being convinced that while at first the effect of equality will be only economic and social it will increasingly lead to greater natural equality among individuals by eliminating all artificial inequalities, the historic products of a false, iniquitous social system.

4. Hostile to all despotism, acknowledging no political form other than the republican form, and totally rejecting any alliance with reaction, it also repudiates all political action whose target is anything except the triumph of the workers' cause over Capital.

5. It recognizes that all the political and authoritarian States of today must scale down their functions to the simple administration of the public services in their respective lands and merge into the universal union of free Associations, both agricultural and industrial.

6. The concrete, final solution to the social question can only be realized on the basis of international workers' solidarity, and the *Alliance* repudiates any policy based on so-called patriotism and national rivalry.

7. It stands for the universal Association of all local associations, through Liberty.

IV. *The Programme of the Slav Section in Zurich*

1. The Slav section, fully accepting the basic statutes of the International Working Men's Association, passed at the first Congress in September 1866 in Geneva, sets itself the special task of propagating revolutionary socialist principles and of organizing populist forces in the Slav countries.

2. It will struggle with equal energy against the tendencies and manifestations both of Pan-Slavism, that is, the liberation of Slav nations with the help of the Russian empire, and Pan-Germanism, that is, liberation at the hands of the bourgeois German civilization which is now trying to organize a huge State allegedly on populist lines.

3. Since we accept the anarchist revolutionary programme, which we believe alone contains the conditions for the real and complete emancipation of the populist masses, and since we are convinced that the existence of any sort of State is incompatible with the freedom of the proletariat, for it would not permit of an international, fraternal union of peoples, we wish to abolish all States. For the Slav nations in particular this abolition is a matter of life and death, as well as being, at the same time, the only means of making peace with peoples of other races, for instance Turks, Hungarians and Germans.

4. Together with the State must perish all that is known as law, the whole structure of law-making and government, from the top downwards, for its sole aim has always been the establishment of the systematic exploitation of the people's labour for the benefit of the ruling classes.

5. The abolition of law and the State would inevitably lead to the abolition of inheritable property and the juridical concept of the family based on such property, for both are inimical to human justice.

6. The abolition of the State, law, property and the juridical concept of the family would alone make possible the

organization of popular life, from the bottom upwards, based on collective work and property, which, by the very force of events, would become accessible and obligatory for all through the completely free federation of private individuals in associations or in autonomous communes, or, if not in communes and not restricted by various regional and national demarcations, in great homogeneous associations united by the similarity of their interests and social aims, so that communes would form nations, and nations mankind.

7. The Slav section, believing in materialism and atheism, will fight against all forms of religious worship, against all official and unofficial Churches, and, showing both in words and in deeds its complete respect for freedom of conscience and the sacred right of everyone to propagate his own ideas, will endeavour to destroy the concept of anything divine in all religious, metaphysical, doctrinal, political and judicial manifestations, in the conviction that this harmful concept was, and still is, the consecration of every sort of slavery.

8. It has the most complete respect for the positivistic sciences; it demands that the proletariat should have all the possibilities for egalitarian, scientific education, without sexual discrimination, but, as the enemy of government, it rejects with horror governing bodies composed of scholars, as being the most treacherous and harmful of all.

9. The Slav section demands for women as well as for men not only liberty, but equality of rights and obligations.

10. The Slav section, while aiming at the liberation of the Slav peoples, in no way contemplates the organization of a special Slav world, hostile to other races through national feeling. On the contrary, it will strive to bring the Slav peoples into the common family of mankind, which the International Working Men's Association has pledged itself to form on the basis of liberty, equality and universal fraternity.

11. In view of this great task—the liberation of popular masses from every sort of tutelage and every form of government—which the International Working Men's Association has taken upon itself, the Slav section will not allow the possibility of the existence among it of any sort of higher authority or government, and it therefore cannot accept any organization other than that of a free federation of autonomous sections.

12. The Slav section does not admit of any official doctrine or any uniform political programme laid down by the general council or by Congress itself. It accepts nothing short of the complete solidarity of individuals, sections and federations in the economic struggle of the workers of all countries against their exploiters. It will particularly strive to introduce Slav workers to all the practical consequences of this struggle.

13. The Slav section recognizes for the sections of all countries: (*a*) the freedom of philosophical and social propaganda; (*b*) political freedom, so long as it does not interfere with the freedom and rights of other sections and federations; (*c*) freedom in the organization of national revolution; (*d*) freedom of association with sections and federations of other countries.

14. As the Jura Federation has proclaimed these principles aloud, and as it is sincerely putting them into practice, the Slav section has joined it.

X REVOLUTIONARY ORGANIZATION AND THE SECRET SOCIETY

Bakunin's letter to Albert Richard is in the collection of the Archives départementales de la Rhône at Lyons, MS 5401, no. 12 It is here translated from the French by Steven Cox. The extract from the letter to Sergej Nečaev is taken from *Archives Bakounine*, vol. IV, 'Michel Bakounine et ses relations avec Sergej Nečaev, 1870–1872' (Leiden, 1972), pp. 111–20. It is here translated from the Russian by Olive Stevens.

I. *From a Letter to Albert Richard, April 1st, 1870*

You're always telling me that 'we agree on the main issues'. Alas, my friend, I am very much afraid that we utterly disagree on those issues. According to your recent letters and the latest news I have had about you, I am bound to assume that you remain more than ever a supporter of centralization and the revolutionary State. Whereas I am more opposed to it than ever, and see no salvation except in revolutionary anarchy, guided on all issues by an invisible collective power — the only dictatorship I accept, because it is the only kind compatible with openness and maximum energy for the revolutionary movement.

Your revolutionary plan can be summed up in these words: As soon as the revolution breaks out in Paris, Paris organizes the provisional revolutionary commune; Lyons, Marseilles, Rouen and other big towns rise simultaneously and immediately send their revolutionary delegates to Paris, where they form a kind of National Convention or Committee of Public Safety for the whole of France. This committee decrees the Revolution, decrees the abolition of the old State, social liquidation, collective ownership — organizes the Revolutionary State with power enough to suppress domestic and foreign reaction.

Isn't this your idea?

Our idea, our plan, is quite the opposite. Firstly, it is not by any means proved that the revolutionary movement is absolutely bound to start in Paris. It is not at all impossible for it to start in the provinces. But let us suppose that in accordance with tradition it is Paris that starts. To our mind, Paris only has one quite negative—meaning frankly revolutionary—step to take, and that step is destruction and liquidation, not organization. If Paris rises and triumphs, it will have the duty and right to proclaim the total liquidation of the political, judicial, financial and administrative State, public and private bankruptcy, dissolution of all the powers, services, functions and forces of the State, incineration or public burning of all papers and public and private deeds. Paris will naturally make haste to organize itself as best it can, in revolutionary style, after the workers have joined into associations and made a clean sweep of all the instruments of labour and every kind of capital and building; armed and organized by streets and *quartiers*, they will form the revolutionary federation of all the *quartiers*, the federative commune. And this commune will have every right to declare that it does not claim the right to govern or organize France, but that it calls on the people and all the communes, either in France or in what until now was called Abroad, to follow its example, for each in their own place to make an equally radical revolution, equally destructive of the State, judicial law and privileged ownership, and after that to come and join in federation with itself, either in Paris or wherever else is agreed. All the French and foreign revolutionary communes will then send representatives to organize the necessary common services and arrangements for production and exchange, to establish the charter of equality, the basis of all liberty—a charter utterly negative in character, defining what has to be abolished for ever rather than the positive forms of local life which can only be created by the living practice of each locality—and to organize common defence against the enemies of the Revolution, together with propaganda, the weapon of revolution, and practical revolutionary solidarity with friends in all countries against enemies in all countries ...

In other words, the revolution should be and should everywhere remain independent of the central point, which must be its expression and product—not its source, guide and cause ...

Anarchy, the mutiny of all local passions and the awakening

of spontaneous life at all points, must be well developed in order for the revolution to remain alive, real and powerful. Once the revolution has won its first victory, the political revolutionaries, supporters of overt dictatorship, advocate the muting of passions, and speak for order, trust and submission to the established revolutionary powers — in this way they reconstitute the State. We, on the other hand, must foment, awaken and unleash all the passions, we must produce anarchy and, like invisible pilots in the thick of the popular tempest, we must steer it not by any open power but by the collective dictatorship of all the allies — a dictatorship without insignia, titles or official rights, and all the stronger for having none of the paraphernalia of power. That is the only dictatorship I accept. But in order for it to take action it must exist, and to that end it must be prepared and organized in advance, for it will not happen of its own accord — or through discussions, disquisitions and debates over principle, or through popular assemblies.

Few allies, but good ones — energetic, discreet, loyal but above all devoid of personal vanity and ambition. Strong men, serious enough and with minds and hearts lofty enough to prefer the reality of power to its egocentric trappings. If you set up this collective, invisible dictatorship, you will triumph, the revolution, properly guided, will triumph. If not, not. If you fall to playing at Committees of Public Safety and official, overt dictatorship, you will be devoured by the reaction that you yourselves will have created.

Dear friend, I admire the generous instincts and lively intelligence of the French workers. But I am very much afraid of their penchant for showing off, for big, dramatic, heroic, rowdy scenes. Many of our friends — yourself included — are making ready to play key roles in the coming revolution — the roles of Statesmen of the Revolution. They count on becoming the Dantons, Robespierres, Saint-Justs of revolutionary socialism — and they are already rehearsing the fine speeches and brilliant strokes which are to astonish the world. They will naturally make the popular masses a stepping-stone — a pedestal for their democratic ambition, their personal glory! To save us all, they will produce dictatorship, government, the State. A ridiculous, woeful illusion. They will create nothing but vanity, serve nothing but reaction—they themselves will be reaction.

Bear in mind, my friend and brother, that the present-day socialist movement—quite opposed in this respect to the political movement which aims only at the domination and glorification of individuals—the movement for popular emancipation does not mean the triumph and dictatorship of individuals. If it is individuals who triumph, we shall no longer have socialism but politics—bourgeois business—and the socialist movement will be lost. If it does not succumb, then self-centred, ambitious, boastful individuals—budding dictators—will bring about a terrible fiasco.

There is only one power and one dictatorship whose organization is salutary and feasible: it is that collective, invisible dictatorship of those who are allied in the name of our principle—and this dictatorship will be all the more salutary and effective for not being dressed up in any official power or extrinsic character.

But in order to form it, really strong men are required, whose minds and hearts raise them above vulgar ambition, and who have enough worthy ambition to want only the triumph of their idea, not their own selves, to prefer real power to the trappings of force, and lastly to realize that our century is the century of collective, not individual power, and that collectivity will crush all those individuals who try to foist themselves upon it.

You are too intelligent a man not to realize all this, but will your heart and character rise to the level of your intelligence? That is the question. What will come uppermost—the love of justice and equality or the desire to cut an historic figure? Will you have the strength to subdue in yourself this Italian charlatanism, which you see as an excellent means of attracting the masses, this mania for posing and thirst for glory that are still haunting you today?

You see, I am talking with all the freedom of a friend and brother who believes that he has a right to speak out because he feels immense affection for you in his heart, and who, although he recognizes a powerful element of individualism in you, relies on your intelligence and your heart, which are far greater than your failings—in other words, a man who has faith in your friendship. If you still retain it after reading this letter, I shall congratulate myself on writing it.

One word more. In one of your letters you told me that I can become the Garibaldi of the social movement. You really have far too good an opinion of me, dear friend. Be assured that I know myself well, and that I find in myself not one of the qualities nor any of the faults necessary to make a hero; and in any case I have not the least desire to make an historic name for myself.

Do you know what all my ambition amounts to? It is great, but it does not aspire to glory or publicity:

It is to help you to form that invisible collective force which alone can preserve and guide the revolution ...

II. *From a letter to Sergej Nečaev, June 2nd, 1870*

The main point that distinguishes my system is that it refutes not only the value, but even the possibility, of any revolution that is not spontaneous or popular and socialist. I am deeply convinced that any other revolution would be dishonest and harmful, and would annihilate both liberty and people, for it would promise the masses new forms of poverty and slavery; and, most important of all, any other revolution has now become impossible and unattainable, and cannot be achieved. In the course of the last seventy-five years of recent history, centralization and civilization, railways, the telegraph system, new weapons and new military organization — generally speaking, administrative techniques, that is the techniques by which the masses are systematically enslaved and exploited and national and all other rebellions cut short, have been so carefully developed, checked by experience and perfected that at this present time the State has been strengthened in all these ways by the most tremendous resources, so that any attempt which is not popular in character, but is at all artificial, and deals in secret plots, sudden assaults, surprises and blows, is bound to wreck itself against the State, which can only be conquered and broken by a spontaneous popular socialist revolution.

And therefore the sole object of a secret society must be not to create an artificial force outside the people, but to arouse, unite and organize spontaneous popular forces; in this way the only possible, the only effective army of the revolution is not outside the people, but consists of the people themselves. It is impossible to rouse the people by artificial means. Popular revolutions are born by the actual force of events or else by the stress of history which flows unseen underground but continually and usually slowly in the popular strata, embracing and penetrating, adding drop after drop, until the time comes when it bursts out from under the ground in a torrent which breaks down all obstacles and destroys everything that stands in the way.

It is impossible to bring about such a revolution artificially. It is not even possible to speed it up at all significantly, although I have no doubt that an efficient and wise organization can cushion the explosion. There are some periods in history when revolutions are quite simply impossible; there are other periods when they are inevitable. In which of these periods do we now find ourselves? I am deeply convinced that we are in a period of universal, inevitable popular revolution. I shall not attempt to prove that I am right in this conviction, as that would take me too far. Besides I do not need to prove this since I am addressing a person and people who, it seems, share this conviction in full. I say that socialist popular revolution is inevitable everywhere, in the whole of Europe. Will it break out soon, and where will it break first—in Russia, or in France, or in some other part of the West? No one can foretell. Maybe it will break out within a year, or in less than a year, or not for ten or twenty years. That is not the point, and the people who are determined to serve the revolution faithfully do not serve it for their own pleasure. All secret societies that really want to be of use to it should first of all rid themselves of all nervousness and impatience. They should not sleep, but, on the contrary, they should be as ready as possible every minute, always on the alert, always able to make use of every fortuitous incident; but at the same time they must be equipped and organized not for a speedy insurrection but for the purpose of long-drawn-out and patient underground work in imitation of your friends the Jesuit fathers.

I will confine myself to discussing Russia. When will the Russian revolution burst forth? We do not know. Many of us, and I confess to having been among them, expected a popular uprising in 1870, but the people did not awaken. Does this mean that the Russian people will forgo a revolution, that the revolution will pass them by? No, such a conclusion is impossible and would be meaningless. There is no way out for our people, and their position is definitely critical both economically and politically, while on the other hand there is the positive incapacity of our government and our State to alter or even at least to alleviate conditions, and this incapacity stems not out of some quality in individuals in the government, but out of the very nature of our State system in particular, and of the State in general. Anyone who realizes this situation cannot fail to conclude that a Russian popular revolution is inevitable. It is not only in the negative sense that it is inevitable, it is also positively inevitable, for there is in our people, in spite of their backwardness, a historically developed ideal, to which they strive consciously or unconsciously. This ideal is the communal ownership of land with complete freedom from any sort of State control or exploitation. This is what the people strove for at the time of the False Dmitri, Stenka Razin and Pugachev, and this is what they strive for now in a continuous series of rebellions that are always being quelled because they are so scattered.

I have pointed out only two main characteristics of the Russian popular ideal, which I cannot describe fully in a few words. A great deal exists in the intellectual strivings of the Russian people which will come to light with the first revolution. For the time being it is enough for me to prove that our people are not a blank sheet of paper on which any sort of secret society, even for instance your communists, can write whatever programme they like. The people have worked out their own programme; maybe three-quarters of it is unconscious, but part of it is conscious, and a secret society should find out and guess what it has to co-operate with, if it wants to be successful.

Undoubtedly a fact that is well known to us is that at the time of Stenka Razin, and also during the Pugachev rising, and indeed whenever a popular uprising succeeded, albeit only for a time, there was one thing our people always did: they seized all the land and brought it under communal

control, sending all the gentry and landowners, tsarist bureaucrats and sometimes the priests to the devil, and organizing
their own free commune. This means that our people already
have in their memory, and as an ideal, one precious element
for the future organization which does not exist among
Western peoples, and that is the *free economic commune*. There
are two basic facts in popular life and popular thought which
we can build on: frequent uprisings and the free economic
commune. There is a third basic fact, and that is the Cossack
world of thieving brigands, which contained in itself a protest
both against the State and against the restrictions of a patriar-
chal society, and, one might say, contains elements of the
first two.

The frequent risings, although always caused by casual
events, nevertheless were due to general conditions and
expressed the deep and widespread dissatisfaction of the people.
They form, as it were, the everyday or natural phenomenon of
Russian popular life. There is not a village in Russia which is
not deeply dissatisfied with its conditions; they all suffer
from poverty, restrictions and changes, and deep within their
collective heart lurks the desire to seize all the gentry's and
kulaks' land, which they are convinced should belong to them.
There is not a village in which an able person could not start a
rising. The only reason why there are not more risings in
villages is because of fear and a consciousness of lack of power.
This consciousness is due to the fact that the communes are
scattered, and there is an absence of real solidarity among
them. If every village knew that it could rise and that at the
same time there would be risings in all the other villages,
one could safely say that there would not be a single village
in Russia that did not rebel. From this arises the first duty,
purpose and aim of a secret society: to arouse in all communes
a consciousness of their unalterable solidarity, and thus to
arouse in the Russian people a consciousness of their greatness
—in a word, to unite the large number of separate peasant
risings into one general popular rising.

I am deeply convinced that one of the chief means of
attaining this aim should be through the free Cossacks in all
parts of the country, and through the enormous number of
vagabonds, both 'holy' and otherwise, through 'pilgrims' and

'*beguny*',[8] thieves and brigands — the whole of that widespread and numerous underground world which, from time immemorial, has protested against State and sovereignty and against a knouto-Germanic civilization. This was expressed in an anonymous broadsheet, 'The background to the Revolutionary Problem', which caused an outburst of indignation among our respectable and vainglorious babblers who consider that their doctrinaire Byzantine chatter is work. In fact the broadsheet was quite right, and can be proved right by the whole of our history. The Cossack robber-brigand and vagabond world played precisely this role of originator and co-ordinator in separate communal risings both at the time of Stenka Razin and of Pugachev; our wandering people are the best and truest channels for a people's revolution, for they foretell popular disturbances, and are the forerunners of popular uprisings, while everyone knows that these wanderers easily become thieves and robbers when opportunity offers. And which of us is not a robber or a thief? Isn't that what the government is? And what about our government and private speculators and businessmen? Or our landowners and merchants? I personally cannot stand either robbery or violence, or in fact anything that constitutes an assault on humanity, but I admit that if I had to choose between the robbery and violence that sits on a throne or makes use of every possible privilege, and the robbery and violence of the people, then I would not have the slightest hesitation in coming down on the side of the latter, which I find natural, essential and even in some ways legal. I admit that from the point of view of real humanitarianism the world of popular brigands is far, far from beautiful. But what is beautiful in Russia? What can be more filthy than our respectable, hierarchical world of middle-class civilization and cleanliness, with its smooth Western façade hiding the most awful debauchery of thought, feeling, attitude and actions, or at the very best a cheerless and aimless emptiness. While on the other hand the lusts of the people spring from nature, strength and life, and contain finally the sacrifice of many centuries of history. There is in them a mighty protest against the fundamental origin of all debauchery against Sovereignty, and in this there is hope for the future. That is why I prefer the violence of the people, and see in it one of the most natural methods of achieving a popular revolution in Russia ...

Whoever wants to preserve his ideal and virgin chastity had better remain in his study, dreaming, thinking and writing dissertations or poetry. Whoever wants to become a real revolutionary activist in Russia should pull off his gloves, for there are no gloves that can preserve him from the Russian mud which goes on for ever in all directions. The Russian world, whether it be the world of State privilege or the people's world, is terrible. Inevitably the Russian revolution will be a terrible revolution. Whoever is frightened of horrors and mud had better get away from this world and this revolution; but whoever wants to serve the revolution should know where it will lead him, and must brace himself and be ready for anything.

It is not an easy business to make use of the world of brigands, and turn it into a tool for a popular revolution and a means of co-ordinating and spreading separate communal risings; I accept this as a necessity, but at the same time I admit that I am completely unfit for such a task. In order to take it on and bring it to a successful conclusion, one must have the nervous strength of a legendary hero, passionate conviction and iron will. Maybe there are such people among your ranks. But people of our generation and with our background are of no use. Going to the brigands does not mean that one should become a brigand and nothing more than a brigand. It does not mean sharing all their ... passions and calamities, nor their aims, feelings and actions which are frequently vile. No, it means instilling a new spirit and arousing a new world outlook in these wild men who are rough to the point of cruelty, but whose nature is fresh and strong, unsubdued and inexhaustible, and therefore open to lively propaganda, so long as this propaganda really is lively and not doctrinaire, and dares to approach them and knows how to. There is still a great deal I can say on this subject if I have occasion to continue this correspondence with you.

I have said that another precious element in the future popular life of Russia is the free economic commune, and this is a really precious element which does not exist in the West.

The Western social revolution will have to create this essential and rudimentary embryo of all future organizations, and its creation will cause the West a very great deal of difficulty. As far as we are concerned, it has already been created. Were there to be a revolution in Russia, were the government and all its bureaucrats to perish, the Russian village would have not the slightest difficulty in organizing itself that very same day. On the other hand Russia will have difficulties unknown to the West. Our communes are very widely separated, hardly know each other, and frequently find themselves opposing each other in the old Russian way. Recently, *because of the government's financial measures*, they have become accustomed to the union of small rural districts, so that the rural district has more and more popular significance, and is becoming canonized popularly, but that is as far as it goes. The rural districts definitely do not know, and do not want to know, anything about each other. But it is essential for the establishment of a revolutionary victory, and for the attainment of liberty in the future for the people, that the small rural districts (*volosti*) should form themselves into larger regions (*uyezdy*) *by their own people's movement*, that these regions (*uyezdy*) should form regions (*oblasti*), and that the regions should themselves unite into a free Russian federation.

It is again the duty of a secret organization to arouse a realization in our communes that this is essential for their own freedom and their own good, and nothing but a secret organization would want to take this on, for the interests of the government and of the government classes would be bitterly opposed to it. How this should be undertaken, and what should be done to instil in the communes the knowledge that this is their road to salvation, the only road to salvation, cannot be discussed at any length here.

Here, my dear friend, are the chief features of the whole programme of the Russian popular revolution, deeply imbedded in the historic instinct and the whole condition of our people. Whoever wants to lead a popular movement must accept all this in full and carry it out. He who wants to impose *his own* plan on the people will make a fool of himself.

The people themselves, as we have seen, because of their ignorance and the way in which they are dispersed, are unable to formulate and bind themselves to a system, and to unite in its name. That is why they need helpers. Where are these helpers coming from? That is the most difficult question in all revolutions. Up till now the helpers in all the Western revolutions have come from the privileged classes, and have almost always turned out to be exploiters. And in this connection too, Russia is again more fortunate than the West. In Russia there is an enormous number of people who are educated and who think, and at the same time have been deprived of any opportunity to have any position or career or to find a way for themselves. At least three-quarters of the young students find themselves in precisely this situation. They are seminarists, children of peasants or the lower middle class, the children of unimportant civil servants and bankrupt gentry — but why should I go on, you know this world better than I do. If we accept the people as our revolutionary army, then this is our general staff, this is precious material for a secret organization.

But this world must really be organized and *filled with moral purpose*. Your system will only corrupt them, and make them traitors to you and exploiters of the people. Remember that in the whole of that world there is very little morality except for the small number of iron-willed, high-principled natures that have emerged from filthy oppression and untold poverty according to Darwin's theory. They are the virtuous, that is, lovers of humanity, and they support all that is just against all that is unjust, and all the oppressed against all the oppressors, only because of the situation; they do this by no means consciously but instinctively. Take a hundred people by lot out of this world, and put them in a situation which would allow them to exploit and oppress the people, and one can be certain that they will exploit and oppress the people without qualm of conscience. Consequently, there is little independent virtue among them. It is necessary to make use of their poverty-stricken position and their involuntary virtue, and by continuous propaganda and the power of organization arouse, educate and strengthen them, making their virtue passionately conscious. But you do exactly the opposite; you follow the Jesuitical teaching and systematically kill all individual, human feelings in them and all their personal sense of justice — as if feeling and justice could be impersonal — and you train them in lies, suspicion, espionage and denunciation, relying far more on the outward fetters with which you have chained them than on their inner virtue. Conditions only have to change and they need only realize that the government can be more terrifying than you can be, and, having been trained by you, they become excellent government servants and spies. The fact, my dear friend, has been proved that an enormous number of your comrades, who were seized by the police, disclosed all they knew about everything and everybody without very much coercion from the government side, and *without having been put on the rack*. If it were only possible for you to change, this sad fact would open your eyes and force you to alter your system.

How can we bring about a moral improvement in this world? How can we rouse it directly and consciously, and strengthen in minds and hearts the sole and overwhelming desire to free all the peoples of the world. It is the strength of this new and unique religion that can stir hearts and create a saving collective strength. This should be the whole content of our propaganda from now on. Our short-term aim should be to create a secret organization, an organization that should at one and the same time create a force to help the people, and become a practical training-ground for the moral education of all its members.

Let us first of all define more precisely the aim and the meaning and purpose of this organization. According to my system, as I have already remarked several times above, it should not form a revolutionary army — we should only have one revolutionary army, the people. The organization should only be the general headquarters of this army, and the organizer not of its own, but of the people's forces, as a link between the people's instincts and revolutionary thought. But revolutionary thought is only revolutionary, alive, active and true, in so far as it expresses, and only in so far as it formulates, popular instincts that have been worked out by history. Any effort to impose *our* ideas on the people which might be opposed to their instincts signifies a desire to enslave them to a new sovereignty. Therefore an organization that sincerely wants only to free popular life must accept the programme which is the fullest expression of the people's strivings. It seems to me that the programme laid out in the first number of *Narodnoye Delo* ['The People's Cause'] completely fulfils this aim. It does not impose any new resolutions, regulations or ways of living on the people, and only unleashes their will and gives a wider opportunity for their self-determination and their social-economic organizations, which should be created by them alone from the bottom upwards, and not from the top downwards. The organization must be sincerely impregnated with the idea that it is the servant and helper of the people, and by no means their ruler, and also not in any circumstances, not even on the pretext of the people's welfare, should it ever be their master.

The organization will be confronted with an enormous task. Not only is there the preparation for a triumphant people's revolution, through propaganda and the co-ordination of popular forces; not only is the force of this revolution to wreck finally and absolutely all present-day existing economic, social and political ways of doing things; but also, having survived the triumph of revolution, it will be necessary to make sure, the day after the people's victory, that there is no establishment of any sort of State control over the people, even one that appears to be revolutionary itself, even yours — because all domination, whatever it might be called, would inevitably inflict the old slavery on the people in a new form. Therefore our organization must be sufficiently strong and vital to survive the first victory of the people — and that is not at all easy — and it should be so conscious of its principle that one could hope that, even in the very midst of revolution, it would not alter its ideas or its character or its direction. Then what should its direction be? What is to be the chief aim and purpose of this organization? *To help the people towards self-determination on the lines of the most complete equality and the fullest human freedom in every direction, without the least interference from any sort of domination, even if it be temporary or transitional, that is without any sort of government control.*

We are the most pronounced enemies of every sort of *official power* — even if it is an ultra-revolutionary power. We are the enemies of any sort of publicly declared dictatorship, we are social revolutionary anarchists. But, you will ask, if we are anarchists, by what right do we want to influence the people, and what methods will we use? Denouncing all power, with what sort of power, or rather by what sort of force, shall we direct a people's revolution? *By a force that is invisible, that no one admits and that is not imposed on anyone, by the collective dictatorship of our organization which will be all the greater the more it remains unseen and undeclared, the more it is deprived of all official rights and significance.*

Imagine yourself in the midst of a triumphant, spontaneous revolution in Russia. The state and with it all forms of social and political organization have been demolished. The people have all risen, and have taken all that they needed and have driven away all their enemies. There are no longer any laws or any domination. An ocean of insurrection has broken through all the dykes. This great mass of people is far from being all one race; on the contrary it consists of a great number of races, and covers the immense spaces of the empire of All the Russias; and these people of All the Russias have begun to live and act by their own initiative because they exist in their own right, and no longer because they are ordered to be something, and everywhere universal anarchy is being itself. A great deal of churned-up mud has got collected among the people, and this is thrown up; at various points many new faces show themselves, brave, clever, without a conscience but with ambition, and these apparently are each striving in their own way to gain the people's confidence and to use it for their own ends. These people bump into each other, struggle and destroy each other. It seems that anarchy is terrible and that there is no way out of it.

But imagine that in the middle of this universal anarchy there were a secret organization, dispersing its members in small groups throughout the empire, but nevertheless firmly united and inspired with a single idea, a single aim, applicable everywhere in different ways according to the circumstances, of course, and acting everywhere along the same lines. These small groups, unknown to anyone as such, would have no officially declared power. But strong in the idea behind them, expressing the very essence of popular instincts, desires and demands in their clear and conscious aims among a crowd of people who would be struggling without any purpose or plan, these groups would finally have the strength of that close solidarity which binds isolated groups in one organic whole, *the strength of mind and energy* of its members, who manage to create round themselves a circle of people who are more or less devoted to the same idea, and who are naturally subject to their influence. These groups would not seek anything for themselves, neither privilege nor honour nor power, and they would be in a position to direct popular movements in opposition to all those who were ambitious but not united and fighting each other, and to lead the people towards the most complete realization of the social-economic ideal and the organization of the fullest popular freedom. This is what I call *the collective dictatorship* of a secret organization.

The dictatorship is free of any self-interest, vainglory and ambition, for it is anonymous, and unseen, and does not reward any of the members that compose the group, or the groups themselves, with any profit or honour or official power. It does not threaten the freedom of the people, because, lacking any official character, it does not take the place of State control over the people, and because its whole aim, laid down for it in the programme, consists of the fullest realization of the liberty of the people.

This sort of dictatorship is not in the least contrary to the free development and the self-determination of the people, nor to its organization from the bottom upward, conformable to the people's customs and instincts, for it influences the people exclusively through the natural, personal influence of its members, who have not the slightest power, are scattered in an unseen web throughout the regions, districts and communes, and, in agreement with each other, try, in whatever place they may be, to direct the spontaneous revolutionary movement of the people towards the plan that has been discussed beforehand and firmly determined. This plan, the plan for the organization of popular liberty, should in the first place have its main premises and aims so firmly and clearly inscribed that all possibility of misunderstanding and straying on the part of the members who are called upon to carry it out is ruled out. Secondly it must be broad enough and sufficiently natural to embrace and accept all the

7

inevitable alterations, arising from a variety of circumstances, and all the various movements developing out of the many facets of the life of the people.

Thus the whole question now consists of this: how should such a secret collective dictatorship and power be organized out of the elements known and available to us. This secret dictatorship would in the first place, and at the present time, carry out a broadly based popular propaganda, a propaganda that would *really* penetrate to the people, and by the power of this propaganda and also by *organization among the people themselves* join together separate popular forces into a mighty strength capable of demolishing the State. In the second place it is to survive the revolution itself, not falling apart and not altering its direction the day after the liberty of the people has been achieved.

Such an organization, and particularly the basic nucleus of this organization, should be composed of the strongest people, *the cleverest and, if possible, the most knowing, that is the wisest in experience*. They must be passionately steadfast and unalterably devoted to the people, and having, if possible, turned aside from all other interests, and renounced once and for all, for the whole of their lives till death itself, everything that entices men, all the material comforts and pleasures of society, and all the satisfactions of vainglory, love of rank and fame, they must be solely and completely overwhelmed with the single passion of liberty for all people. They must be people who would refuse personal historical importance during their lives and even a name in history after their death.

XI THE PARIS COMMUNE AND THE IDEA OF THE STATE

This text was written between July 5th and July 23rd, 1871, and was intended as a preface to the second part of *L'Empire knouto-germanique*; it was entitled 'Preamble to the second instalment'. It was taken from Bakunin's posthumous papers and published, in a somewhat free version, in *Le Travailleur* (Geneva, 1878), by Élisée Reclus, who gave it its title. In 1892 a more correct edition was published in the *Entretiens politiques et littéraires* (Paris). Since the manuscript had been lost, this text was reprinted by James Guillaume in the *Œuvres*, vol. IV (Paris, 1910), pp. 247–75. The present translation, by Geoff Charlton, is taken from the edition prepared by Nicolas Walter (London, CIRA, 1971).

This work, like all the writings which I have published until now—so far there have been few enough—is a product of events. It is the natural continuation of my *Letters to a Frenchman* (September 1870),[7] in which I had the easy and sad privilege of foreseeing and predicting the horrible misfortunes which are today assailing France and, along with her, the whole civilized world; misfortunes against which there has been and remains only one remedy now: *the Social Revolution*.

To prove this truth—from now on indisputable—from the historical development of society and from the very events taking place before our eyes in Europe, in such a way as to make it acceptable to all men of good will, and by all sincere seekers of the truth—and then to set forth frankly without reticence or equivocation the philosophical principles as well as the practical goals which make up, so to speak, the essence of the activist spirit, the basis and the aim of what we call the Social Revolution—such is the object of the present work.

The task which I have set for myself is not easy, I know, and I might be accused of presumption if I brought into this work the least personal conceit. But there is none of that, I can assure the reader. I am neither a scholar nor a philosopher, nor even a writer by profession. I have written very little during my life and I have never done so, as it were, except in self-defence, and only when a passionate conviction compelled me to overcome the repugnance which I feel instinctively for parading my private self in public.

Who am I then, and what is it that compels me to publish this work at the present time? I am a passionate seeker of the truth, and none the less persistent an enemy to the harmful untruths which the *law and order party* (that official representative, privileged and self-seeking, of all the religious, metaphysical, political, legal, economic and social villainies, past and present) still has the arrogance to make use of today so as to brutalize and enslave the world. I am a fanatical lover of freedom, considering it as the unique environment within which the intelligence, dignity and happiness of mankind may develop and increase. I am not speaking of that freedom which is purely formal, doled out, measured and regulated by the State, an everlasting lie which in reality never represents anything but the privilege of a few based on the enslavement of everyone else. Nor do I mean that individualistic, egotistical, malicious and illusory freedom, extolled by the school of J.-J. Rousseau, as by all the other schools of bourgeois liberalism, which considers the so-called rights of everyone, represented by the State as the limit of the rights of each individual, and which in fact leads of necessity and without exception to the reduction of the rights of the individual to zero. No, I mean the only freedom which is truly worthy of that name, the freedom which consists in the full development of all the material, intellectual and moral powers which are found in the form of latent capabilities in every individual. I mean that freedom which recognizes only those restrictions which are laid down for us by the laws of our own nature; so, properly speaking, there are no restrictions, since these laws are not imposed by some outside legislator situated maybe beside us or maybe above us, they are immanent in us and inherent in us and constitute the very basis of all our being, as much material as intellectual and moral. Thus, instead of trying to find a limit for them, we should consider them as the real conditions of and the real reason for our freedom.

I mean that freedom of the individual which, far from stopping as if before a boundary in face of the freedom of others, on the contrary finds in that freedom its own confirmation and extension to infinity; the unlimited freedom of each in the freedom of all, freedom in solidarity, freedom in equality; triumphant freedom, victorious over brute force and the principle of authority which was never anything but the idealized expression of brute force; freedom which, after overthrowing all the heavenly and earthly idols, will establish and organize a new world, that of humanity in solidarity, built on the ruin of all Churches and all States.

I am a convinced supporter of *economic and social equality*, because I know that, outside that equality, freedom, justice, human dignity, morality, and the well-being of individuals, just as much as the prosperity of nations, will never be anything but lies. But, supporter though I may be of freedom, this first condition of humanity, I think that equality must be established in the world by the spontaneous organization of work and of the collective ownership of producers' associations, freely organized and federated in the communes, and by the equally spontaneous federation of these communes, but not by the overriding and enslaving activity of the State.

This is the point which mainly divides the revolutionary socialists or collectivists from the authoritarian communists who are supporters of the absolute power of the State. Their goal is the same: both the one and the other faction equally desire the creation of a new social order based solely on the organization of collective work, inevitably imposed on one and all by the very nature of things, in economic conditions which are equal for all, and upon the collective appropriation of the instruments of labour.

Only the communists imagine they will be able to attain this by the development and the organization of the political power of the working classes, principally of the urban proletariat, with the help of bourgeois radicalism, while the revolutionary socialists, enemies of every tie and every alliance of an equivocal nature, think on the contrary that they will not be able to attain this goal except by the development and organization, not of the political but of the social (and, by consequence, anti-political) power of the working masses as much in the towns as in the countryside, including all the men of good will who, breaking with their past in the upper classes, might sincerely wish to join with them and wholly accept their programme.

From this two different methods are derived. The communists believe they should organize the workers' strength to take over the political power of the States. The revolutionary socialists organized with a view to the destruction, or, if one wants a more polite word, the liquidation, of the States. The communists are supporters of the principle and practice of authority; the revolutionary socialists have no faith except in freedom. Both the one and the other, equally supporters of science which is to destroy superstition and replace belief, differ in the former wishing to impose it, and the latter striving to propagate it; so that human groups, convinced of its truth, may organize and federate spontaneously, freely, from the bottom up, by their own momentum according to their real interests, but never according to any plan laid down in advance and imposed upon the *ignorant masses* by some superior intellects.

The revolutionary socialists think that there is much more practical and intellectual common sense in the instinctive aspirations and in the real needs of the mass of the people than in the profound intelligence of all these doctors and teachers of mankind who, after so many fruitless attempts to make humanity happy, still aspire to add their own efforts. The revolutionary socialists think the opposite: that mankind has allowed itself to be governed long enough, too long, and that the origin of its unhappiness does not reside in this or that form of government but in the very principle and fact of government, whatever kind it may be.

Finally this is the same, already historic, contradiction which exists between the scientific communism developed by the German school and accepted in part by the American and English socialists on the one hand, and the Proudhonism widely developed and pushed right to these, its final consequences, on the other, accepted by the proletariat of the Latin countries* Revolutionary socialism has just attempted its

* It is equally accepted and will be accepted yet more by the essentially non-political instinct of the Slav peoples.

first demonstration, both splendid and practical, in the *Paris Commune*.

I am a supporter of the Paris Commune, which, because it was massacred and drowned in blood by the executioners of monarchic and clerical reaction, has therefore become all the more lively and powerful in the imagination and heart of the European proletariat. I am above all a supporter of it because it was a bold and outspoken negation of the State.

It is a tremendously significant historical fact that this negation of the State should have been manifested particularly in France, which has been until now the country par excellence of political centralization, and that it should have been above all precisely Paris, the historic fountain-head of this great French civilization, which should have taken the initiative. Paris, taking off it own crown and proclaiming its own downfall with enthusiasm so as to give freedom and life to France, to Europe, to the whole world! Paris, affirming once more its historic ability to take the lead, and showing to all the enslaved peoples (and which popular masses indeed are not slaves?) the unique way of emancipation and salvation! Paris, striking a mortal blow at the political traditions of bourgeois radicalism and providing a real basis for revolutionary socialism! Paris, earning once more the curses of all the reactionary gangs of France and Europe! Paris, being buried in its ruins so as to pronounce a solemn contradiction to triumphant reaction; saving by its catastrophe the honour and future of France, and proving to a comforted mankind that, if life, intelligence and moral power have disappeared from the upper classes, they have remained energetic and full of potential in the proletariat! Paris, inaugurating the new era, that of the final and complete emancipation of the masses of the people and of their solidarity, henceforth a matter of fact, across and despite State frontiers. Paris, destroying patriotism and building on its ruins the religion of humanity! Paris, proclaiming itself humanist and atheist: and replacing the fictions of religion by the great realities of social life and faith in science, replacing the lies and injustices of religious, political and legal morality by the principles of freedom, justice, equality and fraternity, these eternal fundamentals of all human morality! Heroic Paris, rational and faithful, confirming its energetic faith in the destinies of mankind even in its glorious downfall and destruction, and leaving that faith much more energetic and lively for the generations to come! Paris, soaked in the blood of its most generous-hearted children — there indeed is mankind crucified by the international and co-ordinated reaction of all Europe, under the immediate inspiration of all the Christian Churches and that high priest of iniquity, the Pope. But the next international and solidarist revolution of the people will be the resurrection of Paris.

Such is the true meaning, and such are the immense beneficial consequences, of the two months of the existence and the fall, for ever memorable, of the Paris Commune.

The Paris commune lasted for too short a time, and it was too much hindered in its internal development by the mortal struggle which it had to maintain against the Versailles reaction, for it to have been able, I do not say even to apply, but to elaborate its socialist programme in theory. Besides, it must be recognized that the majority of the members of the Commune were not strictly speaking socialists and that, if they appeared to be such, it was because they were irresistibly swept forward by the course of events, by the nature of their environment, and by the necessities of their position, and not by their own personal conviction. The socialists, at the head of whom our friend Varlin naturally takes his place, formed in the Commune only a very small minority indeed; they were at the very most only some fourteen or fifteen members. The remainder was composed of Jacobins. But, let it be understood, there are Jacobins and Jacobins. There are the lawyer and doctrinaire Jacobins, like M. Gambetta, whose *positivist* republicanism,* presumptuous, despotic and formalistic, having repudiated the old revolutionary faith and having conserved nothing from Jacobinism except the cult of unity and authority, has surrendered popular France to the Prussians, and later to indigenous forces of reaction; and there are those Jacobins who are openly revolutionary, the heroes and last sincere representatives of the democratic faith of 1793, capable of sacrificing their well-armed unity and authority to the necessities of the Revolution, rather than bow down their consciences before the insolence of reaction. These great-hearted Jacobins, at the

* See his letter to Littré in the *Progrès de Lyon*.

head of whom Delescluze naturally takes his place, a great spirit and a great character, wish for the triumph of the Revolution before all things. And since there is no revolution without the popular masses, and since these masses today have pre-eminently a socialist instinct and can no longer make any other revolution but an economic and social one, the Jacobins of good faith, allowing themselves to be led on more and more by the logic of the revolutionary movement, will end by becoming socialists in spite of themselves.

This was precisely the situation of the Jacobins who took part in the Paris Commune. Delescluze and many others with him signed programmes and proclamations of which the general line and promises were definitely socialist. But since, in spite of all their good faith and good intentions, they were only socialists more through external pressure than through internal conviction, and since they did not have the time or the capacity to overcome and suppress in themselves a mass of bourgeois prejudices which were in contradiction with their more recent socialist outlook, one can understand that, paralysed by this internal conflict, they could never escape from generalities, nor take one of those decisive steps which would break for ever their solidarity and all their connections with the bourgeois world.

This was a great misfortune for the Commune and for themselves; they were paralysed by it, and they paralysed the Commune; but it is not possible to reproach them for it, as though for a fault. Men do not change from day to day, nor do they change their own natures or habits at will. These men proved their sincerity, in letting themselves be killed for the Commune. Who will dare ask more of them?

They are all the more excusable, because the people of Paris, under whose influence they thought and acted, were themselves socialist much more by instinct than by ideology or considered conviction. All their aspirations are to the highest degree and exclusively socialist; but their ideas, or rather the traditional representations of them, are still far from reaching that level. There are still many Jacobin prejudices, many dictatorial and governmental conceptions, among the proletariat of the large cities of France and even among that of Paris. The cult of authority, a fatal product of religious education, that historic source of all the evils, all the depravities and all the servility among the people, has not yet been entirely eradicated from their minds. It is equally true that even the most intelligent children of the people, the most convinced socialists, have not yet succeeded in entirely delivering themselves of it. Rummage in their conscience and you will still find there the Jacobin, the governmentalist, pushed back into some murky corner and, it is true, become very modest, but he is not entirely dead.

Furthermore, the situation of the small number of convinced socialists who formed part of the Commune was extremely difficult. Not feeling themselves sufficiently supported by the great mass of the Parisian population (the organization of the International Association moreover being itself very imperfect, numbering scarcely a few thousand individuals), they had to keep up a daily struggle against the Jacobin majority. And in what circumstances indeed! They had to give bread and work to some hundreds of thousands of workers, organize them, arm them, and at the same time keep an eye on the reactionary manœuvres going on in a huge city like Paris, under siege, threatened with starvation, and exposed to all the dirty tricks of the reactionary faction which had managed to set itself up and maintain itself at Versailles, *with the permission and by the favour of the Prussians*. They had to oppose a revolutionary government and army to the government and army of Versailles—that is, in order to combat monarchic and clerical reaction, they had to organize themselves in reactionary Jacobin fashion, forgetting or sacrificing what they themselves knew were the first conditions of revolutionary socialism.

Is it not natural that, in such circumstances, the Jacobins, who were the strongest because they constituted the majority in the Commune and who besides this possessed to an infinitely superior degree the political instinct and the tradition and practice of governmental organization, had immense advantages over the socialists? What one must surely find astounding is that they did not take more advantage than they did, that they did not give an exclusively Jacobin character to the Paris rising, and that they allowed themselves, on the contrary, to be carried on into a social revolution.

I know that many socialists, very consistent in their theoretical ideas, reproach our Paris friends for not showing themselves sufficiently socialist in their revolutionary practice, while all the loud-mouths of the bourgeois press accuse them on the contrary of having followed their socialist programme only too faithfully. Let us leave these ignominious denunciators from that section of the press on one side for the moment; I should like to make the point to the strict theoreticians of the emancipation of the proletariat that they are unjust to our Paris friends. For between the most precise theories and putting them into practice there is an immense distance which cannot be covered in a few days. Whoever had the good fortune to know Varlin, for instance, to name only one whose death is certain, knows how much the socialist convictions in him and his friends were passionate, considered and profound. These were men whose ardent enthusiasm, devotion and good faith could never have been doubted by any of those who came across them. But precisely because they were men of good faith, they were full of mistrust in themselves when faced with the immense work they had devoted their life and their thought to: they counted for so little! They had moreover that conviction that in the Social Revolution — diametrically opposed in this as in everything else to the Political Revolution — the action of individuals counted for almost nothing and the spontaneous action of the masses should count for everything. All that individuals can do is to elaborate, clarify and propagate the ideas that correspond to the popular feeling, and, beyond this, to contribute by their ceaseless efforts to the revolutionary organization of the natural power of the masses, but nothing beyond that. And everything else should not and could not take place except by the action of the people themselves. Otherwise one would end with political dictatorship, that is to say, the reconstruction of the State, of the privileges, injustices and all oppressions of the State, and one would arrive by a devious but logical path at the re-establishment of the political, social and economic slavery of the popular masses.

Varlin and all his friends, like all sincere socialists, and in general like all workers born and bred among the people, shared to the highest degree this perfectly legitimate prejudice against the continual intervention of the same individuals, against the domination exerted by superior personages; and since they were fair-minded above all things, they turned this foresight, this mistrust just as much against themselves as against all the other individuals.

Contrary to that authoritarian communist type of thinking — in my opinion completely erroneous — that a Social Revolution can be decreed and organized, whether by a dictatorship or whether by a constituent assembly resulting from some political revolution, our friends, the socialists of Paris, thought that it could not be made or brought to its full development except by the spontaneous and continuous action of the masses, the groups and the associations of the people.

Our friends in Paris were a thousand times right. For indeed, where is that head, however brilliant it may be, or if one wishes to speak of a collective dictatorship, were it formed by many hundreds of individuals endowed with superior faculties, where are those brains powerful enough and wide-ranging enough to embrace the infinite multiplicity and diversity of the real interests, aspirations, wishes and needs whose sum total constitutes the collective will of a people, and to invent a social organization which can satisfy everybody? This organization will never be anything but a Procrustean bed which the more or less obvious violence of the State will be able to force unhappy society to lie down on. That is what has always happened until now, and it is precisely this old system of organization by force that the Social Revolution must put an end to, by giving back their complete freedom to the masses, groups, communes, associations, individuals even, and by destroying once and for all the historic cause of all the violent acts, the power, and the very existence, of the State. The State must carry away in its fall all the injustices of the juridical law with all the lies of the various religions, this law and these religions never having been anything but the enforced consecration (as much ideological as actual) of all the violence represented, guaranteed and licensed by the State.

It is clear that freedom will never be given to mankind, and that the real interests of society, of all the groups and local organizations as well as of all the individuals who make up society, will only be able to find real satisfaction when there are no more States. It is clear that all the so-called general interests of society, which the State is alleged to represent and which in reality are nothing but the constant and general negation of the positive interests of the regions, communes, associations and the largest number of individuals subjected to the State, constitute an abstraction, a fiction, a lie, and that the State is like one great slaughter-house, and like an immense graveyard where, in the shadow and under the pretext of this abstraction, there come all the real aspirations, all the living initiatives of a nation, to let themselves be generously and sanctimoniously sacrificed and buried. And since no abstraction ever exists by itself or for itself, since it has neither legs to walk on, nor arms to create with, nor stomach to digest this mass of victims which it is given to devour, it is plain that, in exactly the same way that the religious or heavenly abstraction, God, represents in reality the very positive and very real interests of a privileged caste, the clergy (its terrestrial counterpart), so the political abstraction, the State, represents the no less real and positive interests of the class which is principally if not exclusively exploiting people today and which is moreover tending to swallow up all the others, the bourgeoisie. And just as the clergy is always divided and today is tending to divide itself all the more into a very powerful and a very rich minority and a majority which is very subordinate and rather poor, so, in the same way, the bourgeoisie and its diverse social and political organizations in industry, agriculture, banking and commerce, just as in all the administrative, financial, judicial, university, police and military functions of the State, is tending to weld itself further each day into a truly dominant oligarchy and a countless mass of creatures who are more or less vainglorious and more or less fallen, living in a perpetual illusion and pushed back inevitably more and more into the proletariat by an irresistible force, that of present-day economic development, and reduced to serving as blind instruments of this all-powerful oligarchy.

The abolition of the Church and of the State must be the first and indispensable condition of the real emancipation of society; after which (and only after which) it can, and must, organize itself in a different fashion, but not from top to bottom and according to an ideal plan, dreamt up by a few wise men or scholars, or even by force of decrees put out by some dictatorial force or even by a national assembly, elected by universal suffrage. Such a system, as I have already said, would lead inevitably to the creation of a new State, and consequently to the formation of a governmental aristocracy, that is, an entire class of people, having nothing in common with the mass of the people. Certainly, that class would begin again to exploit the people and subject them under the pretext of the common good or in order to save the State.

The future social organization must be made solely from the bottom upwards, by the free association or federation of workers, firstly in their unions, then in the communes, regions, nations and finally in a great federation, international and universal. Then alone will be realized the true and life-giving order of freedom and the common good, that order which, far from denying, on the contrary affirms and brings into harmony the interests of individuals and of society.

It is said that the harmony and universal solidarity of the interests of individuals and of society will never be capable of realization in practice because society's interests, being contradictory, are not in a position to balance one another by themselves or even to come to some sort of understanding. To such an objection I will reply that, if up to the present day the interests have never anywhere been in mutual harmony, that was because of the State, which has sacrificed the interests of the majority to the profit of a privileged minority. That is why that notorious incompatibility and that struggle of personal interests with those of society is nothing less than a political deception and lie, born out of the theological lie which imagined the doctrine of original sin so as to dishonour man and destroy in him the sense of his own worth. This same false idea of the conflict of interests was also sown by the dreams of metaphysics which, as is known, is a close relative of theology. Not appreciating the sociability of human nature, metaphysics regards society as a mechanical aggregate of individuals, of a purely artificial kind, suddenly brought together in the name of some contract, either formal or secret, freely entered into or else under the influence of a higher power. Before uniting themselves in society, these individuals, endowed with a kind of immortal soul, enjoyed complete freedom.

But if the metaphysicians assert that men, above all those who believe in the immortality of the soul, are free beings outside society, we arrive inevitably then at this conclusion: that men cannot unite in society except on condition that they repudiate their freedom, their natural independence, and sacrifice their interests, first personal and then local. Such a renunciation and such a sacrifice of oneself must be, on that argument, all the more pressing as society becomes more numerous and its organization more complex. In such a case the State is the expression of all the individual sacrifices. Existing under such an abstract form, and at the same time such a violent one, it continues, as goes without saying, to obstruct individual freedom more and more in the name of that lie which is known as the 'public good', although it evidently only represents exclusively the interest of the ruling class. The State, in this way, appears to us as an inevitable negation and an annihilation of all freedom, all interest, individual as well as general.

We see here that in the metaphysical and theological systems everything is linked and explained self-consistently. This is why the logical defenders of these systems can and indeed must, with an easy conscience, continue to exploit the popular masses by means of Church and State. Cramming their pockets and slaking all their foul desires, they can at the same time console themselves with the thought that they are taking all this trouble to the glory of God, for the victory of civilization and for the eternal happiness of the proletariat. But we others, not believing either in God or in the immortality of the soul, nor in the individual freedom of the will, we assert that freedom must be understood in its completest and widest sense as the goal of the historic progress of mankind. By a strange, though logical, contrast, our idealist opponents of theology and metaphysics take the principle of freedom as the foundation and basis of their theories so as to conclude quite simply with the indispensability of the enslavement of men. We others, materialist in theory, we tend in practice to create and to make durable a rational and noble idealism. Our enemies, religious and transcendental idealists, come down to a practical, bloody and vile materialism in the name of the same logic, according to which each development is the negation of the basic principle. We are convinced that all the richness of the intellectual, moral and material development of man, just like his apparent independence — that all this is the product of life in society. Outside society, man would not only not be free, but he would not be transformed into a real man at all, that is to say, into a being who has self-consciousness, who alone thinks and speaks. The combination of intelligence and collective work has alone been able to force man to leave the state of savagery and brutality which constituted his original nature or indeed his starting-point for further development. We are profoundly convinced of this truth that the whole life of men — interests, trends, needs, illusions, stupidities even, just as much as the acts of violence, the injustices, and all the actions which have the appearance of being voluntary — represent only the consequence of the inevitable forces of life in society. People cannot admit the idea of interdependence, yet they cannot repudiate the reciprocal influence and the correlation between phenomena in the external world.

In nature itself, that marvellous interrelationship and network of phenomena is certainly not attained without struggle. Quite the contrary, the harmony of the forces of nature only appears as the actual result of that continual struggle which is the very condition of life and movement. In nature and also in society, order without struggle is death. If order is natural and possible in the universe, it is so solely because this universe is not governed according to some system imagined in advance and imposed by a supreme will. The theological hypothesis of a divine system of laws leads to an evident absurdity and to the negation not only of all order, but of nature itself. Natural laws are not real except in so far as they are inherent in nature, that is to say they are not fixed by any authority. These laws are only simple manifestations or else continual fluctuations of the development of things and of combinations of these very varied, transient, but real facts. Together this all constitutes what we call 'nature'. Human intelligence and its capability for science observed these facts, controlled them experimentally, then reunited them in a system and called them laws.

But nature itself knows no laws. It acts unconsciously, representing in itself the infinite variety of phenomena, appearing and repeating themselves in an inevitable way. That is why, thanks to this inevitability of action, universal order can and indeed does exist.

Such an order also appears in human society, which apparently evolves in a supposedly non-natural manner, but actually submits to the natural and inevitable course of events. Only, the superiority of man over the other animals and the faculty of thinking brought to his development an individual characteristic—which is quite natural, let it be said in passing—in the sense that, like everything that exists, man represents the material product of the union and action of forces. This individual characteristic is the capacity for reasoning, or indeed that faculty for generalization and abstraction, thanks to which man can project himself through thought, examining and observing himself like an alien and external object. Raising himself above his own level through the medium of ideas, just as he raises himself from the surrounding world, he arrives at the representation of perfect abstraction, absolute nothingness. And that absolute is nothing less than the faculty of abstraction, which scorns everything that exists and, arriving at complete negation, there comes to rest. It is already the final limit of the highest abstraction of thought: that absolute nothingness is God.

That is the meaning and the historic basis of every theological doctrine. Not understanding the nature and the material causes of their own thoughts, not taking account of the conditions even or of the natural laws which are peculiar to them, these first men and societies certainly could not suspect that their absolute notions were only the result of the faculty of conceiving abstract ideas. That is why they considered these ideas taken from nature as if they were real objects, before which nature itself would cease to have any reality. They took it into their heads afterwards to worship their own fictions, their impossible notions of the absolute, and to grant them all kinds of honour. But they had the need, in some fashion, to represent and make tangible the abstract idea of nothingness or of God. To this end, they inflated the concept of divinity and endowed it into the bargain with all the qualities and powers, good and evil, which they only came across in nature and in society.

Such was the origin and historic development of all religions, beginning with fetishism and ending with Christianity.

We hardly have the intention of plunging into the history of religious, theological and metaphysical absurdities and still less of speaking of the successive unfolding of all the incarnations and divine visions created by centuries of barbarism. Everybody knows that superstition always gives birth to frightful sufferings and causes the flow of streams of blood and tears. Let us say only that all these sickening aberrations of poor mankind were historical events, inevitable in the normal growth and evolution of social organisms. Such aberrations engendered in society the fatal idea, dominating the imagination of men, that the universe was supposedly governed by a supernatural force and will. Centuries succeeded centuries, and societies became accustomed to this idea to such an extent that they finally destroyed within themselves every tendency towards a further progress, and every capacity they had to reach it.

First the ambition of a few individuals, then a few social classes, erected slavery and conquest into a vital principle, and implanted more than any other this terrible idea of the divinity. Since when all society was impossible without those two institutions as a base, the Church and the State. These two social scourges are defended by all the dogmatists.

Scarcely had these institutions appeared in the world than all of a sudden two castes were organized: that of the priests, and the aristocracy, who without losing any time did the job of inculcating deeply into that enslaved people the indispensability, usefulness and sanctity of the Church and the State.

All that had as its goal the changing of brutal slavery into legal slavery, provided for and consecrated by the will of the Supreme Being.

But did the priests and the aristocrats really believe sincerely in these institutions, which they sustained with all strength in their own particular interest? Were they not merely liars and deceivers? No, I believe that they were at the same time both believers and impostors.

They believed too, because they took a natural and inevitable part in the aberrations of the mass, and only later, in the age of the decadence of the ancient world, did they become sceptics and shameless deceivers. Another reason allows us to consider the founders of States as sincere people. Man always believes easily in whatever he desires, and in what does not contradict his interests. Even if he is intelligent and informed, the same thing happens: through self-love and his desire to live with his neighbours and profit by their respect, he will always believe in whatever is pleasant and useful. I am convinced that, for example, Thiers and the Versailles government were forced at great cost to convince themselves that, in killing several thousand men, women and children in Paris, they were saving France.

But if the priests, augurers, aristocrats and middle-class citizens, of ancient and modern times, were able sincerely to believe, they nevertheless remained impostors. One cannot in fact admit that they believed in every absurdity that constituted faith and politics. I am not even speaking of the age when, according to the words of Cicero, 'two augurers could not look each other in the eye without laughing'. Afterwards, even in the time of general ignorance and superstition, it is difficult to suppose that the inventors of daily miracles were convinced of the reality of these miracles. One can say the same thing of politics, which may be summed up in the following rule: 'It is necessary to subjugate and exploit the people in such a way that they will not complain too greatly of their fate, nor forget to submit, nor have time to think of resistance and rebellion.'

How then, after this, can we imagine that people who turned politics into a profession and knew its aim—that is to say injustice, violence, lies and murder, in the mass or in isolation —might believe sincerely in the political art and the wisdom of the State as the creator of social contentment? They cannot have arrived at such a degree of stupidity despite all their cruelty. Church and State have been the great schools of vice in every age. History bears witness to their crimes; at all places and at all times the priest and the statesman have been the conscious, systematic, implacable and bloody executioners of the people.

But how, all the same, can we reconcile two things which are apparently so incompatible: deceivers and deceived, liars and believers? Logically, this seems difficult; however, in fact—that is to say in practical life—these qualities occur together very often.

In the great majority of cases people live in contradiction with themselves, and under perpetual misapprehensions; they generally do not notice it, that is until some extraordinary event brings them back from their habitual sleep and compels them to take a look at themselves and around themselves.

In politics as in religion, men are only machines in the hands of the exploiters. But robbers and robbed, oppressors and oppressed, all live one alongside the other, governed by a handful of individuals whom it is convenient to consider as the true exploiters. These are the same people, free of all pre-judices, political and religious, who consciously maltreat and oppress. In the seventeenth and eighteenth centuries, until the explosion of the Great Revolution, as in our own day, they ruled in Europe and did pretty well as they pleased. We must believe that their domination will not prolong itself much further.

While the principal leaders deceive and lead the people astray quite consciously, their servants, or the minions of the Church and State, apply themselves with zeal to uphold the sanctity and integrity of these odious institutions. If the Church, according to the pronouncements of the priests and of the majority of statesmen, is necessary for the salvation of the soul, the State in its turn is also necessary for the conservation of peace, of order and of justice, and the dogmatists of all the schools must shout, 'Without Church and Government there will be neither civilization nor progress.'

We need not discuss the problem of eternal salvation because we do not believe in the immortality of the soul. We are convinced that the most harmful of things for humanity, for truth and progress, is the Church. And how could it be other-wise? Is it not to the Church that the care of perverting the younger generations, above all the women, falls? Is it not the Church which, through its dogmas and lies, its stupidity and shame, tends to destroy logical reasoning and science? Does the Church not attack the dignity of man, in perverting in him the notion of rights and justice? Does it not give back as a corpse that which is living, does it not lose freedom, is it not the Church which preaches slavery of the masses in perpetuity for the benefit of tyrants and exploiters? Is it not the Church, this implacable Church, which tends to perpetuate the reign of darkness, ignorance, poverty and crime?

And if the progress of our century is not a deceptive dream, it must get rid of the Church.

XII THE POLITICAL THEOLOGY
OF MAZZINI

The first of these two texts is Bakunin's *Réponse d'un International à Mazzini*, written in 1871 after the crushing of the Paris Commune; it is taken from *Archives Bakounine*, vol. I, 1, 'Michel Bakounine et l'Italie, 1871–1872. Première partie. La polémique avec Mazzini' (Leiden, 1961), pp. 3–12. The second text is an extract from the second part of *La théologie politique de Mazzini*, written in the same year, but not published in Bakunin's lifetime. It was published in the same volume of the *Archives Bakounine*, pp. 120–24. They are here translated from the French by Steven Cox.

I

If there is one man who is universally respected in Europe and whose more than forty years of active, single-minded dedication to a great cause have really deserved that respect, it is Mazzini. He is incontestably one of the noblest, purest personalities of this century—I would even say the greatest, if greatness were compatible with the stubborn pursuit of error.

Unfortunately, from the very outset, the Italian patriot's revolutionary programme had at its core an essentially false principle which, after paralysing and nullifying his most heroic efforts and most ingenious schemes, was bound sooner or later to lure him into the ranks of reaction. That principle is a dual idealism, both metaphysical and mystical, grafted on to the patriotic ambition of the statesman. It is the cult of God and of divine and human authority, it is faith in the messianic destiny of Italy as queen of nations, Rome as capital of the world, it is the political lust for State grandeur and glory, necessarily based upon hardship for the people. Lastly, it is that religion of all dogmatic and absolutist minds, that passion for uniformity which they call unity and which is the graveyard of liberty.

Mazzini is the last high priest of an obsolescent religious, metaphysical and political idealism.

Mazzini reproaches us for not believing in God. We, on the other hand, reproach him for believing, or rather we do not so much reproach as simply deplore his belief. We infinitely regret that, as a result of this intrusion of mystical sentiment and ideas into his awareness, activity and life, he should have been impelled to take his stand against us in the ranks of all the enemies of popular emancipation.

For after all, there is no denying it any longer. Who now stands beneath the banner of God? From Napoleon III to Bismarck, Empress Eugénie to Queen Isabella, and between them the Pope, gallantly offering his mystic rose to each in turn, it is all the emperors, all the kings and all the official, officious, noble or otherwise privileged world of Europe, meticulously catalogued in the Almanach de Gotha; it is all the swollen blood-suckers of industry, commerce and banking; the established teachers and all the servants of the State — police great and small, gendarmes, jailers and executioners, not to mention the priests who now constitute the black police of the soul, on the State's behalf; it is the generals, those humane defenders of public order, and the kept editors of the press, pure representatives of all the official virtues. This is the army of God.

This is the banner beneath which Mazzini now stands, probably very much in spite of himself, but hamstrung by the logic of his idealistic convictions, which force him if not to bless everything they bless, then at least to curse everything they curse.

And in the opposite camp, what is there? There is revolution, there are the bold defiers of God, divine order and the principle of authority, but also, and for the selfsame reason, the upholders of a human order and human liberty.

The young Mazzini, divided between two opposite currents, was both priest and revolutionary. But in the long run, as might have been expected, the inspirations of the priest stifled the instincts of the revolutionary, and everything he thinks, says and does today is permeated by the most unadulterated reaction, amid great rejoicing in the enemy camp and sorrow in our own.

But we have other things to do than feel sorry for ourselves; all our time belongs to the struggle. Mazzini has thrown down the gauntlet, and it is our duty to pick it up, so that it may not be said that our reverence for a man's past services has made us bow our heads to falsehood.

There is no pleasure in making up one's mind to attack a man like Mazzini, a man whom one is bound to respect and love even while fighting him, for if there is one thing that nobody would dare call in question it is the lofty disinterestedness, immense sincerity and no less immense passion for the good in this man whose incomparable purity shines out so brightly amid the corruption of the century. But piety, legitimate though it may be, must never turn to idolatry, and if there is one thing more sacred than the greatest man in the world it is truth, justice and the obligation to defend the sacred cause of humanity.

This is not the first time that Mazzini has hurled his accusations and condemnations, not to mention his insults and slanders, into our faces. Last year, in a letter to his friend and fellow-idealist the illustrious Quinet, he bitterly castigated the materialist, atheist attitudes of modern youth. That was his right, and a logical outcome of his misfortune in always having tied his noblest aspirations to the fictive existence of an impossible absolute Being, an absurd, mischievous phantom, created by the childish imagination of peoples departing from the animal state. After being successively revised, corrected and enriched by the creative fantasy of poets, then gravely defined and systematized by the abstract speculations of theologians and metaphysicians, it is fading today, like the true phantom it is, before the high wind of popular awareness matured by historical experience, and before the still more pitiless analysis of real science. And since the illustrious Italian patriot has had the misfortune to entrust all his most revolutionary thoughts and deeds to the protection of this fictitious Being from the start of his long career, and to shackle his whole life to it, even to the point of sacrificing the true emancipation of his beloved Italy to it, is it any wonder that he now rails against the new generation which draws its inspiration from another spirit, another morality and another love than his own, and turns its back on his God?

Mazzini's bitterness and rage are natural. To be at the forefront of the European revolutionary movement for more than thirty years, only to feel his control slipping away and the movement taking a direction in which his petrified convictions prevent him not only from guiding but even following; to remain alone, abandoned, unappreciated and now himself incapable of appreciating what is going on right under his nose! For a great soul, a proud intelligence and sweeping ambition like his, at the end of a career totally dedicated to the service of humanity, it is a tragic, cruel position.

So when the saintly old man launched his thunderbolts from the heights of his idealist isolation, we made hardly any reply. We respected that powerless but grievous rage. And yet there was no shortage of arguments, not only for refuting his reproaches but also for turning them against him.

He says that we are materialists and atheists. We have nothing to reply to that, for so we are, and in so far as a feeling of pride is possible for poor individuals who rise like the waves, only to disappear into the vast ocean of the collective life of human society, we glory in it, because atheism and materialism are truth, or rather the real basis of all truth, and because it is truth we want above all, regardless of the practical consequences, and nothing but the truth. Furthermore, we do have this faith—that despite all appearances to the contrary and despite the timid reservations of political and sceptical caution, truth alone can create the practical good of men.

This then is our first article of faith, and we shall force you, our illustrious master, to admit that we too have a faith. Except that it never looks back, but only forward.

Not content with pointing out our atheism and materialism, however, you conclude that we can have neither love for men nor respect for their dignity; that all the great issues which have made the noblest hearts beat faster through the ages— liberty, justice, humanity, beauty, truth—must be completely alien to us, and that while we eke out our miserable random existence, crawling rather than walking on the earth, we can know no other concerns than the satisfaction of our coarse and sensual appetites.

Had anyone but you made that remark, we should call him a shameless slanderer. To you, our respected and unjust master, we shall say that you are making a woeful error. Do you want to know how much we all love those great and beautiful things which you refuse to let us recognize and love? Then let us tell you that we love them so much that we are sick and tired of seeing them everlastingly dangling in your heaven, which has stolen them from earth, as so many eternally unattainable symbols and promises. We are not satisfied with the shadow of these things any longer—we want the substance.

And this is our second article of faith, illustrious master. We believe in the possibility, in the necessity of that attainment on earth; we are also convinced that all the things that you worship as heavenly longings will necessarily lose their mystical divinity by becoming human, earthly realities.

When you call us materialists, you believe that you have said it all, and conclusively condemned and crushed us. And do you know how this error arises? It is because your matter and ours are two things, two utterly different concepts. Your matter is a fictitious Being, like your God, your Devil and your immortal soul. Your matter is of the basest grossness, is the brutally inert, an impossible being, just as impossible as the pure, immaterial, absolute spirit which resembles it in never having existed outside the fanciful speculations of theologians and metaphysicians, those unique creators of the one and the other. The history of philosophy has now disclosed the quite simple process of that unconscious creation and the genesis of the fatal historical illusion which has battened like a dreadful nightmare on the downtrodden spirit of generations of human beings.

The first thinkers, who were necessarily theologians and metaphysicians because the terrestrial spirit is built so that it always starts out with a great many stupidities, falsehood and error before arriving at a portion of the truth (which is no great recommendation for the *sacred traditions of the past*)— the first thinkers, I say, extracted from all the real beings they knew—themselves included, of course—everything which seemed to them to constitute their power, movement, life and intelligence, and they called this by the generic name of *spirit*; then they gave the rest, the formless, inert residue which they assumed must remain after the extractive operation performed unconsciously on the real world by their own spirit, the name of *matter*. After which it surprised them that this *matter*, which, like this spirit, existed only in their imagination, should seem so inert and mindless in the presence of their God of pure spirit.

For our own part, we freely admit that we do not know your God, but neither do we know your matter; or rather we know that both are equally Non-Beings, created *a priori* by the fanciful speculation of the naive thinkers of earlier centuries. What we understand by the words *material* and *matter* is the totality, the entire range of real beings, known and unknown, from the simplest organisms to the constitution and operation of the brain of the greatest genius; the noblest sentiments, the greatest thoughts, heroic deeds, acts of devotion, duties as well as rights, sacrifice as well as selfishness, even the transcendental mystical aberrations of Mazzini, together with the manifestations of organic life, chemical properties and reactions, electricity, light, warmth and the natural attraction of physical bodies, constitute in our view so many different but no less closely interdependent variations on that totality of real beings which we call *matter*.

And notice that we do not consider this totality as a kind of absolute and eternally creative substance, as the pantheists do, but as an eternal *derivative*, produced and incessantly reproduced anew by the conjunction of an infinity of actions and reactions of all kinds and by the continual transformation of the real beings who are born and die in its depths.

So as not to protract this metaphysical dissertation, I shall state, in conclusion, that we describe as *material* everything that is, everything that occurs in the real world, within as well as beyond mankind, and we apply the word *ideal* exclusively to the products of the cerebral activity of man; but since our brain is a completely material structure, and consequently all its functions are just as material as the interactions of all other things, it follows that what we call matter or the material world by no means excludes but necessarily embraces the ideal.

There is a fact which might well be worth the consideration of our Platonic antagonists: How is it that in general the materialist theorists turn out in practice to be so much more broadly idealistic than themselves? In the long run, nothing could be more logical and natural than that fact. You will agree that every development implies in a sense the negation of its point of departure; well, the materialists start out from the conception of matter to arrive at—what?—the idea. Whereas the idealists, starting out from the absolute pure idea and for ever repeating the ancient myth of original sin, which is only the symbolic expression of their own sad destiny, eternally fall back, both in theory and practice, upon the matter which they can never shake off, and look at their matter!—brutish, ignoble and mindless, created by their own imagination as the obverse or *alter ego* of their *ideal self*.

Again, the materialists, always adapting their social theories to the real developments of history, consider bestiality, cannibalism and slavery as the first points of departure in the progressive movement of society, but what are they looking for, what do they want? The emancipation and complete humanization of society. Meanwhile the idealists who take the immortal soul and free will as the basis of their speculations inevitably arrive at the cult of public order, like Thiers, and of authority, like Mazzini—in other words, at the consecration and organization of perpetual serfdom. So that it clearly follows that while theoretical materialism necessarily leads to practical idealism, the only possible realization of idealist theories lies in the most crass practical materialism.

Where were the materialists and the atheists yesterday, for all to see? In the Paris Commune. And what about the idealists, the believers in God? In the National Assembly at Versailles. What did the men of Paris want? The final emancipation of mankind, through the emancipation of labour. And what does the triumphant Assembly of Versailles seek now? Its final degradation under the double yoke of the spiritual and temporal power. The materialists, contemptuous of hardship, danger and death, want to go forward, because they see the triumph of humanity gleaming before them; and the idealists, running out of breath, no longer seeing anything but red bogeys before them, want to drag mankind back, at any cost, into the mud it is trying so hard to leave. Compare and judge!

With the doctrinaire, imperative tone characteristic of all founders of new religions, Mazzini asserts and assumes that the materialists are incapable of love, or of pledging their existence to the service of great things. In so saying he is only proving that as a consistent idealist and despiser of humanity in the name of the God whose prophet he genuinely believes himself to be, he has never begun to understand human nature and the historical developments of society, and that if he is not ignorant of history, he singularly fails to understand it.

His reasoning is the reasoning of all theologians. If there was no God-the-creator, he says, the world with all its wonderful laws could not have existed, or else would be nothing but a dreadful chaos, in which all things would be governed not by a providential and divine purpose but by the frightful chance and anarchic collision of blind forces. There would be no purpose in life, and everything would be material, brutish and accidental. For without God there would be no coherence in the physical world and no *moral law* in human society; and without moral law, no motherland, no Rome, no Italy, for if Italy exists as a nation it is only because she had a providential cosmic mission to fulfil, and she could only have been charged with this mission by God, who in his fatherly concern for the queen of nations has gone so far as to trace out with his own divine forefinger the frontiers perceived and described by the prophetic genius of Dante.

In subsequent articles, I shall attempt to prove against Mazzini:

1. That had there been a creator-God, the world could never have existed.

2. That if God had made the laws of the natural world — which to our mind embraces the entire world, both physical and human or social — what we call the natural physical and social laws could likewise never have existed. Like all political States subordinated and dominated from the top downward by arbitrary lawgivers, the world would provide the spectacle of the most revolting anarchy. It could not exist.

3. That the *moral law* whose existence we materialists and atheists acknowledge much more thoroughly than is possible for the idealists of any school, Mazzinians or non-Mazzinians, is only a truly moral law, a real, logical, powerful law, and a law which is bound to triumph over the aspirations of all the idealists in the world because it stems from the very nature of human society, a nature whose real roots must be sought not in God but in the animal.

4. That the idea of a God, far from being essential to the establishment of that law, has never done anything but disturb and distort it.

5. That all Gods, past and present, have owed their original existence to the fantasies of men barely out of the cradle of primitive bestiality; that belief in a supernatural or divine world constitutes an historically inevitable aberration in the past growth of our mind; and that, to borrow a saying of Proudhon's, men, deceived by a kind of optical illusion, have only ever worshipped in their Gods their own reversed and monstrously exaggerated image.

6. That divinity, once established on its heavenly throne, has become the scourge of humanity and the ally of every tyrant, charlatan, tormentor and exploiter of the popular masses.

7. Lastly, that the disappearance of the divine phantoms, a necessary precondition of the triumph of humanity, will be one of the inevitable consequences of the emancipation of the proletariat.

As long as Mazzini stuck to insulting the young students who, in the deeply corrupt and decadent setting of the present-day bourgeoisie, are alone in displaying some enthusiasm for great issues, truth and justice; as long as he confined his onslaughts to the German professors such as Moleschott and Schiff, among others, who commit the terrible crime of teaching true science in the Italian universities, and as long as he amused himself with denouncing them to the Italian government as disseminators of subversive ideas in the land of Galileo and Giordano Bruno, the silence enjoined by piety and pity could still be maintained. Youth is vigorous and the professors are learned enough to look after themselves.

But now Mazzini has gone too far. Always in good faith, and always inspired by a fanatical but genuine idealism, he has committed two crimes which are unpardonable both in our own view and in that of the whole of European socialist democracy.

At the very moment when the heroic populace of Paris, in its noblest hour, was being massacred in its tens of thousands, women and children and all, in defence of the most humane, the most just and highest cause that history has ever seen, *the cause of the emancipation of workers all over the world*; at the moment when the hideous coalition of all the obscene reactionaries who today are celebrating their victorious blood-bath at Versailles, not content with the mass-murder and imprisonment of our brothers and sisters of the Paris Commune, is also spewing out all the slanders which only a boundless viciousness can imagine, Mazzini, the great Mazzini, the pure democrat, turns his back on the cause of the proletariat, forgets everything but his mission as priest or prophet, and weighs in with his own outrages also! He has the audacity to deny not only the justice of their cause but also their sublime, heroic dedication, and portrays the people who gave up their lives for the deliverance of all the world as a common mob, ignorant of all moral law and obeying only savage, self-seeking urges.

This is not the first time that Mazzini has insulted and slandered the people of Paris. In 1848, after the memorable June days which inaugurated the era of proletarian organization and of the socialist movement in Europe, Mazzini published a very angry manifesto, castigating the workers of Paris and socialism at the same time.[9] Against the workers of 1848, devoted, heroic and sublime as their children in 1871 and, like them, massacred, Mazzini parroted all the slanders summoned up by Ledru-Rollin and his so-called red republican cronies to palliate their ludicrous, shameful impotence in the world's eyes, and perhaps their own.

Mazzini condemns socialism; whether as priest or as messianic envoy of the supernal master he is bound to condemn it, since socialism, seen from the moral viewpoint, is the advent of *human respect* to replace the voluntary bondage of *divine worship*, while seen from the practical scientific viewpoint it is the proclamation of that great principle which, once instilled in the awareness of the people, has become the sole starting-point both for the researches and growth of positivist science and for the revolutionary action of the proletariat.

Here is that principle, summed up in all its simplicity: 'Just as in the material world proper, inorganic matter (mechanical, physical, chemical) is the determinant of organic matter (vegetable, animal, mental or cerebral), so in the social world, which in any case can only be considered as the highest-known level of the material world, the development of economic forces has always been and still continues to be the determinant of all religious, philosophical, political and social developments.'

It will be realized that this theory entails nothing less than the most daring overthrow of all the theories, scientific as well as moral, and of all the religious, metaphysical, political and juridical ideas which constitute the overall belief of all idealists past and present. It is a revolution a thousandfold more powerful than the one which from the Renaissance and especially from the seventeenth century onward overthrew the scholastic doctrines, those bulwarks of the Church, together with absolutist monarchy and the feudal nobility and replaced them by the metaphysical dogmatism of so-called pure reason, so conducive to the dominion of the latter-day privileged class, and notably of the bourgeoisie.

If the overthrow of scholastic barbarism caused a truly dreadful turmoil in its time, we must understand what upheavals are bound to be caused in our own day by the overthrow of doctrinaire idealism, the last refuge of all the privileged oppressors and exploiters of humanity.

The exploiters of idealistic beliefs feel their closest interest threatened, and the disinterested, fanatical but sincere upholders of this dying idealism—men like Mazzini—see all religion, all the illusion of their lives, destroyed at one stroke.

Since the beginning of his public career, Mazzini has never ceased to repeat to the proletariat of Italy and Europe the following words, which sum up his religious and moral catechism: 'Be moral, worship God, accept the moral law I bring you in his name, help me to establish a republic founded on the (impossible) union of reason and faith, divine authority and human liberty, and you shall have power and glory, and furthermore prosperity, liberty and equality.'

Socialism, on the other hand, speaking with the voice of the International, tells them 'that the economic subjection of the man of labour to the monopolizer of the means of labour, that is, the sources of life, lies at the bottom of servitude in all its forms, of all social misery, mental degradation and political dependence; and that, for this reason, the economic emancipation of the working classes is the great end to which every political movement ought to be subordinate as a simple means.'

This is the basic thinking of the *International Working Men's Association*, in all its simplicity.

We understand that Mazzini was bound to condemn it, and this is the second crime for which we reproach him, although we realize that in doing so he was obeying his conscience as priest and prophet.

But while paying tribute to his indisputable sincerity, we must point out that by combining his invectives with those of all the European reactionaries against our ill-fated brothers, the heroic defenders of the Paris Commune, and his ex-communications with those of the National Assembly and the Pope against the rightful claims and international organization of the workers of the entire world, Mazzini has made a final break with revolution and joined the ranks of international reaction.

In the succeeding articles I shall examine his grievances against our praiseworthy Association one by one, and attempt to expose the inanity of the religious and political doctrines of the prophet.

II

The reflection of a reflection! the incarnation of a shadow! Yes, for if this idealism, these preconceived ideas that the idealists call *inspired or innate** are not creations of the human brain, then what are they? And how does it create them? By *ideally* reproducing the real world, natural as well as social, which surrounds it.

To consider the origin of human ideas (and I know of no other kind, from the materialist point of view) would mean deviating from my intended plan in these articles, but in order to elucidate the sense of my indictment of the *absolutist idealism* of Mazzini, I must draw attention here and now to the yawning gap which separates idealists from materialists in terms of their appreciation of the *value* or the *nature* of ideas.

---

* In the following articles, referring to God and the soul, I shall necessarily reach the point of inquiring into the law of the formation of ideas in the human brain.

In the sphere of strictly scientific ideas and developments in what have come to be called the positive sciences, the difference has now become almost non-existent. There was a time, in the days of scientific barbarism, when theological versions of astronomy, physics and chemistry were practised. In Germany, metaphysical natural science was still the rule during the whole of the first half of this century, under the aegis of great names like Oken, Schelling and Hegel. Those days are over, and nowadays, when it comes to serious scientific discussion, the faithful themselves — the fiercest idealists and famous scholar-converts like MM. Dumas and Leverrier and so many others who professed a highly profitable Christianity at the time of the Empire, and under the special protection of the Empress Eugénie — straight away shed their idealist beliefs, hypocritical or sincere, and become materialists like ourselves, forgetting the very existence of a God who can and must falsify all the calculations of the human spirit and the natural development of things, and finding themselves compelled to follow only the most rigorously scientific principles and to accept no syntheses which cannot be demonstrated by the analysis of concrete facts.

True, Mazzini protests loudly against this betrayal, which he undoubtedly sees as cowardice. Alone among all the idealists vanquished by science, he remains upright and defiant. In the name of Socrates and Humboldt (poor Humboldt, how astonished he would be to find himself enlisted among the idealists of science), Phidias and Michelangelo, Aeschylus and Byron, Mazzini speaks out against these 'fumbling youngsters of science who style themselves materialists'* and informs them, as if it were news, that experimentation is only one aspect of science and that, to make it whole, synthesis is required. So far so good, overlooking the gratuitous impertinence, and we fully share his opinion: experiment and analysis of data are not enough, synthesis is absolutely necessary in order for science to be complete. But the immediate question is, where does that synthesis come from, and what is it based on?

'Experimentation', Mazzini continues, 'neither creates nor reveals, but verifies those facts which it is able to collect — the

* Giuseppe Mazzini, *Dal Concilio a Dio*.

hypotheses which are the discoveries of intuition, unlooked-for, spontaneous revelations produced by the rapid and intense concentration of all the faculties upon a given point.'

Thus far we are in full accord. Let us read on:

And those facts themselves, girdled and explained by hypothesis, by revelation, demonstrate its truth; properly observed, interpreted and classified, they need a principle, a pre-accepted concept of Law. Synthesis, that inborn power, transcends the human spirit and casts its light down on the path, where it would otherwise grope, uncertain and impotent, entombed in a labyrinth of facts, viewpoints and meanings, which differ according to their relations with other facts. Harmony between the order of things and the human mind pre-exists all experimentation, which is of no use unless it is accepted and defined.

This is where the chasm begins to yawn between us. Mazzini is a very subtle dialectician, and is extremely adept at smuggling such misleading glosses into the truest accounts that, if they are not spotted at once, truth turns imperceptibly into falsehood, the real into the absurd.

Thus he is quite correct when he says that without the art of devising scientific hypotheses, without the intuitive eye which is the special gift of great geniuses, brains of a fortunate cast, which divine the connections between things or facts even prior to normal analysis and experiment, the scientists would have made only the most meagre progress. He is correct when he says that anybody who wanted to study nature without bringing to that study a (mentally) fixed concept of what we call the laws of nature, anybody who intended to research, analyse and experiment with things or facts without being guided in his researches by some kind of synthesis, either scientifically proven or the strictly hypothetical fruit of an imagination trained and moulded by previous scientific study, anybody who had neither method nor even the idea of what he wanted and what he should be looking for, would inevitably lose himself amidst a multitude of facts, as in an inextricable labyrinth.

It comes down to knowing what is meant by the words *intuition, hypothesis* and *synthesis*. Mazzini provides a good definition of the first: '*It is the rapid and intense concentration of all the faculties upon a single point.*' This faculty is to be found among men at all stages of development, and even among animals, and civilization often causes men to lose it. In animals it is called instinct. The life of the savage is filled with intuition. In the narrow confines of his unvarying existence, half hunting, half fighting, he divines rather than reasons. He has an intuition for place, he divines the approach of an enemy or of game, where a civilized man still sees and hears nothing. But it cannot be said that intuition is innate: the *faculty* of intuition is innate, which is to say, built into the system of the animal as well as the man; but in order for that faculty to become real intuition, both in animals and human beings it needs to be developed through the experience of living. Very young animals and children are totally devoid of it.

Civilization, on the other hand, by dividing man's attention among too great a number of interests, occupations and objectives, often makes him lose this faculty of intuition to a surprising extent. In order for him to regain it, it now becomes necessary for him to be in the grip of some powerful urge, good or bad, but one which concentrates all his faculties on the achievement of a single end, whatever its nature. Great geniuses are always possessed by some overriding mental urge which draws all their intellectual and moral being towards a single goal; consequently they are always full of intuition, and the more it is used the stronger and more unerring it becomes.

The intuition of scholars creates *scientific hypotheses*. It was through intuition that Galileo and Newton hit upon their greatest discoveries. It is said that the former only needed to watch a chandelier swinging in a church, the latter to see an apple fall, in order suddenly to divine the laws of the motion of celestial bodies. Here we have unquestionable proof of genius, for how many men have seen chandeliers swinging or apples falling without ever discovering anything! And yet it is noticeable that these two great men did not experience these magnificent flashes of intuition until their later years, when minds passionately and exclusively dedicated to science had already been moulded by the study and unremitting practice of science. What they had the good fortune to find, they had undoubtedly been seeking for a long time, guided by all the previous discoveries and syntheses built up by science, so that their seemingly spontaneous insights were in fact only the sudden culmination of long and probably laborious mental exertions. Notice too that they were not satisfied with the evidence of strong intuitions, and that in their own eyes their great discoveries were only hypotheses until they had been demonstrated and verified by mathematical calculation and physical experiment.

A hypothesis which has not been verified by analysis and experiment remains nothing more than a plain probability, and it only becomes a scientific truth after standing the test of those two *criteria* of all truth which Mazzini so scornfully dismisses. Every new hypothesis which is scientifically proved produces a new *synthesis*, a new idea which is genuinely scientific because, with scrupulous accuracy and without the intrusion of individual whims (which may be more or less ingenious, but are alien to science), it reflects the proper logic of facts, the system of interconnections and the order by which things and facts actually develop in the real world — *the system of the laws of nature*.

Among the various scientific syntheses there is a natural grouping, hierarchy and subordination which faithfully reflects the grouping, hierarchy and subordination of natural phenomena, and we can imagine a higher synthesis, unique, supreme and embracing all the universe, which would subsume all the more or less inferior, more limited syntheses as its hierarchically subordinate parts. We may dimly imagine it, in an utterly abstract way, devoid of any content or real object, but we shall never be able to realize it for the simple reason that our senses, hence our imagination, and hence too our thinking, will never really be able to embrace more than a tiny fraction of the universe.

This is what grates on Mazzini, as it did on all of us in our younger days, and this is what made all of us more or less idealists. We felt so infinite, thanks to our juvenile fancy and the ardour of the young blood pounding in our veins, that even the vastness of the visible world seemed too narrow for us. We looked on it with disdain, and soared high away to — where? — into the void of abstraction, into Nothingness. Which we tried our best to fill with phantasmagorical creations and the dreams of our drunken imagination. But a closer look showed us that the fantasies and dreams which seemed so infinite and lavish were nothing but pale reflections as well as monstrous exaggerations of that real world which we dismissed so scornfully, and we realized eventually that by flying so high into the void we were not enriching ourselves but instead impoverishing heart and mind alike, and that we were becoming not more powerful but powerless. We finally realized that by playing, just like children, at peopling with dreams that immense void, that God, that Nothingness created out of our own power of abstraction or negation, the predominant faculty of our brain, we were abandoning society and putting all our real existence at the mercy of the prophets, tyrants and religious, political and economic exploiters of the divine idea on earth, and that by seeking out an ideal liberty isolated from the conditions of the real world we were condemning ourselves to the most dismal, shameful slavery.

We realized that in order to fulfil our earthly destiny — and we acknowledge no other — we must centre all our thoughts and efforts solely on the emancipation of human society on earth. But how was it to be emancipated without science, in other words without real knowledge of the conditions or laws of development of real things on earth? Therefore we ought and want to acknowledge those laws. But it is real science we want, not the idealistic, religious or metaphysical flights which lure us back to the impotence of ancient times. Since experiment, the properly controlled and scrutinized evidence of our senses, is a necessary condition of real science, we must abandon the idea of knowing anything which is beyond the range of our senses. Therefore not only must we renounce understanding, grasping or even imagining the infinite vastness of the Universe, but we must also give up the idea of knowing about the greater part of our visible world: that starry sky which itself forms only an imperceptible point in the infinity of space baffles our investigations. We shall never know anything, or hardly anything, about it. Like it or not, then, we must be satisfied with knowing a little about our own solar system, and must assume that it is in harmony with the infinite Universe, for if that harmony did not exist, then either it would have to be established or our world would perish. We already know this world in terms of advanced mechanics, and we are beginning to know it in physical, chemical and geological terms. Our science will have difficulty in going much further.

If we want more concrete information, we must stick to our earthly globe. We are at home here, and nothing is inaccessible to our questing mind, which finds no other limitations than the infinite diversity of detail which no observation or science could ever exhaust. We know that just like all other planets, as well as all suns, our terrestrial globe was born in time, and that in an indefinite number of centuries it is doomed to perish, as everything in existence is born and perishes, or rather is transformed.

Fiery, gaseous matter at first, how did it condense, cool and take shape? Through what vast series of geological evolutions did it pass before its surface produced all this infinite abundance of organic life, from the simplest vegetable cell to man? How was it transformed and how will it continue to develop in the history of our social world? Finally, what end are we pursuing, driven by that supreme and inescapable law of unceasing transformation, and what are the means we must use to achieve that end?

These are the only questions accessible to us, the ones we must always be making new efforts to resolve, on pain of disowning our humanity.

XIII ON MARX AND MARXISM

The first of these four texts is an extract from the *Lettres à un Français sur la crise actuelle*, published in *Œuvres*, vol. IV, (Paris 1910), pp. 62–7. The *Lettre à la Liberté*, never sent off and not published until 1910, is taken from *Archives Bakounine*, vol. II, 'Michel Bakounine et les conflits dans l'Internationale, 1872' (Leiden, 1965), pp. 147–68. The third extract is from an unfinished manuscript entitled *Écrit contre Marx*, also not published at the time, and now printed in the same volume of the *Archives Bakounine*, pp. 201–4. The last text is an extract from Bakunin's only book in Russian, *Gosudarstvennost' i anarchija* ['Statism and anarchy'], subtitled 'The struggle between the two factions in the International Working Men's Association'; it was published in Switzerland in 1873 by a Russian group affiliated to Bakunin. The present text is taken from *Archives Bakounine*, vol. III, 'Étatisme et anarchie, 1873' (Leiden, 1967), pp. 145–9. The first three extracts are here translated from the French by Steven Cox; the fourth extract is translated from the Russian by Olive Stevens.

I

[The basic principle of modern communism] was first expressed by Babeuf, towards the end of the great Revolution, with all the apparatus of ancient civicism and revolutionary violence which characterized that era, and it was adapted and reproduced in miniature about thirty years ago by M. Louis Blanc in the slim pamphlet on *The Organization of Labour* in which that worthy citizen, a great deal less revolutionary and far more lenient with bourgeois failings than Babeuf, did his best to gild and sweeten the pill, so that the bourgeois should swallow it without suspecting that they were taking a deadly poison. The bourgeois were not deceived and, exchanging brutality for courtesy, expelled M. Blanc from France. In spite of which, with a constancy that one is bound to admire, M. Blanc remains the sole advocate of his economic system and goes on believing that the entire future is contained in his little pamphlet on the organization of labour.

Since that time, the idea of communism has found its way into more capable hands. Herr Karl Marx, the undisputed leader of the German socialist party—a powerful mind backed by deep learning, and a man of whom it may be said without flattery that his whole life has been exclusively dedicated to the greatest cause of the present day, that of the emancipation of labour and the worker—Herr Marx, who is also beyond question if not the sole then one of the principal founders of the International Working Men's Association, has given serious attention to the development of the communist idea. His great work *Das Kapital* is not a fantasy or an *a priori* concept hatched in a single day out of the mind of a young man more or less ignorant of the economic condition of society and the prevailing system of production. It is based on very detailed and extensive knowledge and analysis in depth of that system and its conditions. Herr Marx is a mine of statistical and economic information. His book on capital, although unfortunately bristling with metaphysical formulae and subtleties which make it inaccessible to the vast majority of readers, is positivist and realist to the highest degree, in the sense that it accepts no logic but the logic of facts.

Having lived almost exclusively for about thirty years in the midst of German workers, refugees like himself, and with a circle of friends and more or less intelligent disciples belonging by birth or contact to the bourgeois world, Herr Karl Marx naturally came to the point of forming a school, a kind of small-scale communist Church, made up of fervent believers and scattered all over Germany. Although restricted in numerical terms, this Church is expertly organized, and thanks to extensive contacts with working men's associations in all the key points of Germany it is already a force to be reckoned with. Herr Marx naturally enjoys a position close to supreme authority in the Church, and it has to be admitted in all fairness that he is adept at handling his little army of fanatical supporters so as continually to enhance his prestige and his power over the imagination of the German workers.

Herr Marx's idea of communism permeates all his writings, and was equally apparent in the proposals advanced last year by the General Council of the International Working Men's Association, seated in London, at the Basel Congress,[10] as well as in the proposals he intended to table at the Congress which was to have taken place in September of this year and which had to be suspended as a result of the war. Herr Karl Marx, member of the General Council in London and corresponding secretary for Germany, enjoyed great — and admittedly legitimate — influence in that Council, so it can certainly be assumed that the proposals made by the General Council at the Congress stemmed mainly from the system and collaboration of Herr Marx.

This was how the English citizen Lucraft, a member of the General Council, produced the idea at the Basel Congress that all the land in a country should become *State property*, and that its cultivation should be controlled and administered by State officials, which, he added, 'will only be possible in a democratic and socialist State, in which it will be the people's task to be vigilant over the State's administration of the national land'.

This was how, when the proposal to abolish the right of inheritance was debated at the same Congress — a proposal which won an overall majority in the voting — all the members of the General Council, all the English delegates and the great majority of the German delegates voted against abolition, for the special reason, expressed by citizen Eccarius on behalf of the General Council, that 'once the collective ownership of land, capital and in general all the instruments of labour is recognized and established in any country, the abolition of the right of inheritance will lose its point, because the law is bound to collapse of its own accord, there being nothing left to inherit'. But by a strange paradox, this same Eccarius, speaking in the name of this same General Council, made a counter-proposal in favour of instituting a provisional *inheritance tax* on behalf of the working masses, which indicates that the General Council does not expect collective ownership to be established now, by means of revolution, but gradually, by means of successive political deals with the bourgeois property-owners.

The delegates of the German Working Men's Associations, who were making their first appearance in force at an

International Congress, also tabled a new proposal — together with the delegates from German Switzerland — quite in accord with their Eisenach programme,[11] and aiming at nothing less than the introduction of *the principle of national and bourgeois politics* into the programme of the International. This proposal of *direct legislation by the people* as the absolutely necessary preliminary to achieving social reforms was put forward by citizen Bürkli of Zurich, and cordially supported by citizens Goegg, Rittinghausen, Bruhin and Liebknecht. It gave rise to quite a heated debate, at the height of which citizen Liebknecht, one of the chief leaders of the German social democratic party, stated that it was *reactionary* to refuse to discuss this question, which was an extremely legitimate and urgent one, since in its previous Congresses, and particularly at Lausanne in 1867, the Association itself had asserted that the political question was inseparable from the social, and lastly, that if this question did not seem important in Paris, Vienna and Brussels, where the social question could not be dealt with in its political form and conditions, it was important for countries where that possibility did exist.

Thanks to the opposition of the French, Italian, Spanish, Belgian and some of the French Swiss delegates, this question was dropped. It did not arise again at the Basel Congress. *Inde irae.*

II. *A Letter to the Editorial Board of* La Liberté

Zurich, October 5th, 1872

Gentlemen,

Having published the verdict of excommunication which the Marxist Hague Congress has just passed against myself, in all fairness you will surely publish my reply. Here it is.

The triumph of Herr Marx and his followers has been complete. Certain of a majority which had been a long time in preparation and which was organized with great skill and care, if without much respect for the principles of Morality, Truth and Justice which are so often to be found in their speeches and so seldom in their actions,[12] the Marxists have shed their masks and, in the typical manner of power-loving men, always in the name of that popular sovereignty which in future will serve as a stepping-stone for all pretenders to control of the masses, they have boldly ordained the enslavement of the people of the International.

If the International were less deeply rooted, if it was based, as they imagine, only on the organization of centres of control, instead of on the real solidarity of the actual interests and aspirations of the proletariat of every country in the civilized world, regardless of any governmental tutelage, the decrees of that dismal Hague Congress, the all too pliant and faithful embodiment of Marxist theory and practice, would have been enough to kill it. They would have brought down both ridicule and odium upon that fine association, in whose foundation I would like to add that Herr Marx played an intelligent, vigorous part.

A State, a government, a universal dictatorship! The dream of a Gregory VII, a Boniface VIII, a Charles V or a Napoleon, recurring under new guises but always with the same pretensions, in the camp of socialist democracy! Is it possible to imagine anything more absurd, but also more loathsome?

To claim that even the most intelligent and best-intentioned group of individuals will be capable of becoming the mind, soul and guiding and unifying will of the revolutionary moment and economic organization of the proletariat of every land is such an outrage against common sense and historical experience that one can only wonder how a man as clever as Herr Marx could have conceived it.

The Popes at least had the excuse of the absolute truth which they said the Holy Ghost had given into their hands, and which they were bound to believe. Herr Marx has no such excuse, and I shall not insult him by thinking that he imagines himself to have scientifically invented something approaching absolute truth. But granted that the absolute does not exist, there can be no infallible dogma for the International and consequently no official political or economic theory, and our congresses should never aspire to the role of ecumenical councils proclaiming compulsory principles for all adherents and believers.

There is only one law binding all the members, individuals, sections and federations of the International, a law which constitutes its one true basis. In all its scope, consequences and applications, it is *the international solidarity of workers in all jobs and all countries in their economic struggle against the exploiters of labour*. It is the real organization of that solidarity through the spontaneous action of the working classes, and the absolutely free federation — all the stronger for being free — of the working masses of all tongues and nations, not their unification by decree and under the aegis of any government, which constitutes the real, living unity of the International.

Who can doubt that it is out of this increasingly widespread organization of the militant solidarity of the proletariat against bourgeois exploitation that the political struggle of the proletariat against the bourgeoisie must rise and grow? The Marxists and ourselves are unanimous on this point. But now comes the question that divides us so deeply from the Marxists.

We think that the policy of the proletariat must necessarily be a revolutionary one, aimed directly and solely at the destruction of States. We do not see how it is possible to talk about international solidarity and yet to intend preserving States — unless in some dream of the universal State, meaning universal slavery, the dream of the great emperors and popes — because by its very nature the State is a breach of that solidarity and therefore a permanent cause of war. Nor can we conceive how it is possible to talk about the liberty of the proletariat or the real deliverance of the masses within and by means of the State. State means dominion, and all dominion involves the subjugation of the masses and consequently their exploitation for the sake of some ruling minority.

We do not accept, even in the process of revolutionary transition, either constituent assemblies, provisional governments or so-called revolutionary dictatorships; because we are convinced that revolution is only sincere, honest and real in the hands of the masses, and that when it is concentrated into those of a few ruling individuals it inevitably and immediately becomes reaction. That is our belief, but this is not the moment to expand on it.

The Marxists profess quite different ideas. They are worshippers of State power, and necessarily also prophets of political and social discipline and champions of order established from the top downwards, always in the name of universal suffrage and the sovereignty of the masses, for whom they save the honour and privilege of obeying leaders, elected masters. The only kind of emancipation the Marxists accept is what they expect to come out of their so-called People's State (*Volksstaat*).[13] They are so unopposed to patriotism that their International flies the flag of Pan-Germanism all too often. Between the policies of Bismarck and Marx there may well be a marked difference, but between the Marxists and ourselves there is a chasm. They are for government, we, for our part, are anarchists.

It is these two main attitudes which today split the International into two camps. On the one side Germany, practically alone; on the other, to a greater or lesser degree, Italy, Spain, the Swiss Jura, a large part of France, Belgium, Holland, and soon the Slav peoples. These two trends clashed at the Hague Congress, and, thanks to the cunning of Herr Marx and the utterly artificial organization of that Congress,[14] the German trend won.

Does this mean that the crucial question was resolved? It was not even properly debated; the majority voted like a well-drilled regiment and crushed all debate beneath its vote. The contradiction therefore looms more menacingly than ever, and Herr Marx himself, despite the intoxication of victory, certainly does not imagine that he can be rid of it so cheap. And even if he had momentarily entertained such a foolish hope, the united protest of the Jura, Spanish, Belgian and Dutch delegations (not counting Italy, which did not even bother to send delegates to such a blatantly rigged Congress), that protest, so moderate in form but all the more forceful and significant in essence, must soon have disabused him.

In itself, that protest is clearly only a very feeble precursor of the storm of opposition which will break in every country truly imbued with the principles and passion of social revolution. And that whole storm will have been raised by the Marxists' fatal preoccupation with making the political question a plank of the International, and a binding principle.

In fact, no rapprochement is now possible between these two trends. Only the praxis of social revolution, great new historical experiments and the logic of events might eventually

lead them to a common solution, and, convinced as we are of
the value of our own principle, we hope that the Germans
themselves—the workers of Germany, not their leaders—
will then join us at last to raze those people's prisons which
are called States and to pass sentence on politics, which is
in fact nothing but the art of subduing and fleecing the
masses.

But what is to be done today? Since solution and rapprochement in the political sphere are impossible, we must
mutually tolerate one another by leaving each country the
undisputed right to follow the political trends that suit it
best and seem best adapted to its particular situation. It will
consequently be necessary to set aside the political planks of
the International and to seek the unity of that great Association solely in the sphere of economic solidarity. That solidarity
unites us, whereas political questions fatally divide us.

It is certain that neither the Italians, the Spaniards, the
Jurassiens, the Belgians, the Dutch, the Slavonic peoples—
those historic enemies of Pan-Germanism—nor even the
proletariat of England and America will ever knuckle under
to the political directives now being imposed on the German
proletariat by its leaders' ambitions. But even supposing that
the new General Council lays an interdiction on all these
countries because of their disobedience, and that a new
Marxist ecumenical council excommunicates them and
declares them expelled from the International, will all this
diminish the economic solidarity which necessarily and
naturally exists between the proletariat of Germany and of all
these other countries? If the German workers go on strike or
revolt against either the economic tyranny of their bosses or
the political tyranny of a government which is the natural
protector of capitalists and other exploiters of popular labour,
will the proletariat of all those countries excommunicated by
the Marxists stand by with arms folded and remain casual
spectators of the struggle? No, it will give what money it has,
and more, all its blood to its brothers in Germany, without
stopping to inquire what political system they expect to be
delivered by.

And this is where the true unity of the International lies:
it is in the common aspirations and spontaneous action of the

popular masses of every land, not in any government, and not in any uniform political theory imposed on these masses by some General Congress. This is so obvious that a man needs to be blinded by the lust for power in order not to realize it.

If I try hard, I can understand how despots crowned or uncrowned could have dreamed of world power, but what is to be said when a friend of the proletariat, a revolutionary who claims that he genuinely supports the emancipation of the masses, proceeds to set himself up as controller and supreme arbiter of every revolutionary movement which may break out in every country, and dares to dream of subjecting the proletariat of all those countries to a single approach hatched out of a single brain—his own!

I believe that Herr Marx is a very serious if not very honest revolutionary, and that he really is in favour of the rebellion of the masses, and I wonder how he manages to overlook the fact that the establishment of a universal dictatorship, collective or individual, a dictatorship which would create the post of a kind of chief engineer of world revolution, ruling and controlling the insurrectionary activity of the masses in all countries, as a machine might be controlled—that the establishment of such a dictatorship would in itself suffice to kill revolution and warp and paralyse all popular movements. What man, what group of individuals, no matter how great their genius, would dare to think themselves able to embrace and understand the plethora of interests, attitudes and activities, so various in every country, province, locality and profession, whose vast totality, united but not standardized by a great common aspiration and by a few basic principles which have now entered into the collective awareness of the masses, will constitute the future social revolution?

And what are we to think of an international congress which, allegedly in the interest of that revolution, imposes on the proletariat of the entire civilized world a government vested with dictatorial powers and exercising the inquisitorial, pontifical right of suspending regional federations and debarring whole nations in the name of a so-called official principle which is nothing but Herr Marx's own thinking, transformed into absolute truth by the vote of a rigged majority?[15] What are we to make of a congress which,

doubtless to rub in its folly, relegates that dictatorial government to America, after packing it with men who may be very
honest but are also obscure, relatively ignorant and completely unknown to that congress? Our opponents the bourgeois
must be right after all when they jeer at our congresses and
claim that the International Working Men's Association
fights old tyrannies only to establish a new one, and that its
worthy substitute for existing absurdities is the creation of
another!

For the honour and the very salvation of the International,
should we not therefore make haste to proclaim that the ill-
fated Hague Congress, far from being the expression of the
aspirations of the entire European proletariat, and despite
its disguise of bogus rectitude, was in fact nothing but the
unhappy outcome of deceit, intrigue and an outrageous
breach of faith, as well as of the authority which had unfortunately been granted to the defunct General Council for
too long? This was a congress not of the International but of
the General Council, whose Marxist and Blanquist members
made up about a third of the total number of delegates,
together with their following of well-disciplined Germans on
the one hand and a few unsuspecting Frenchmen on the other,
and went to The Hague not to discuss the right conditions for
the emancipation of the proletariat but to gain the upper
hand in the International.

Herr Marx, abler and more astute than his Blanquist
allies, tricked them, just as Herr von Bismarck once tricked
the diplomats of the French Empire and Republic. The
Blanquists had obviously gone to the Hague Congress in the
hope—probably fostered by Herr Marx himself—of being
able to take control of the French socialist movement by way
of the General Council, and counted on remaining influential
members of the Council. Herr Marx does not like sharing,
but it is more than likely that he had made specific promises
to his French colleagues, without whose co-operation he
would not have had his majority at the Hague Congress. But
once having used them he politely showed them the door, and
in accordance with a scheme arranged in advance between
himself and his real friends, the Germans in America and
Germany, he shipped off the General Council to New York,

leaving his former friends the Blanquists in the highly un-comfortable situation of conspirators fallen victim to their own conspiracy. Two such setbacks at such brief intervals do little credit to the French spirit.

But surely Herr Marx was deposing himself by shipping the administration off to New York? Not at all. No one will insult him by supposing that he took that administration seriously, or that he would trust the fate of the International to untried, feeble hands, when he sees himself in a sense as its father and slightly too much as its master. His ambition may involve him in doing it a great deal of damage, it is true, but he cannot want to see it destroyed—and would it not bring certain destruction to vest those dictatorial powers in incompetents? How are we to resolve this problem?

It is resolved very easily for those who know or guess that in the shadow of the official New York administration another has been established, anonymous, and made up of the irresponsible, obscure but all the more powerful so-called agents of that administration in Europe, or rather of the secret but real power of Herr Marx and his followers. This was the whole object of the Hague intrigue. It explains the calmly triumphant attitude of Herr Marx, who thinks that he will now have the entire International in his pocket—and unless he is sorely deceiving himself he has good reason for rejoicing, for by savouring the divine luxury of secret power he will be able to foist all its awkward attributes on to that wretched General Council in New York.

One only has to glance over one of the September issues of the *Volksstaat*, the principal organ of the German Social Democratic Workers' Party, to be convinced that these really are Herr Marx's intentions. With typical German naivety and clumsiness, a semi-official article in this paper, which derives its inspiration direct from Herr Marx, lists all the reasons that caused him and his closest friends to move the administration of the London International to New York. There were two main reasons for staging the coup.

The first was the impossibility of reaching an understanding with the Blanquists. If Herr Marx is riddled with the Pan-Germanic instincts which have made such headway in Germany since the conquests of Herr von Bismarck, the

Blanquists are French patriots above all. Knowing nothing about Germany, and caring less, in true French style, they might well have left its absolute control to Herr Marx, but on no account would they have conceded control of France, which they are naturally saving for themselves. And it is just this dictatorship in France that Herr Marx, true German that he is, particularly craves, even more than he craves the dictatorship of Germany.

No matter what material or political successes the Germans may gain over France, morally and socially they will always feel inferior. This irrepressible feeling of inferiority is the perpetual source of all the jealousy and animosity aroused in them by the very name of France, and also of all the irrational and secret envy. A German does not believe that his world-standing is high enough as long as his reputation, glory and name go unrecognized in France. Acceptance by French and especially by Parisian opinion has always been the burning secret ambition of every German of note. And to control France, and through France the opinion of the entire world, what fame, and above all what power!

Herr Marx is far too intelligent and far too vain and ambitious a German not to have realized this, so he has used every conceivable means to woo French revolutionary and social opinion. It seems that he partly succeeded, since the Blanquists fell for it at first, although it was also their own ambitions which made them sue for alliance with this pretender to the dictatorship of the International; thanks to his almighty protection, they became members of the London General Council.

They must have been in full accord at first, for as authoritarian, power-loving men they were united by their common loathing of the rest of us, who are irreconcilable enemies of all power and all government, and therefore also of the man who was to be ensconced in the International. Yet the alliance could not last long, for with Herr Marx unwilling to share his power and the Blanquists unable to concede the dictatorship of France, their friendship was bound to be short-lived. So it was that even before the Hague Congress, while there was still every appearance of the most tender affection between them, Herr Marx and his cronies had made up their minds to expel the Blanquists from the General Council. The *Volksstaat* bluntly admits this, adding that since it was impossible to remove them as long as the General Council remained in London, it was decided to transfer the latter to America.

The other reason, similarly admitted by the *Volksstaat*, was the open insubordination of the English workers. This admission must have pained Herr Marx, for it reveals a great setback. Apart from his economic scholarship, incontestably very serious and profound, and in addition to his equally remarkable and incontrovertible skills as a political intriguer, Herr Marx has always had two strings to his bow in the campaign to attract and overmaster his compatriots. The first was French, and consisted of a fairly awkward imitation of the French spirit, the second English, involving a much more successful affectation of the practical reason of the English. Herr Marx has spent more than twenty years in London among the English workers, and as is usually the case with the Germans, who at heart are ashamed of their own country and assume and rather clumsily exaggerate the customs and language of their adoptive country, Herr Marx likes to show that he is more English than the English. I hasten to add that during the years in which he has applied his remarkable intelligence to studying the economic situation in England he has acquired a very detailed, thorough knowledge of all the economic relationships between labour and capital in that country. All his writings bear witness to this fact, and if we overlook an element of Hegelian jargon which he has been unable to shed, it will be found that under the specious pretext that because all other countries are more backward from the viewpoint of capitalist production they are necessarily equally backward from that of social revolution, Herr Marx has seen only its English aspects. He could be taken for an Englishman talking only to the English.

This certainly constitutes no great recommendation from the standpoint of internationalism, but it might at least have been concluded that Herr Marx must wield a legitimate and salutary influence over the English workers; and in fact a very close intimacy and great mutual trust do seem to have existed for many years between himself and a fair number of outstandingly active English workers, which led everybody to believe that in general terms he enjoyed considerable authority in England, and this could not fail to enhance his prestige on the Continent. Therefore it was with confidence as well as impatience that the entire International awaited the moment when, thanks to his forceful, clever propaganda, the million workers who today constitute the formidable association of the trades unions would come over, bag and baggage, into our own camp.

This hope is about to be at least partially realized. Already an English Federation formally affiliated to the International has been created. But the odd thing is that the first action of this Federation was openly to break all ties with Herr Marx, and if one studies the disclosures of the *Volksstaat*, and especially the harsh words and insults incautiously aimed by Herr Marx at the English workers at the Hague Congress,[16] one comes to the conclusion that the proletariat of Great Britain absolutely refuses to bow its head under the yoke of the socialist dictator of Germany. To pay court to a people for over twenty years, only for it to end like this! To ring all the changes on praise for the English workers, to set them up as examples for the proletariat of all other countries, then suddenly to have to round on them and accuse them of selling out to reaction! What a mishap, and what a downfall—not for the English workers, but for Herr Marx.

But a fully merited downfall. Herr Marx had been misleading the English members of the General Council for too long. By playing partly on their ignorance of Continental affairs and partly on their regrettable indifference to those affairs, he had managed to make them swallow whatever he wanted for years. There seems to have been a tacit understanding between Herr Marx and these English members, by which Herr Marx was not to interfere in specifically English matters, or not to do so without their consent, while they left him in control of the International on the Continent, where it did not greatly concern them. In fairness to these citizens, it must be supposed that they had the utmost confidence in the loyalty and fairmindedness of Herr Marx.

We know now the extent to which Herr Marx had abused

that confidence. We know that all the business of the International, or rather all the intrigues fomented and conducted in our great association in the name of the General Council, were contrived and guided by a close-knit circle around Herr Marx, made up almost exclusively of Germans and exercising the functions of a kind of executive committee. This committee knew everything, decided everything and undertook everything, while the other members, who made up the great majority of the Council, knew absolutely nothing. The respect they enjoyed was so far-reaching as to spare them the trouble of signing their names to the General Council's circulars; their names were signed for them, so that until the very last minute they had not the slightest idea of all the abominations for which they were being made unwittingly responsible.

It is obvious how such a favourable situation could be turned to advantage by men like Herr Marx and his friends — far too able politicians to be baulked by scruples. I doubt if there is any need to explain the objective of the great intrigue. It was to establish the revolutionary dictatorship of Herr Marx in Europe, by means of the International. Herr Marx — a new Alberoni — felt himself bold enough to conceive and execute such a plan. As for the methods, I must say that he spoke of them quite offhandedly, disparagingly and insincerely in his final speech in Amsterdam. It is true, as he said, that he cannot summon up armies, finance, *chassepots* or Krupp cannon to subjugate the world. But on the other hand he has a remarkable genius for intrigue, and unrelenting determination; he also has a sizeable number of agents at his diposal, hierarchically organized and acting in secret under his direct orders; a kind of socialist and literary freemasonry in which his compatriots, the German and other Jews,[17] hold an important position and display zeal worthy of a better cause. Lastly he has had the great name of the International, which exercises such magical power on the proletariat of every country, and which he has been too long permitted to use for the furthering of his ambitious plans.

Herr Marx opened his campaign in 1869, and stepped it up in 1871. Until the Basel Congress of September 1869 he had managed to conceal his intentions. But when the resolutions of that Congress aroused his rage and apprehensions, he ordered a general all-out attack by all his underlings against the men he was now beginning to hate for their unflinching opposition to his principles and his dictatorship. He opened fire against my friends and myself, successively, but especially against myself, first in Paris, then in Leipzig and New York, and finally in Geneva.[18] Instead of shells, the Marxist artillery shot mud at us. It was a deluge of foul idiotic abuse.

I knew as early as spring 1870 — because M. Utin (a little Russian Jew who is striving to build for himself a reputation in that poor Geneva International by every possible underhand means) had been telling anybody who was willing to listen — that the latter had received a confidential letter from Herr Marx instructing him to collect all the facts against me — meaning all the tall stories and all the accusations, as unpleasant as possible, and with the merest shreds of proof — adding that if these shreds were plausible they were to be used against me at the next Congress. This was the origin of the notorious trumped-up charge based on my past contacts with the unfortunate Nečaev, contacts which I am still forbidden to talk about and which have just been used by the Marxists on the commission of inquiry to dictate to the Marxist Hague Congress a prefabricated verdict of expulsion.

In order to give the measure of the good faith of Marxist agents and journals, perhaps I may tell another anecdote. I am so inured to being systematically and regularly libelled in nearly every issue of the *Volksstaat* that I do not usually bother to read the rubbish it churns out against myself, but it happens that friends have shown me an article which seems worthy of mention here, all the more so because it appears very apt for bringing out Herr Marx's loyalty and veracity. This respectable Leipzig journal, the official organ of the German Social Democratic Party, seems to have set out to prove that I am nothing less than a paid agent of the Russian government. To this end it has published some quite extraordinary information, such as that my late compatriot Alexander Herzen and I used to receive considerable subsidies from a Pan-Slavist committee set up in Moscow under the direct supervision of the St Petersburg government, and that after Herzen's death I had the good fortune to find my allowance doubled. Obviously I have nothing to say in face of such conclusive facts.

In the *Volksstaat* No. [71] of [September 4th, 1872] the following anecdote appears: In 1848, when Bakunin was in Breslau, where the German democrats had made the blunder of taking him fully into their confidence, unaware that he was a Pan-Slavist propagandist, a Cologne newspaper, the *Neue Rheinische Zeitung*, edited by Herren Marx and Engels, published a message from Paris in which it was said that Mme George Sand had expressed herself in a highly disquieting manner on the subject of Bakunin, saying that he was not to be trusted, that nobody knew what he was or what he wanted, that he was, in a word, a very equivocal person, etc., etc. The *Volksstaat* adds that Bakunin never made any reply to such a blunt accusation, that instead he had disappeared and gone to ground in Russia after the publication of this message, and that he had not surfaced again until 1849 in Germany, to take part, probably as an agent provocateur, in the Dresden rising.

Now here are the true facts. Herren Marx and Engels had in fact published this *message from Paris* against myself, which only goes to show that they were already motivated by tender affection for me, and by that same spirit of loyalty and justice that distinguishes them today. I do not think it necessary to relate the facts which won me this expression of good will, but here is what I do believe I should add, since the *Volksstaat* has forgotten or neglected to mention it: In 1848 I was younger, more impressionable and consequently much less long-suffering and indifferent than I am today, and immediately I read this message from Paris in Herren Marx and Engels's paper I hastened to write a letter to Mme George Sand, who was far more revolutionary at that time than she appears to be today, and for whom I had expressed my most sincere and lively admiration. This letter, in which I asked for an explanation of the comments attributed to her, was delivered by my friend Adolphe Reichel, today a musical director in Berne. Mme Sand replied in a charming letter, expressing the firmest friendship for myself. At the same time she sent

Herren Marx and Engels a strong letter indignantly calling them to account for having dared to misuse her name in order to libel her friend Bakunin, for whom she felt both affection and esteem. For my own part, I had asked a friend of mine, a Pole called Koscielski, who was going to Cologne on private business, to ask the editors of the *Neue Rheinische Zeitung* either for a public retraction or else for satisfaction, in my name. Under this dual pressure, these gentlemen proved most pleasant and accommodating. They published the letter which came to them from Mme Sand—a letter which was highly deleterious to their *amour-propre*—and they appended a few lines in which they expressed their regret at the insertion, *in their absence*, of an unfounded message attacking the honour of their 'friend Bakunin', for whom their hearts too were filled with affection and esteem. After such a statement— which the *Volksstaat* can locate in one of the issues of the *Neue Rheinische Zeitung* for July or August of 1848, as well as in the memory of Herren Marx and Engels, who will certainly not be so impolitic as to repudiate it—I obviously have no need to ask any other satisfaction of them. As for my alleged disappearance to Russia, these gentlemen know better than anybody that I did not leave Germany until 1850, when after a year of enforced residence in the fortress of Königstein I was transferred in irons to Prague, then to Olmütz, before being moved to St Petersburg, still in irons, in 1856.

I find it extremely distasteful to be forced to bring up all these stories. I do so today for the first and last time, in order to show the public the kind of men I am obliged to contend with. Their relentless hounding of myself, when I have never made any personal attack on them, have never even talked about them and deliberately refrained from replying to their own unsavoury assaults—this persistent hatred which has constrained them to slander and defame me in all their private correspondence and in all their journals ever since my escape from Siberia in 1861 seems to me such an extra-ordinary phenomenon that I have not managed to understand it to this day. Their activities against myself are not only hateful and repellent, they are also foolish. How is it that it has not occurred to these gentlemen that by assailing me with this incredible intensity they have done a lot more for my

reputation than I myself could have done, for all the disgusting
stories which they spread about all over the world with this
impassioned hatred will naturally collapse under the weight
of their own absurdity. But my name will remain, and to
this name, which they will have contributed so much to making
known in the world, will attach the real, legitimate glory of
having been the pitiless and irreconcilable adversary, not of
their own persons, which matter very little to me, but of their
authoritarian theories and ridiculous and detestable pretensions to world dictatorship. So if I were a boastful, vain, ambitious man, far from bearing any grudge against them for all
these attacks I should have felt infinitely grateful, for by
doing their worst to denigrate me they have achieved what
has never been my intention or inclination—they have made
my name.

In March 1870, still in the name of the General Council
and with the signatures of all its members, Herr Marx launched
a defamatory circular against me, published in French and
German and addressed to the regional Federations.[19] I only
heard about this circular about six or seven months ago, on
the occasion of the trial of Bebel and Liebknecht, when it
appeared and was read out in evidence against them. In this
memorandum apparently directed exclusively against myself
and whose full details are still unknown to me, Herr Marx
recommends *underground work* in the International, among
other things, to his friends; then he turns on me, and together
with a number of other pleasantries produces the accusation
that I have set up a sinister secret society inside the International, with the obvious intention of destroying it. But what
struck me as the height of absurdity was that while I was
quietly living in Lausanne, a long way from all the sections
of the International, Herr Marx was accusing me of con-
ducting a terrible intrigue—see how mistaken it can be to
judge others by oneself—aimed at shifting the General
Council from London to Switzerland, with the obvious
intention of setting up my personal dictatorship there. The
circular ended with a very learned and quite conclusive
demonstration of how essential it was then—but no longer,
apparently—to keep the General Council in London, a town
which Herr Marx saw as the natural centre and true capital

of world trade, prior to the Hague Congress. It seems to have been superseded ever since the English workers rebelled against Herr Marx, or rather since they discerned his dictatorial ambitions and his all too clever means of furthering them.

But it was after September 1871, at the time of the famous London Conference,[20] that the decisive, open campaign against us began — as open as it could be, coming from men as autocratic and cautious as Herr Marx and his circle. The disaster in France seems to have raised high hopes in Herr Marx, while at the same time the triumphs of Herr von Bismarck — whom Herr Engels, Herr Marx's *alter ego* and closest friend, describes in a semi-official letter now in front of me as a very useful servant of social revolution[21] — made him extremely envious. As a German he was extremely proud of them, as a socialist democrat he consoled himself and Herr Engels with the thought that in the long run this triumph of the Prussian monarchy was bound sooner or later to turn into that of the great republican and popular State whose *patron* he is, but as an individual he was cut to the quick at the prospect of anybody but himself causing such a furore and rising to such heights.

I appeal to the memory of all those who happened to see or hear the Germans during the years 1870 and 1871. Anyone who took the pains to sort out their basic thinking from the contradictions of an equivocal way of speaking will agree with me that with a very few exceptions, not only among the radicals but also among the vast majority of the social democrats themselves, side by side with the very grief they felt at the sight of a republic succumbing to a despot, there was general satisfaction at seeing France fallen so low and Germany risen so high. Even among those of them who fought most courageously against the flood of patriotism which had overwhelmed the whole of Germany, even in the minds of Herren Bebel and Liebknecht, who paid and are still paying with their liberty for their strong protestations against Prussian barbarism and on behalf of the rights of France, there were noticeable traces of triumphant nationalism. For instance, I recall one of the September 1870 issues of the *Volksstaat* printing the following comment, which I cannot reproduce verbatim, not having the relevant issue to hand, but which made too deep an impression on me for me to have forgotten its sense and general tone: 'Now that, as a result of the defeat of France, *the initiative of the socialist movement has moved from France to Germany*, great duties confront us.'[22]

These words sum up all the thinking, hopes and ambitions of the Marxists. They seriously believe that the recent German military and political triumph over France marks the beginning of a great age in history, and that it now falls to Germany to play the leading world role in every respect — doubtless for the very salvation of the world. France and all the Latin peoples *have been*, the Slavs *are not yet*, and in any case are too barbaric to get anywhere by themselves, without German help; today, only Germany *is*. The outcome is a threefold attitude on the part of the Germans. For the Latin peoples, 'once intelligent and powerful, but today sunk into decadence', they feel a kind of pitying respect tinged with indulgence; they are polite with them, or rather they try to be, because politeness does not come naturally or habitually to the Germans. For the Slavs they affect disdain, but there is a great deal of fear in that disdain, and their underlying feeling is one of hatred, the hatred of the oppressor for the man he oppresses, in dread of a terrible rebellion. For their own part, finally, they have become extremely presumptuous and self-infatuated, which does not make them any more lovable, and they imagine that they mean something and are capable of something under the unitary — Herr Engels would probably say *revolutionary* — yoke of their Pan-Germanic emperor.

What Herr von Bismarck has done for the political and bourgeois world, Herr Marx claims to be doing today for the socialist world, among the proletariat of Europe: replacing French initiative by German initiative and dominion. And since, according to him and his disciples, no German thought is more advanced than his own, he concludes that the time has come for its theoretical and political triumph within the International. This is the main and in fact the only purpose of the conference he convoked in London in September 1871.

This Marxist thinking is developed explicitly in the famous Manifesto of the German communists, drafted and published by Herren Marx and Engels in 1848. It is the theory of the emancipation of the proletariat and the organization of labour by the State. It seems that at the Hague Congress Herr Engels, taken aback by the unfavourable impression produced by the reading of a few excerpts from this Manifesto, lost no time in asserting that this was an obsolete *document*, a theory discarded by themselves. If he said this, he was wanting in sincerity, because the Marxists had set about distributing the document nation-wide on the very eve of that Congress. In any case, it is reproduced word for word, with all its principal points, in the programme of the German Social Democratic Party. The main issue, which crops up again in the manifesto produced by Herr Marx in 1864 in the name of the provisional General Council and was withdrawn from the programme of the International by the Geneva Congress, is *the seizure of political power by the working class*.

It is understandable that indispensable men like Herren Marx and Engels should support a programme whose retention and advocacy of political power is an open invitation to ambition. Since there is to be political power there will inevitably be subjects, got up as citizens, true, in proper republican style, but subjects all the same, and as such compelled to obey, for without obedience no power is possible. It will be objected that it is not men who are to be obeyed, but the laws which they themselves have made. My answer is that everybody knows the way the people make laws in the freest and most democratic — but politically oriented — countries, and what is meant by their obedience to those laws. Anybody who is not determined to take fiction for reality will have to admit that even in those countries the people obey laws made not by themselves but in their name, and that obedience to those laws never means anything except submission to some custodial and governmental minority, in other words freedom to be slaves.

There is another expression in that programme which is deeply antipathetic to us revolutionary anarchists who unconditionally advocate full popular emancipation, and that is the designation of the proletariat, the world of the workers, as *class* rather than as *mass*. Do you know what this means? Nothing more or less than a new aristocracy, that of the urban and industrial workers, to the exclusion of the millions who make up the rural proletariat and who, in the previsions of the German social democrats, will in effect become subjects of this great so-called popular State. *Class, power* and *State*, these three terms are inseparable, each of them necessarily implying the other two, and summed up in aggregate by these words: *the political subjugation and economic exploitation of the masses.*

The Marxist belief is that just as in the past century the bourgeois class overthrew the aristocratic class, replacing and slowly absorbing it into its own body and sharing with it the domination and exploitation of the workers in town and country alike, so the urban proletariat of today is appointed to overthrow the bourgeois class, absorb it and share with it the domination and exploitation of the rural proletariat, that last parish of history, except that in future it will be for the latter to rise up and demolish all classes, all dominion and all powers—in other words, all States.

Thus they do not reject our programme out of hand. They only blame us for wanting to hasten and overtake the slow march of history and for disregarding the positivist law of successive evolutions. Having had the typically German audacity to proclaim, in works devoted to the philosophical analysis of the past, that the bloody defeat of peasant rebellions in Germany and the rise of despotic States in the sixteenth century constituted a great revolutionary advance, today they have the nerve to be content with establishing a new despotism, to the alleged advantage of the urban workers and the detriment of the rural.

It is the same German temperament and the same logic which draw them directly and inevitably towards what we call *bourgeois socialism* and towards the conclusion of a new political pact between the (sometimes unwillingly) radical bourgeoisie and the *intellectual*, respectable, in other words *bourgeois-influenced* minority of the urban proletariat, to the exclusion and detriment of the mass of the proletariat, both rural and urban.

This is the true meaning of workers' candidacies to the parliaments of existing States and of the seizure of political power by the working class. For, even from the standpoint of that urban proletariat who are supposed to reap the sole reward of the seizure of political power, surely it is obvious that this power will never be anything but a sham? It is bound to be impossible for a few thousand, let alone tens or hundreds of thousands of men to wield that power effectively. It will have to be exercised by proxy, which means entrusting it to a group of men elected to represent and govern them, which in turn will unfailingly return them to all the deceit and sub-servience of representative or bourgeois rule. After a brief flash of liberty or orgiastic revolution, the citizens of the new State will wake up slaves, puppets and victims of a new group of ambitious men.

It may well be imagined how and why astute politicians should be so passionately attached to a programme which offers such broad scope to their ambitions; but for serious workers, men whose hearts contain the living flame of solidarity with their companions in slavery and hardship throughout the world, and who wish to emancipate themselves not to the detriment but by the emancipation of all, so as to be free with all men and not so as to become tyrants in their turn — for workers of good faith to become attached to such a programme, this is what it is far harder to understand.

I therefore firmly believe that inside a few years the German workers themselves, recognizing the fatal consequences of a theory which can reward only the ambitions of their bourgeois leaders or else of a handful of workers trying to climb on their backs and become bourgeois dominators and exploiters in their own turn, will reject it in scorn and anger and embrace the true programme of workers' emancipation, the programme of the destruction of States, with the same enthusiasm now being shown by the workers of the great Mediterranean countries, France, Spain and Italy, as well as of Holland and Belgium.

In the meantime we fully acknowledge their right to take the path which best suits themselves, providing they allow us the same freedom. We even acknowledge the likelihood that their whole history, nature, state of civilization and entire present situation force them to take this path. Let the German, American and English workers strive to seize political power, if that is their pleasure. But let them allow the workers in other lands to take equally vigorous steps towards the destruction of all political authority. Liberty for all and mutual respect for that liberty—these, I say, are the essential conditions for international solidarity.

But Herr Marx obviously wants nothing to do with that solidarity, since he refuses to acknowledge that liberty. And in vindication of his refusal he has a very special theory, although it is no more than a logical extension of his entire system. The political State in every country, he says, is always the product and faithful reflection of its economic situation; to change the former, one has only to change the latter. This is the whole secret of political evolutions, according to Herr Marx. He pays no heed to other elements in history, such as the effect—obvious though it is—of political, judicial and religious institutions on the economic situation. He says that 'hardship produces political slavery—the State', but does not allow for the converse: 'Political slavery—the State—reproduces and maintains hardship as a condition of its existence, so that in order to destroy hardship the State must be destroyed.' And the strange thing is that the man who forbids his opponents to condemn political slavery, the State, as an *actual* cause of hardship should be instructing his friends and disciples in the German Social Democratic Party to consider the seizure of political power and liberties as the absolutely essential precondition for economic emancipation.

Herr Marx also utterly ignores one highly important element in the historical development of humanity, and that is the individual temperament and character of all races and peoples, which are themselves the product of a host of ethnographic, climatological and economic, as well as historical, causes but which, once established, exert a considerable influence over the destinies and even the development of a country's economic forces, outside and independent of its economic conditions. Among these elements and so to speak natural characteristics, there is one whose effect is absolutely crucial in the individual history of every people, and that is the intensity of the instinct of rebellion, and hence of liberty, with which it is endowed or which it has preserved. This instinct is a totally primordial, animal factor; it occurs to varying degrees in every living creature, and the energy and vitality of each is measurable by its intensity. In man, and in conjunction with the economic needs that constrain him, it becomes the most powerful of all agents of human emancipation. And since it is a matter of temperament, not of intellectual and moral culture, although it usually appeals to both of these, it sometimes happens that civilized peoples have only a slight degree of it, either because it has been used up in their earlier development, or because the very nature of their civilization has drained it, or else because from the dawn of history they have had a smaller share of it than others.

In a previous publication,* I have attempted to show that this is just the plight of the German nation. It does possess many other sterling qualities which make it quite a respectable nation—it is hardworking, thrifty, rational, studious, thoughtful, learned, very argumentative and yet in love with hierarchic discipline, and very far-ranging: the Germans are not greatly attached to their own country, travel far and wide to earn their living, and easily—if not always successfully, as I have already observed—adopt the morals and customs of their foster-countries. But with all these undoubted advantages, the one they lack is the love of liberty, the instinct of rebellion. They are the most resigned and obedient people in the world. Furthermore, they have another great fault, which is the spirit of acquisition, slow, systematic absorption and domination that makes them the greatest single threat to the liberty of the world, and never more so than at this moment.

This was aristocratic and bourgeois Germany throughout its past, and this is the Germany of today. Can the German proletariat, the age-old victim of both, be said to be sympathetic to the conquering spirit discernible today in the higher levels of the nation? In concrete terms, certainly not. For a conquering people is necessarily a slave people, and the slave is always the proletariat. Conquest is therefore totally opposed to its interests and its liberty. But it is imaginatively sympathetic, and will continue to be so as long as it fails to realize that the Pan-Germanic, republican and so-called popular State promised for the more or less imminent future

---

* *L'Empire knouto-germanique.* I have published only the first part, and intend to publish the rest in the near future.[23]

I

would be nothing less than a new form of grevious servitude if it were ever to materialize.

Until the present moment, at any rate, it appears not to have understood this, and none of its leaders, orators or publicists have yet felt inclined to explain. Instead they are all doing their best to lead the German proletariat along a path in which it can find only the censure of the world and its own enslavement, and as long as it follows their lead and pursues this dreadful illusion of the popular State it is certain that it will never hold the initiative in the social revolution. That revolution will come to it from outside, probably from southern Europe, and only then will the German people succumb to the universal infection, unlock their passions and overthrow the dominion of their tyrants and so-called emancipators.

The reasoning of Herr Marx leads him to an entirely different conclusion. Taking only the strictly economic question into account, he tells himself that the most advanced countries, and consequently those most capable of producing social revolution, are the ones where modern capitalist production has reached its highest point of development. It is they, and they alone, which are the civilized countries, and they which are meant to initiate and control that revolution, which will consist either of the gradual or violent expropriation of the present landowners and capitalists or of the appropriation of all land and capital by the State. In order to be able to carry out its great economic and social mission, this State will have to be very far-reaching, very powerful and highly centralized. It will administer and supervise agriculture by means of its appointed managers, who will command armies of rural workers organized and disciplined for that purpose. At the same time it will set up a single bank on the ruins of all existing banks, as the sleeping partner of all labour and national trade.

It is understandable that at first sight such an apparently simple plan of organization might catch the imagination of workers more eager for justice and equality than for liberty, and foolishly imagining that either can exist without it — as if it were possible to rely on others, and particularly on rulers, no matter how elective and popularly controlled they claim to be, to seize and consolidate liberty! In fact, this would be a barracks regime for the proletariat, in which a standardized mass of men and women workers would wake, sleep, work and live by rote; a regime of privilege for the able and the clever; and for the Jews, lured by the large-scale speculations of the national banks, a wide field for lucrative transactions.

At home it will mean slavery, abroad, unremitting warfare, unless all the people of the 'inferior' Latin and Slavonic races, the former weary of bourgeois civilization, the latter barely familiar with it and instinctively despising it, were to resign themselves to bowing under the yoke of an essentially bourgeois nation and a State which will be all the more despotic for styling itself 'popular'.

Social revolution as envisaged and longed for by the Latin and Slav workers is infinitely broader than that which is promised by the German or Marxist programme. There is no question for them of the grudgingly measured, long-term emancipation of the working classes, they foresee the complete and real emancipation of the entire proletariat not just of a few but of all nations, civilized or not, because the new unconditionally popular civilization must begin with this act of universal emancipation. And the first password can only be *liberty*, not that political liberty advocated and recommended by Herr Marx and his supporters as a preliminary objective, but the *broad human liberty* which, by destroying all the dogmatic, metaphysical, political and judicial chains which now encumber the entire world, will give the world — collectives and individuals alike — full autonomy of action and development, and rid it once and for all of guides, supervisors and protectors.

The second password is *solidarity* — not the Marxist solidarity, organized from the top downwards by some form of government and imposed either by trickery or force on the popular masses; not that solidarity of all which denies the liberty of all and which by the same token becomes a lie, a fiction, the direct equivalent of slavery; but the solidarity which is instead the confirmation and realization of all liberty, drawing its strength not from any political law but from man's own collective nature, according to which no man is free if all the men around him and all those who have the slightest influence on his life are not equally free. This truth finds magnificent expression in Robespierre's *Rights of Man*, which proclaims that *the enslavement of the least of men is the enslavement of all*.

The solidarity we are asking, far from being produced by some artificial or authoritarian organization, can only be the spontaneous outcome of social life, both economic and moral, the outcome of free federation of common interests, aspirations and inclinations. Its basic essentials are *equality, collective labour*, made binding upon all not through legal pressure but the pressure of things, and *collective ownership*; its guiding lights are *experience*, which means the practice of collective life, and *science*; its final objective is the *constitution of mankind*, and therefore the downfall of all States.

It is this ideal, not divine or metaphysical but human and *practical*,* which is the only solution to the modern aspirations of the Latin and Slav peoples. They want the whole of liberty, the whole of solidarity, the whole of equality; in other words, they want nothing but humanity and will not be

---

* Practical in the sense that it will be far less difficult to realize than the Marxist idea, which, next to the poverty of its objective, still has the serious drawback of being absolutely impracticable. This will not be the first time that able, reasonable men, the advocates of *practical, feasible* things, are recognized as Utopians, while those who are now called Utopians become the practical men of tomorrow. The absurdity of the Marxist system consists precisely in the hope that by inordinately narrowing the scope of the socialist programme in order to get it accepted by the bourgeois radicals, it will transform the latter into unconscious and involuntary servants of social revolution.

This is a big mistake: all historical experience shows that an alliance concluded between two different parties always benefits the more backward —the more advanced party is inevitably weakened because the alliance diminishes and distorts its programme and destroys its moral strength and self-confidence; whereas when a backward party lies, it always finds itself closer than ever to its own truth. We ought not to overlook the example of Mazzini, who in spite of his republican austerity has spent his whole life in transactions with royalty and has always finished up as its dupe, for all his genius. As for myself, I have no hesitation in saying that all the Marxist flirtations with bourgeois radicalism—reformist or revolutionary—can have no other outcome than the demoralization and disorganization of the nascent power of the proletariat, and therefore the further consolidation of the established power of the bourgeois.

satisfied with less, even on a temporary, transitional basis. The Marxists will call their hopes fanciful, and have been doing so for some time, but they will not be diverted from their objective and will never exchange the splendour of that objective for the bourgeois shoddiness of Marxist socialism.

The communalist insurrection in Paris ushered in the social revolution. What makes that revolution important is not really the weak experiments which it had the power and time to make, it is the ideas it has set in motion, the living light it has cast on the true nature and goal of revolution, the hopes it has raised, and the powerful stir it has produced among the popular masses everywhere, and especially in Italy, where the popular awakening dates from that insurrection, whose main feature was the revolt of the Commune and the workers' associations against the State. Through this insurrection, France has won back her reputation at a single stroke, and Paris, capital of world revolution, has regained her glorious initiative in the teeth and under the guns of the Bismarckian Germans.

Its general effect was so striking that the Marxists themselves, who saw all their ideas upset by the uprising, found themselves compelled to take their hats off to it. They went even further, and proclaimed that its programme and purpose were their own, in face of the simplest logic and their own true sentiments. This was a truly farcical change of costume, but they were bound to make it, for fear of being overtaken and left behind in the wave of feeling which the rising produced throughout the world.

So one had to admire the courage as well as the ability of Herr Marx when, two months later, he had the audacity to convene a conference of the International in London so as to present his wretched programme to it. That audacity can be explained by two factors. First, the Paris of the people was decimated, and the whole of revolutionary France momentarily reduced to silence, with very few exceptions. Second, the great majority of those who went to London to represent France were Blanquists, and I think I have adequately explained the causes which made the Blanquists look to an alliance with Herr Marx, who, instead of meeting opposition from these authoritarian representatives of the Paris

Commune in London, received strong backing from them at that time.

In any case we know how that Conference was rigged; it was packed with Herr Marx's hand-picked cronies, plus a few dupes. The Conference voted for everything it suited him to propose, and the Marxist programme, transformed into official truth, was imposed on the entire International as an obligatory principle.

But once the International had an official truth it had to have a government to maintain it. This was Herr Marx's second proposal; it was voted as the first. From then on the International found itself shackled to the mind and will of the German dictator. He was given the right of censorship over all the publications and all sections of the International. The pressing need for secret correspondence between the General Council and all the regional councils was acknowledged, and Herr Marx was also granted the right to send secret agents to all countries so as to intrigue on his behalf and sow dissension to the greater glory of Herr Marx. In other words, he was vested with full secret power.

In order to guarantee his peaceful enjoyment of it, Herr Marx decided that there was yet another step that must be taken. He had to destroy the public reputation of the opponents of his dictatorship, and he did me the honour of putting my name at the top of the list. Consequently he formed the heroic resolve of breaking me. He therefore sent for his little confederate and compatriot Utin in Geneva, and, although he held no officially delegated powers, Utin seems to have gone to London for the sole purpose of spreading all kinds of slanders and smears about me in open conference. I still do not know what he said, but I judge it by the following fact. On his return to Spain, citizen Anselmo Lorenzo Asprillo, a delegate of the Spanish Federation, was questioned by some friends of mine and wrote them the following message:

'If Utin was telling the truth, Bakunin must be a scoundrel; if he lied Utin must be a scoundrelly slanderer.'

And remember that all this occurred completely without my knowledge and that I only found out about it through that reply from Señor Asprillo, which did not reach me until April or May.

A circular from the General Council, now transformed into an official government, finally informed the stunned International of the *coup d'état* it had just undergone.

I think that Herr Marx, in the first flush of a triumph too easy to be secure and of the dictatorial power vested in himself, had been so blinded by it that he did not realize what a terrible storm his coup was bound to raise in the independent regions of the International. The honour of the first revolt belongs to the Jura Federation.

III

The policy of Herr von Bismarck is that of the present day, while the policy of Herr Marx, who sees himself at the very least as his successor and continuator, is that of the future. And when I say that Herr Marx considers himself Herr von Bismarck's successor, I am far from misrepresenting Herr Marx. If he did not see himself in that light, he would not have allowed Herr Engels, the repository of all his thoughts, to write that Herr von Bismarck serves the cause of social revolution. He serves it now in his own fashion, and Herr Marx will serve it later in another. It is in this sense that he will continue Herr von Bismarck's policy in future, as he admires it today.

We shall now examine the particular nature of Herr Marx's policy. And first we shall note the essential points on which it differs from Herr von Bismarck's. The principal—one might say the only—point is that Herr Marx is a democrat, an authoritarian socialist and a republican, while Herr von Bismarck is a Pomeranian Junker, an aristocrat and a monarchist. The difference is therefore very great, very significant, and equally sincere on either side. In this respect there is no possible point of contact or agreement between the two. Quite apart from all the unimpeachable pledges which Herr Marx has given to the cause of social democracy throughout his life, his very position and ambition offer a certain guarantee. In a monarchy, no matter how liberal, or even in a conservative Republic in the style of M. Thiers, there can be no place and no role for Herr Marx—still less in the Prusso-German Empire founded by Herr von Bismarck, with a militarist, religious, bugbear emperor at its head and all the barons and bureaucrats of Germany as its protectors. Before taking power, Herr Marx will have to sweep all this away. Thus he is perforce a revolutionary.

This is where Herr Marx differs from Herr von Bismarck — in the form and conditions of government. One is an aristocrat and monarchist, the other a democrat, a republican, and a social democrat and socialist republican into the bargain.

Let us now see where they coincide. Ultimately, *it is in the worship of the State*. There is no need for proof in Herr von Bismarck's case — he provides his own. He is a Statist and nothing but a Statist, through and through. But neither do I see it as a very exacting task to prove that the same applies to Herr Marx. He is so in love with government that he even wanted to institute it in the International Working Men's Association, and he idolizes power so much that he wanted and still intends today to impose his own dictatorship on ourselves. This seems to me quite sufficient to identify his personal leanings. But his socialist and political programme reflects these very faithfully. The supreme objective of all his efforts, as evinced by the basic statutes of his party in Germany, is the establishment of a great *People's State* (*Volksstaat*).

But whoever says State necessarily implies a particular, limited State, which may well include many different peoples and countries if it is a large one, but which excludes even more. Because, short of dreaming of the universal State, as Napoleon and Charles V did, or as the papacy dreamed of the universal Church, and in spite of all the international ambitions which consume him today, Herr Marx will have to be satisfied with ruling a single State, not several States at once, when the bell sounds for the realization of his dreams — if ever it does sound. Consequently, State means *a* State, and *a* State confirms the existence of *several* States, and *several* States means rivalry, jealousy, and incessant, endless war. The simplest logic bears this out, and so does the whole of history.

It is in the nature of the State to disrupt human solidarity and in a sense to deny humanity. The State can only preserve itself in all its integrity and strength if it sets itself up as the ultimate, absolute goal, at least for its own citizens, or to put it bluntly its own subjects, since it cannot impose itself as such on other States' subjects. The inevitable outcome is a break with human solidarity in the universal sense and with universal reason, brought about by the birth of State solidarity and State reason. The principle of political or State morality is very simple. Since the State is the supreme goal, then everything that conduces to the growth of its power is good, and anything contrary to it, no matter how human, is bad. This morality is called *patriotism*. The International, as we have conceived it, is the negation of patriotism and consequently the negation of the State. So if Herr Marx and his friends in the German socialist democratic party could succeed in introducing the principle of the State into our programme, they would kill the International ...

Lastly, no matter how efficient its organization of public upbringing and education, censorship and police may be, the State cannot be sure of its own self-preservation without an armed force to defend it against its own *internal enemies*, against the discontent of its people. The State is the minority government, from the top downward, of a vast quantity of men who differ widely in terms of cultural level, the nature of the regions or localities they inhabit, position, occupation, interests and aspirations, and unless this minority is endowed with the omniscience, ubiquity and omnipotence which the theologians attribute to their God, even if it is elected a thousand times over by universal suffrage and supervised by popular institutions in all its actions, it cannot possibly know or take account of everybody's needs or satisfy the most legitimate and pressing interests with equal fairness. There will always be malcontents, because there will always be sacrifices.

Furthermore the State, like the Church, is a great maker of living sacrifices. It is an arbitrary creature in whose breast all the positive, living, individual or local interests of the people mingle, clash, destroy and absorb each other into the abstraction known as the common interest, the *public good* or the *public welfare*, and where all real wills are dissolved into the other abstraction that bears the name of *the will of the people*. It follows that this alleged will of the people is never anything but the sacrifice and dissolution of all the real wants of the population, just as this so-called public good is nothing but the

sacrifice of their interests. But in order to impose this omnivorous abstraction on millions of men, it has to be represented
and upheld by some real being and some living force. Well,
that being and force have always existed. In the Church,
they are called the clergy, in the State, the upper or ruling
class.

In Herr Marx's People's State, so we are told, there will
be no privileged class. Everybody will be equal, not only from
the judicial and political but also from the economic standpoint. This is the promise at any rate, although judging
by the means of action and the path it is intended to follow,
I very much doubt whether it can ever be honoured. So there
will be no more class, but a government, and, please note, an
extremely complicated government which, not content with
governing and administering the masses politically, like all the
governments of today, will also administer them economically,
by taking over the production and *fair* sharing of wealth,
agriculture, the establishment and development of factories,
the organization and control of trade, and lastly the injection
of capital into production by a single banker, the State. All
this will require vast knowledge and a lot of heads brimful
of brains.[24] It will be the reign of the *scientific mind*, the most
aristocratic, despotic, arrogant and contemptuous of all
regimes. There will be a new class, a new hierarchy of real or
bogus learning, and the world will be divided into a dominant,
science-based minority and a vast, ignorant majority. And
then let the ignorant masses beware!

IV

Lassalle first of all proved to [the workers] that under existing
conditions it is impossible for them to become free, and that
they cannot even obtain the slightest alleviation in their lot,
which is bound to become worse. Secondly he affirmed that as
long as a bourgeois State exists, bourgeois economic privileges
will be impregnable, and this brought him to the conclusion
that to obtain real freedom, freedom founded on economic
equality, *the proletariat must seize control of the State*, so that,
instead of the State being opposed to the proletariat and on the
side of the exploiting class, the State will be in favour of the
proletarian masses and against the bourgeoisie.

How can we seize control of the State? There are only two ways of doing this: either by a political revolution, or by a legal national agitation in favour of peaceful reforms. Lassalle, being a German and a Jew, a scholar and a rich man, advised the second method.

Accordingly, and with this aim in mind, he formed a sizable, mainly political, party of German workers, and organized it as a hierarchy, subject to firm discipline and his own dictatorship, in fact doing what Herr Marx has wanted to do with the International for the past three years. Marx's attempt was unsuccessful, but Lassalle's was a complete success. As the first and foremost aim of the party he put peaceful agitation by all peoples for the universal rights of electing government representatives and authorities. Having won this right by way of legal reform, the people would have to send only their representatives to the national parliament which would turn a bourgeois government into a people's government by a series of decrees and laws. The first business of a people's government would be to allow unlimited credit to producers' and consumers' worker associations, which would only then be in a position to compete with bourgeois capital and would, in a short time, conquer it and swallow it up. When the swallowing-up process is over, there will then come a period in which society will be radically reorganized.

This is Lassalle's programme, and it is also the programme of the Social Democratic Party. Actually it belongs not to Lassalle, but to Marx, who described it fully in the famous *Manifesto of the Communist Party* produced by him and Engels in 1848. There is also a clear reference to it in the first *Address to the International Association*, written by Marx in 1864, in the words: 'the first duty of the working class consists of winning political power for itself,' or, as it says in the *Manifesto of the Communist Party*, 'the first step towards the workers' revolution must consist of raising the proletariat to government level. The proletariat must concentrate all the tools of production in the hands of the government, that is the proletariat, raised to government level.' ...

We have already on many occasions expressed our deep aversion to the theories of Lassalle and Marx, recommending the workers to adopt at least as their first and foremost aim, if not their final ideal, *the establishment of a people's government*, which, as they explain, will be no other than 'the proletariat raised to the level of government'.

One may well ask whether the proletariat would be in the position of a ruling class, and over whom would it rule? This means that yet another proletariat would emerge, which would be subject to the new sovereignty and the new State. For instance, the Marxists, as is well known, are not well disposed towards the peasant rabble, who, being on the lowest cultural level, would doubtless be governed by the urban and factory proletariat; or, if one were to look at this problem from the national point of view, considering Germans and Slavs, then presumably, for the same reason, Slavs would be in a condition of slavery to a triumphant German proletariat, and therefore in the same situation as the lowest class is now to its own bourgeoisie.

If there is a State, then there is inevitably supremacy, and therefore slavery: a State without open or veiled slavery is inconceivable — that is why we are opposed to the State.

What does raising the proletariat to the level of government mean? Surely the whole proletariat is not going to head the administration? There are about forty million Germans. Does it mean that all forty million will be members of the government? Will all the people be rulers, and will there be no one to be ruled? In that case there will be no government and no State, but if there is a State, then there are subjects, that is, slaves.

This dilemma in the Marxist theory can easily be solved. A people's administration, according to them, must mean a people's administration by virtue of a small number of representatives chosen by the people. The universal right of each individual among all the people to elect so-called representatives and members of the government, that is the final word of the Marxists and of the democratic school, and it is a deception which would conceal the despotism of a governing minority, all the more dangerous because it appears as a sham expression of the people's will.

Therefore, whichever way you look at this question, you reach the same sad result: that the vast majority, the great mass of people, would be governed by a privileged minority. But this minority, say the Marxists, will consist of workers. Well, perhaps *former* workers, who would stop being workers the moment they became rulers or representatives, and would then come to regard the whole blue-collared world from governmental heights, and would not represent the people but themselves and their pretensions in the government of the people. Anyone who does not see this does not know anything about human nature.

But those who would be chosen would be burning with conviction, and would also be trained socialists! The expression 'scholarly socialist', or 'scientific socialist', which one is always meeting in the writings and speeches of the Lassallists and Marxists, itself proves that this sham people's government would be no other than the completely despotic rule of the masses by a new and very small aristocracy of actual or alleged 'scholars'. The people are no 'scholars', and therefore they are as a whole to be freed from the toils of government, and as a whole they are to make up the herd that is governed. What a splendid freedom!

The Marxists realize the contradiction in this, and, realizing that the governing of educated people is the most difficult, humiliating and despicable thing in the world, and will be a real dictatorship, whatever democratic form it will take, console themselves with the thought that this dictatorship will be temporary and short-lived. They say that its only concern and purpose will be to educate and raise the people, both economically and politically, to the stage at which all administration will soon become unnecessary, and the State, having lost all of its political, that is sovereign, character, will itself turn into a completely free organization of economic interests and communes.

This is the real contradiction. If their State is really going to be a people's government, then why should it abolish itself, and if its abolition is essential for the real emancipation of the people, then how dare they call it a people's government? By the polemic we have used against them, we have made them realize that liberty or anarchy, that is the free organization of the working masses from the bottom up, is the final aim of social development, and that any State, including their people's State, is a yoke, as it gives birth to despotism on the one side and slavery on the other.

They say that this sort of governmental yoke, this dictatorship, is an essential step leading to the attainment of complete freedom for the people; and that anarchy or freedom is the aim, but the State or dictatorship is the means. Therefore in order to emancipate the masses they must first be enslaved.

On this contradiction we must for the time being end our argument. They affirm that only dictatorship, *theirs* of course, can create a popular will. We reply that no dictatorship can have any other aim except to perpetuate itself, and that it is capable of instilling and fostering only slavery in the masses that endure it. Liberty can only be created by liberty, that is by mass rebellion and the free organization of the working masses from the bottom upwards.

GLOSSARY OF NAMES

ALBERONI, Giulio (1664–1752). Spanish cardinal, minister of Philip V. He tried to make Spain the dominant force in Europe, and was exiled after his failure.

BABEUF, François-Noël (Gracchus) (1760–97). French revolutionary. Editor of *Le Tribun du peuple* (1794–6), in which he promulgated his egalitarian ideas. He organized a conspiracy against the Directory, with the aim of establishing a revolutionary dictatorship which was to enforce communism. On its discovery he was condemned to death.

BARBÈS, Armand (1809–70). French revolutionary, with Blanqui one of the insurrectional leaders of the republican secret societies under the July monarchy. Twice condemned to lifelong imprisonment.

BAUER, Bruno (1809–82). German theologian, philosopher and historian, the acknowledged leader of the Young Hegelians and a prominent contributor to Ruge's *Hallische Jahrbücher*. He denied the historical reality of the Bible, rejected Christianity and, developing a dialectical atheist theory from Hegel's system, became one of the most important humanists of modern times.

BAZAROV, the central figure in Turgenev's famous novel *Fathers and Children* (1861), prototype of 'young Russian' nihilism.

BEBEL, August (1840–1913). German socialist, member of the International, one of the founders and leaders of the German Social Democratic Workers' Party.

BLANC, Louis (1811–82). French socialist, member of the Provisional Government in 1848. In his *L'Organisation du travail* (1839) he proposed the establishment of so-called *ateliers nationaux*, national workshops designed to achieve full employment through public recognition of the 'right to work'.

BLANQUI, Louis-Auguste (1805–81). French revolutionary socialist, one of the greatest revolutionary figures of the nineteenth century. He developed the technique of armed insurrection by small groups and advocated an interim dictatorship for the post-revolutionary period. He was nicknamed *l'Enfermé* on account of having spent a great deal of his life in prison.

BORKHEIM, Sigismund Ludwig (1825–85). German publicist. While living in Baden, he took part in the revolutionary movement of 1848-9, after which he lived in London. He was a personal friend of Marx and attacked Bakunin, whom he took to be the incarnation of pan-Slavism, on several occasions.

BRUHIN, J. Casper Aloïs (born 1824). Swiss publicist, from 1869 chairman of the Basel sections of the International.

BUONARROTI, Filippo (1761–1837). Italian revolutionary socialist who took an active part in the French Revolution. He participated in the conspiracy of Babeuf, about which he wrote his famous book *Conspiration pour l'égalité dite de Babeuf* (1828), thus setting the babouvist trend in European socialism. Escaping Babeuf's fate, he continued his underground activities and organized secret societies throughout Europe until his death.

BÜRKLI, Karl (1823–1901). Swiss socialist, Fourierist, founder and president of the Zurich section of the International.

CABET, Étienne (1788–1856). French socialist. In his *Voyage en Icarie* (1839) he sketched the outlines of an egalitarian society. After the revolution of 1848 he left France to found colonies in the United States, which, however, failed.

CAFIERO, Carlo (1846–92). Italian revolutionary. In 1871 he had an important confidential correspondence with Engels, who was Corresponding Secretary for Italy of the General Council, but after his visit to Bakunin in May 1872 he rallied to collectivism and subsequently became one of the most prominent men in Italian and international anarchism.

CAVAIGNAC, Louis-Eugène (1802–57). French general, Chief of State in 1848. He put down the June Insurrection in Paris (1848). In the Presidential elections of 1849 he was beaten by Louis Napoleon.

ČERNIŠEVSKIJ, Nikolaj Gavrilovič (1828–89). Russian philosopher and radical publicist. As an editor of the journal *The*

Contemporary and author of the novel *What to do?*, which he wrote after his imprisonment in 1862, he had a profound influence on revolutionary circles in Russia.

COMTE, Auguste (1798–1857). French philosopher. Formerly the secretary of Saint-Simon, he became the founder of positivism.

CONSIDÉRANT, Victor (1808–93). French socialist, founder of the Fourierist school and editor of its periodicals *La Phalange* and *La Démocratie pacifique*. After founding Fourierist colonies in Texas, he returned to Paris in 1869.

DELESCLUZE, Louis-Charles (1809–71). French radical publicist. He participated in the revolutions of 1830 and 1848. Member of the Committee of Public Safety and military delegate of the Paris Commune, he was killed in the barricade fighting of the last week.

DOBROLJUBOV, Nikolaj Aleksandrovič (1836–61). Russian radical philosopher and publicist who, like Černiševskij, profoundly influenced Russian revolutionary circles in the 1860s.

ECCARIUS, Johann Georg (1818–89). German socialist, who from 1847 onwards lived as an émigré in London. Member of the Communist League. Member of the General Council of the International (1862–72) and its General Secretary (1867–71), delegate to all congresses and conferences of the International.

ENFANTIN, Barthélémy-Prosper (1796–1864). French Saint-Simonist, one of the founders of the Saint-Simonian Church, of which he became the high priest.

FANELLI, Giuseppe (1827–77). Italian revolutionary, originally an associate of Mazzini and the Italian federalist Pisacane. In 1866 he took part in Garibaldi's campaign against Austria. After 1865 he was closely linked with Bakunin and his secret societies. In November 1868 he departed for Spain as a special emissary of Bakunin, and his journey was to result in the foundation of the Spanish International.

FOURIER, Charles (1772–1837). French socialist. His theory was based on the principles of association among free individuals, liberated in all respects from the stress of forced labour. He proposed the creation of so-called *phalanstères*, co-operatives in which every individual would find his place according to his own abilities and wishes.

GAMBETTA, Léon (1838–82). French lawyer, republican statesman, member of the Government of National Defence (1870).

GARIBALDI, Giuseppe (1807–82). The famous Italian patriot who organized an army to struggle for Italy's independence and unification. He participated in the First Congress of the League for Peace and Freedom (1867).

GOEGG, Amand (1820–97). German democratic publicist, member of the League for Peace and Freedom and of the International; delegate to its Basel Congress (1869).

GUILLAUME, James (1844–1916). Swiss collectivist, a close friend of Bakunin. Until his departure for Paris in 1878, he was the driving force of the Jura Federation and edited its important papers *Le Progrès*, *La Solidarité* and the *Bulletin de la Fédération jurassienne de l'AIT*. He also played an important part in the anti-authoritarian International of Saint-Imier, after having been one of the leaders of the collectivist minority at the Hague Congress (1872).

HEPNER, Adolf (1846–1923). German social democrat, an editor of the *Volksstaat* and a delegate to The Hague Congress of 1872.

HERWEGH, Georg Friedrich (1817–75). German poet and democrat. His political poetry, of which the *Gedichte eines Lebendigen* (1841) was the most celebrated collection, made his fame in radical circles. He took an active part in the revolution in southern Germany in 1848.

HERZEN, Aleksandr Ivanovič (1812–70). Russian revolutionary democrat and publicist, a friend of Bakunin. In 1847 he emigrated to Western Europe, where he founded the free Russian press and edited the *Bell* and the *Polar Star*, among other important papers.

HESS, Moses (1812–75). German publicist, one of the founders and editors of the *Neue Rheinische Zeitung*, the famous radical newspaper in Cologne. He was one of the first to draw communist conclusions from the confrontation of Left Hegelian ideas and French socialism, and in this had a lasting influence on Marx and Engels. After 1842 he lived in Paris. After the foundation of the First International he became one of Bakunin's bitterest enemies.

KARAKOZOV, Dmitrij Vladimirovič (1840–66). Russian revolutionary. As a student in Moscow in 1865 he joined the revolutionary circle of Išutin. In 1866 he was hanged after an abortive attempt on the life of Alexander II.

KOŚCIELSKI, Wladislaw (1818–95). Polish democrat who took part in the Polish revolutionary movement of 1848. He served as an intermediary between Bakunin and the *Neue Rheinische Zeitung* (1848).

LASSALLE, Ferdinand (1825–64). German socialist and publicist, founder of the General Association of German Workers (1863). From his Hegelian philosophical theories he derived the idea of the *Volksstaat* (People's State), which deeply influenced the German working-class movement.

LEDRU-ROLLIN, Alexandre-Auguste (1807–74). French republican and democrat, member of the Provisional Government in 1848. In 1849 he emigrated to England.

LIEBKNECHT, Wilhelm (1826–1900). German socialist, member of the Communist League and of the International. One of the founders and leaders of German social-democracy, editor of the *Volksstaat*.

LITTRÉ, Émile (1801–81). French linguist and positivist philosopher, author of the *Dictionnaire de la langue française*.

LORENZO, Anselmo (1841–1915). Spanish revolutionary socialist, anarchist. One of the organizers of the International in Spain.

LUCRAFT, Benjamin (1809–97). British trade unionist, member of the Executive Committee of the Reform League. Member of the General Council of the International (1864–71), from which he withdrew on the occasion of the Paris Commune.

MALTMAN BARRY, Marry (1842–1909). British publicist, conservative. Member of the General Council, confidential agent of Marx.

MAZZINI, Giuseppe (1805–72). Italian revolutionary republican, one of the outstanding leaders of the Italian national liberation movement. As a member of the abortive Provisional Government in 1849, he was forced to emigrate, but continued organizing his secret societies. He sharply attacked the Paris Commune and the International in 1871.

MURAV'EV, Michail Nikolaevič (1796–1866). Russian general, governor of Poland. He massacred the Polish insurgents of 1863.

NEČAEV, Sergej Gennad'evič (1847–82). Russian revolutionary socialist. After participating in the student movement in St Petersburg in 1868–9, he organized a secret society, which was discovered after he had assassinated a member. He collaborated with Bakunin in Switzerland in 1869–70, until the latter broke with him. Extradited to Russia by the Swiss government in 1872, he died in prison.

OGAREV, Nikolaj Platonovič (1813–77). Russian revolutionary democrat, publicist and poet, close friend of Herzen and Bakunin. An émigré since 1856, he took part in the foundation of the Free Russian Press by Herzen and contributed to his reviews.

PROUDHON, Pierre-Joseph (1809–65). French anarchist. According to his ideas, the economy should be based on the principles of free association; the State was to be eliminated and replaced by a free federation of free associations. His federalist theories, in particular, profoundly influenced Bakunin.

QUINET, Edgar (1803–75). French philosopher, *littérateur* and liberal historian.

RECLUS, Élisée (1830–1905). French anarchist and famous geographer. From 1865 he was a member of Bakunin's 'Fraternité' and in 1868 belonged to the socialist minority that withdrew, with Bakunin, from the League of Peace and Freedom. After his participation in the Paris Commune he was exiled and continued his anarchist activities in the

Swiss Jura. Until his death he remained one of the most influential anarchist theoreticians.

REICHEL, Adolf (1820–1896). German musician. Bakunin met him in Dresden in 1842 and they remained friends until Bakunin's death, at which time Reichel was living in Berne.

RICHARD, Albert (1846–1925). French socialist, one of the leaders of the Lyons section of the International, member of Bakunin's secret Alliance. With Bakunin, he took part in the insurrection in Lyons in 1870.

RITTINGHAUSEN, Moritz (1814–91). German revolutionary democrat, participated in the revolution of 1848, contributor to the *Neue Rheinische Zeitung*. Member of the International and of the German Social Democratic Workers' Party. He was an advocate of direct legislation.

RUGE, Arnold (1802–80). German philosopher and democrat, edited from 1838 to 1842 the Left Hegelian papers *Hallische Jahrbücher* and afterwards the *Deutsche Jahrbücher*. After their suppression he published, jointly with Marx, the *Deutsch-Französische Jahrbücher*.

SAINT-SIMON, Claude-Henri de (1760–1825). French socialist. He opposed the principle of *laissez-faire* and advocated a planned economy based on large-scale industry and banking. His theories influenced the French workers' movement in the first half of the nineteenth century.

SCHIFF, Moritz (1823–96). German physician, lecturer at the University of Florence, where Bakunin met him in 1865.

SORGE, Friedrich Adolf (1828–1906). German socialist. He participated in the revolution in Germany in 1848, and in 1852 emigrated to the U.S.A., where he became an important member of the International. A friend of Marx and Engels, he was a delegate at the Hague Congress of 1872 and subsequently a member of the ephemeral General Council in New York.

STRAUSS, David Friedrich (1808–74). German theologian and philosopher. His *Leben Jesu* (1833), in which he criticized the Gospels and exposed the Christian dogma as a sophisticated symbolization of religious myths, caused a universal sensation. When Bakunin read the book he was still a Right Hegelian, but it had a deep and lasting influence on him.

SUMNER, Charles (1811–74). American statesman, Chairman of the Committee of the U.S. Senate for Foreign Affairs. He was a champion of Negro political rights.

UTIN, Nikolaj (1845–83). Russian revolutionary, an émigré after 1863. One of the founders of the Russian section of the International in Geneva, he violently opposed Bakunin.

VARLIN, Louis-Eugène (1839–71). French revolutionary socialist, trade unionist, one of the organizers of the French International. A member of the Paris Commune, he was killed in the street-fighting.

WEITLING, Wilhelm Christian (1808–71). German tailor, who lived abroad after 1835. He was one of the outstanding leaders of the revolutionary secret societies in the 1830s and 1840s and, in the words of Engels, is to be regarded as the founder of German communism. In 1843 he was arrested in Switzerland and handed over to Prussia, but after his release in 1844 he was again deeply involved in the revolutionary movement in London, Brussels and, from the end of 1846, America. His principal work is *Garantien der Harmonie und Freiheit* (1842).

EXPLANATORY NOTES

1. Countess Zoja Sergeevna Obolenskaja, whom Bakunin had met at Naples in the spring of 1866, had become a member of his secret society, the 'Fraternité internationale'. It is to its programme that Bakunin refers. Of the original complete programme, the manuscript entitled 'Principles and Organization of the International Brotherhood' is reproduced as section IV of the present volume.

2. In the first months of 1866 Bakunin continued working on the organization of his international secret society, and, in particular, spent much time on its one existing section, or 'family', to use his term. This group in Naples published secretly an Italian programme and was subsequently linked up with, and had an influence on, the federalist democratic movement in southern Italy. In this, Bakunin was successful in counteracting the national-revolutionary ideology and enormous prestige of Mazzini and Garibaldi, and this success led in 1871 to the foundation of the Italian Federation of the International, with a Bakuninist programme.

3. In a leading article in the *Bell* (see note 4) of May 1st, 1866, Herzen had severely condemned the attempt on the life of Tsar Alexander II on April 4th of that year; he described its author, Dmitrij Karakozov, as a madman and a fanatic.

4. In 1857 Alexander Herzen published the first issue of *Kolokol* ['the Bell'], printed by the Free Russian Press, originally in London and after 1865 in Geneva. This journal, in which Nikolaj Ogarev was a close collaborator, was the first organ of the Russian opposition and had for many years a profound influence on democratic and revolutionary circles both in Russia and among émigrés. This, however, faded when a new and more radical wave of émigrés arrived in Europe in the 'sixties. The Russian publication, which at different periods came out once a week, once or twice a month, or at even longer intervals, lasted till 1867, while a French translation appeared in Brussels from 1862 to 1865. In 1868–9

the Russian edition was replaced by a French one, also printed in Geneva.

5. He means, of course, the International Working Men's Association, the First International.

6. The principal act of the Third Congress of the International, held at Brussels in September 1868, was the vote on the question of land property. A resolution was carried in which it was stated that mines, railways, means of communication, arable soil, etc., must be converted into the common property of society.

7. The *Lettres à un Français sur la crise actuelle* were written by Bakunin on the outbreak of the Franco-Prussian War, which, in his opinion, had placed the revolutionary question at the top of the agenda. They were published anonymously in September 1870, in an edition prepared and adapted by James Guillaume; the complete original text was published only in 1910.

8. *Beguny*: members of an orthodox sect that originated in the second half of the eighteenth century. According to their creed, Antichrist ruled in the world, and particularly through the persons of the Russian tsars; consequently, they considered all laws unacceptable to the true believers.

9. In fact, Bakunin is referring to Mazzini's speech of February 1852, in which the latter attacked French socialism at a moment when, after the *coup d'état* of December 1851, arrests, incarcerations and deportations were heavily affecting the French workers' movement. Proudhon, too, wrote at the time that Mazzini, by this ignominious speech, had definitely gone over to the camp of the enemies of the revolution.

10. In July and August 1869, the General Council discussed at its meetings the question of the right of inheritance, which was to be dealt with at the Fourth Congress of the International at Basel in September. Marx drew up a resolution, presented at the Congress by Georg Eccarius, in which he stated that the laws of inheritance were not the cause but the effect, the juridical consequence, of the existing economic organization of society based upon private property in the means of production. The disappearance of the right of inheritance would be the natural result of a social change superseding private property in the means of production: but its abolition could

never be the starting-point of such a social transformation; it would tend merely to lead the working class away from the true point of attack against present society. It would be a thing false in theory and reactionary in practice. Marx then considered changes in the laws of inheritance in the context of a state of social transition, where the present economic base of society was not yet transformed, but where the working masses had gathered enough strength to enforce transitory measures calculated to bring about an ultimate radical change of society. Changes of the laws of inheritance formed only part of a great many other transitory measures tending to the same end. The transitory measures, as to inheritance, could only be: (a) Extension of the inheritance duties already existing in many states, and the application of the funds hence derived to purposes of social emancipation; (b) Limitation of the testamentary right of inheritance, which—as distinguished from the intestate or family right of inheritance—appears an arbitrary and superstitious exaggeration even of the principles of private property themselves.

In Basel, another proposal was submitted by a Commission of the Congress, of which Bakunin was a member. Neither this nor the General Council's resolution obtained an absolute majority; the latter one was even defeated.

11. At the Congress of Eisenach in August 1869, Bebel and Liebknecht founded the German Social Democratic Party, which stood in opposition to the Lassallians' General German Workers' Association and was backed by Marx and Engels. In 1875, at the Gotha Congress, both organizations merged into the single German Social Democratic Workers' Party.

12. In the Provisional Rules of the International, drawn up by Marx in 1864, it is stated that the International and all societies and individuals adhering to it 'will acknowledge truth, justice and morality as the basis of their conduct towards each other, and towards all men, without regard to colour, creed or nationality'.

13. Contrary to Bakunin's suggestion, Marx did not accept the idea of a *Volksstaat* at all, while Lassalle, on the other hand, though a Hegelian, could not understand the dialectical process of the 'withering away' of the Marxist State. Marx's disciples Bebel and Liebknecht had adopted the *Volksstaat*

from Lassalle and they included this concept in the 1869 founding programme of the German Social Democratic Party. At the time that Bakunin wrote these words, Marx's rejection of the idea was not known; in 1875 he sharply criticized the new programme carried at the Gotha Congress, but his comment was suppressed by the German party leaders and did not appear until 1891. From Bakunin's point of view, however, there was no great fundamental difference between Marx's 'transitional State', which in 1870 he still called the 'dictatorship of the proletariat', and Lassalle's *Volksstaat*, which was to be the goal of German Social Democracy.

14. Bakunin refers to the fact that a large number of the delegates who made up the Marxist majority at the Hague Congress did not represent any organization of the International.

15. Among the different measures increasing the power of the General Council that were voted at The Hague Congress was the right to suspend federal branches, sections, councils and committees, and even entire federations of the International. At the same time it was declared that the General Council would be obliged to execute the resolutions of the Congresses and to see to the strict observance, in every country, of the principles and the general statutes and rules of the International.

16. This is an allusion to a remark made by Marx at the Hague Congress when questioned on the validity of the mandate delivered to Maltman Barry, a member of the General Council supporting Marx. The latter said that no fault had been found in Barry or in his mandate. As to the accusation that Barry was not a recognized leader of English working men, he answered that that was an honour, for almost every recognized leader of English working men had sold himself to the bourgeoisie or the government.

17. One frequently finds expressions of anti-Jewish sentiment in Bakunin's writings and letters, especially after 1869, when he was attacked by Moses Hess. His apparent anti-Semitism is often explained by the fact that his great opponents and most of his slanderers were Jews, including Marx, Hess, Borkheim and Utin. But though this may have contributed to his feelings, it is difficult, and probably impossible, to

find a full explanation for them. It is to be remembered that anti-Semitism was current in nineteenth-century Russia, perhaps even in an important part of European socialism— Edmund Silberner once noted that Marx's and Bakunin's opinions on Jews had much in common. The regrettable anti-Jewish remarks do not strengthen Bakunin's arguments; on the other hand, they do not invalidate them.

18. In October 1869 Bakunin was slanderously attacked by Moses Hess in the Paris daily *Le Réveil*. In the first half of 1870 Sigmund Borkheim took over the attack, adding some new details, in a series of articles published by the Leipzig *Volksstaat*, of which Wilhelm Liebknecht was the editor-in-chief. At the same time, the German-language paper the *Arbeiter-Union*, appearing in New York and drawing upon European sources, accused Bakunin of being a Russian spy.

19. On March 28th, 1870, Marx wrote his famous *Communication confidentielle*, which was sent to his friend Kugelmann and subsequently to the leaders of the German Social Democratic Party. Bakunin never saw the exact contents of this document, which was not published until 1902, and only knew of its existence because it was mentioned in the trial of Liebknecht, Bebel and Hepner held at Leipzig in March 1872.

20. The London Conference of the International was held from September 17th to 23rd, 1871, with only nine delegates of the sections attending, and thirteen members of the General Council. The most important question on the agenda concerned the attitude of the International towards political action by the proletariat. In spite of the objection that this was a question of principle to be treated only by a Congress, Marx easily succeeded, because of his obvious majority, in carrying through a resolution, the final part of which read:

'Considering, that against this collective power of the propertied classes the working class cannot act, as a class, except by constituting itself into a political party, distinct from and opposed to all old parties formed by the propertied classes;

'That this constitution of the working class into a political party is indispensable in order to ensure the triumph of the Social Revolution and its ultimate end—the abolition of classes;

'That the combination of forces which the working class has already effected by its economic struggles ought at the same time to serve as a lever for its struggles against the political power of landlords and capitalists —

'The Conference recalls to the members of the International:

'That in the militant state of the working class, its economic movement and its political action are indissolubly united.'

21. In a letter to Carlo Cafiero, Friedrich Engels had stated that Bismarck and Victor Emmanuel had both rendered an enormous service to the revolution by bringing about political centralization in their respective countries.

22. Bakunin's assertions are based on an article published in the *Volksstaat* of September 11th, 1870. The organ of the German Social Democratic Party quoted a letter written by Marx to the German party leadership, dated July 20th, 1870, in which he said among other things: 'The French need to be overcome. If the Prussians are victorious, the centralization of State power will be useful to the centralization of the German working class. Moreover, German ascendancy will transfer the centre of gravity of the European workers' movement from France to Germany, and it is sufficient to compare the movement in both countries, from 1866 up till now, to see that the German working class is superior to the French, considered both theoretically and from the viewpoint of organization. On a world scale, the ascendancy of the German proletariat over the French proletariat will at the same time constitute the ascendancy of *our* theory over Proudhon's.'

23. Immediately after Bakunin's participation in the abortive rising at Lyons in September 1870, and his flight from there, he started writing a large manuscript in which he summarized his philosophical and political theories in the light of the situation created by the outcome of the Franco-Prussian War. It was originally to bear the title *La Révolution sociale ou la dictature militaire*, but this was changed to *L'Empire knouto-germanique et la Révolution sociale*. In fact only its first part was published during Bakunin's lifetime, in April 1871. Later on, various extracts were taken from the manuscript and printed separately, as, for instance, the well-known pamphlets *The Paris Commune and the Idea of the State* (1878) and *God and the State* (1882). Eventually most of the text was published in vols.

II–IV of the *Œuvres* (1907–10), but the work still awaits publication in complete form.

24. An allusion to a remark made by the American delegate to The Hague Congress, Sorge, Marx's trusted representative. Against anti-authoritarian attacks, he declared (clearly referring to the author of *Das Kapital*), 'We wish to have not only a head, but a head with plenty of brains.'

BIBLIOGRAPHICAL NOTE

There is no complete edition of Bakunin's works in any language. The most important collections are *Œuvres*, 6 vols. (covering the period from 1867 to 1872), Paris 1895–1913; *Gesammelte Werke*, 3 vols. (1865 to 1873), Berlin 1921–4; *Sobranie Sočinenij i Pisem* ['Collected Works and Letters'], 4 vols. (1828 to 1861), Moscow 1934–5. In 1895 there was published in Stuttgart a large collection of his letters, edited by M. Dragomanov, under the title *Michail Bakunins Sozialpolitischer Briefwechsel mit Alexander Iw. Herzen und Ogarjow*; the original Russian text was published in Geneva in 1896.

An edition of Bakunin's complete works, under the title *Archives Bakounine*, is now in progress. It is edited and annotated by Arthur Lehning and published in Leiden. The four volumes that have appeared are:

    I. 'Michel Bakounine et l'Italie, 1871–1872': Première partie, 'La Polémique avec Mazzini' (1961); Deuxième partie, 'La Première Internationale en Italie et le conflit avec Marx' (1963);

    II. 'Michel Bakounine et les conflits dans l'Internationale, 1872. La Question germano-slave, le communisme d'État' (1965);

    III. 'Gosudarstvennost' i anarchija. Étatisme et anarchie, 1873' (1967);

    IV. 'Michel Bakounine et ses relations avec Sergej Nečaev, 1870–1872' (1971).

Selections in English include *Marxism, Freedom and the State*, London 1950. Two more extensive collections are G. Maximoff, ed., *The Political Philosophy of Bakunin*, Glencoe, Illinois, 1953; and S. Dolgoff, ed., *Bakunin on Anarchy*, New York 1972.

The most important biographical works are Max Nettlau, *The Life of Michael Bakounine. Michael Bakunin. Eine Biographie*, translated into French from the German and published in London in 1896–1900 (3 vols., hectographed); and Jurij Steklov, *Michail Aleksandrovič Bakunin. Ego žizn' i dejatel'nost*

[' ... His Life and Works'], 1814–1876, 4 vols., Moscow–Leningrad 1926–7. The standard biography in English is E. H. Carr, *Michael Bakunin*, London 1937, also available in paperback.

Other useful references may be found in James Guillaume, *L'Internationale. Documents et souvenirs, 1864–1878*, 4 vols., Paris 1905–10; Max Nettlau, *Der Anarchismus von Proudhon zu Kropotkin. Seine historische Entwicklung in den Jahren 1859–1880*, Berlin 1927 (especially Chapters 2, 3, 11, 12); G. D. H. Cole, *A History of Socialist Thought*, vol. II, London 1954 (Chapter 9); E. Lampert, *Studies in Rebellion*, London 1957 (Chapters 3 and 4); Franco Venturi, *Roots of Revolution*, London 1960, New York 1966 (paperback) (Chapters 2 and 17).